AZUSA REIMAGINED

ENCOUNTERING TRADITIONS

Rumee Ahmed, Randi Rashkover, and Jonathan Tran, Editors

AZUSA REIMAGINED

A Radical Vision of Religious and Democratic Belonging

KERI DAY

STANFORD UNIVERSITY PRESS
Stanford, California

STANFORD UNIVERSITY PRESS
Stanford, California

©2022 by the Board of Trustees of the Leland Stanford Junior University.
All rights reserved.

Printed in the United States of America on acid-free, archival-quality paper

Library of Congress Cataloging-in-Publication Data

Names: Day, Keri, author.

Title: Azusa reimagined : a radical vision of religious and democratic belonging / Keri Day.

Other titles: Encountering traditions.

Description: Stanford, California : Stanford University Press, 2022. | Series: Encountering traditions | Includes bibliographical references and index.

Identifiers: LCCN 2021037168 (print) | LCCN 2021037169 (ebook) | ISBN 9781503615236 (cloth) | ISBN 9781503631625 (paperback) | ISBN 9781503631632 (ebook)

Subjects: LCSH: Apostolic Faith Mission (Los Angeles, Calif.)—History. | African Americans—California—Los Angeles—Religion. | Revivals—California—Los Angeles—History—20th century. | Pentecostalism—United States—History—20th century. | Racism—Religious aspects—Christianity. | Capitalism—Religious aspects—Christianity. | Democracy—Religious aspects—Christianity.

Classification: LCC BX6194.A7 D39 2022 (print) | LCC BX6194.A7 (ebook) | DDC 289.9/30979494—dc23

LC record available at https://lccn.loc.gov/2021037168

LC ebook record available at https://lccn.loc.gov/2021037169

Cover image: Fire flame, Nejron Photo | shutterstock

Cover design: Rob Ehle

Typeset by Kevin Barrett Kane in 10/14 Minion Pro

TO
Ariella Rose

TABLE OF CONTENTS

ACKNOWLEDGMENTS

It is always hard for me to write the acknowledgements section because I am always afraid someone will be left out.

This book project began stirring inside of me while I was a visiting professor at Yale University Divinity School in 2016. While having dinner with a good friend, Marlon Millner, the conversation about scholarship on Pentecostalism began. There would be countless conversations over the next year that Marlon and I would have that helped me see why I needed to write about the Azusa Revival from my unique vantage point as a black feminist-womanist scholar. I am indebted to Marlon for generously offering his time, encouragement, energy, and knowledge on scholarship in Pentecostal studies. Without these early conversations, I would not have begun writing this book. Thanks so much, Marlon.

As I began research for this book, I realized that I needed to be in conversation with a top scholar in Pentecostal studies, particularly on the Azusa Revival. And so I turned to Dr. David Daniels. I would not have been able to write this book without becoming a student of David. We have had many conversations over the last few years about this book in a number of places, including accidently bumping into each other at a couple of conferences and taking time to do lunch in order to talk about my unfolding project. David would send me essays and articles to clarify questions and arguments I was thinking through. It has been pure joy to learn from David, and much of my historical research is indebted to his generous guidance.

Although I was not in direct contact with her, I want to acknowledge the extensive scholarly work of Dr. Estrella Alexander. Her various books were of tremendous help as I wrote about the women of Azusa. I do believe her labor of love in clarifying the role of women at Azusa and in black Pentecostalism will serve as an invitation for other black women to write about these movements in new and fresh ways.

A final person who was instrumental as I wrote this book was Dr. J. Cameron Carter. This book was written over five years, and I lectured on most of the chapters in many universities, divinity schools, and seminaries. One important conversation I had with "Jay" was in his home as he and his wife graciously hosted me as the Pauli Murray / Nannie-Helen Burroughs Lecturer at Duke Divinity School in 2018. My conversation with him helped me clarify what I meant when I referred to Azusa as a "lawless" community. Our rich sharing together was invaluable. Thanks, Jay, for your friendship and conversation in this area.

Where would I be without my students? Specifically, my course The Idea of Pentecost was instrumental as I thought about the ideas I present in this book. Students of different theological and ideological viewpoints in this course pushed me, debated with me, and affirmed why this was a worthy project. I can't name all thirty-one students but know that I deeply appreciate each of you.

I am grateful that my home institution, Princeton Theological Seminary, gave me a sabbatical so that I could finish this manuscript. Waking up to write most days was a sweet joy.

My editor is the best—Uli Guthrie, you have become my friend and my writing coach. Thanks so much.

I want to thank my mother and father, Connie Woods and Wilbur Day, and their respective spouses for their continued support. I am also grateful for my close friends: Tamura Lomax, Cece Jones-Davis, and Shively Smith, women who always hold me down.

To my husband, Austin Moore, who is my best friend and biggest cheerleader, you're the best. You give me good love. And finally, the newest member of my family, my sweet baby daughter, Ariella Rose, whom this book is dedicated to. You are the best of who I am and will ever be. May this book allow you to see your Pentecostal heritage anew so that you may be able to work toward justice, care, and belonging.

AZUSA REIMAGINED

Introduction

SUBVERSIVE BEGINNINGS

I AM A CHILD OF PENTECOSTALISM. My spiritual world did not begin with sophisticated theological vocabularies or coherently formulated propositions about God. I was not familiar with refined systems of theological speech that neatly explain elusive spiritual realities. I was not taught to think of faith only as an exercise of the intellect. My childhood Pentecostal community was adamant that spiritual experiences should not be reduced to *this* kind of rational grammar.

My small childhood church—a tiny gray brick building filled with blue-clothed pews—was wary of words alone being able to capture religious experiences and spiritual truths. We depended on divine encounters that were unpredictable, even unimagined. These divine encounters were gorgeously messy, always involving our bodies, tears, shouts, dances, screams, trembles, and ecstasy. We were children of providential dis-order, disordering all expectations and rules around religious worship and divine encounter. My small Pentecostal community lived inside a liminal space between divine revelation and divine mystery.

There is beauty and ugliness in any community, and my childhood church was no different. We were filled with contradictions. While we imagined ourselves as premillennial adherents, withdrawing from the political order of the world in order to wait on the return of Christ to correct all of the world's wrongs, we nevertheless used politically informed speech about the world and felt that our speech mattered to ongoing social problems. While we allowed women to teach and preach freely in our worship services, with full recognition that they were essential to the flourishing of the church, my church also kept women off the pulpit and did not support women at top-tier levels of ministry such as ordained ministry. While our forms of worship and ways of experiencing the divine were highly democratic, breaking many rules of liturgical order, our community nevertheless upheld very moralistic positions that ignored and dismissed people's agency to live authentic and honest lives. Concerns about social transformation tacitly occupied our minds, although we often imagined ourselves embodying the opposite of this-world concerns.

As a teenager, I wanted my church to relate itself publicly to major issues such as racism, poverty, sexual trauma, gender justice, and more. I wondered what my Pentecostal faith had to say about these urgent issues of the day. As I entered graduate school, non-Pentecostal scholars introduced me to essays, books, and articles on how early Pentecostalism engaged its political and economic worlds—an unfamiliar history to me. Learning this history, *my* history, opened up my religious imagination to possible Pentecostal futures that await articulation. As a scholar with my imagination now opened, it became increasingly important for me to excavate early Pentecostalism's social and political witness.

This book tells the story of *one* early Pentecostal church—the Apostolic Faith Mission—and how its religious life promoted economic and democratic transformation. This church's religious life is important for historical and contemporary reasons. It was the Apostolic Faith Mission that sparked the Azusa Street Revival of 1906, which in turn helped spread Pentecostalism in the United States and around the world. Pentecostalism is now the fastest-growing Christian religious movement worldwide, and in large part it began at Azusa. Apostolic Faith Mission is therefore key to understanding how Pentecostal communities, and religious communities more broadly, might shape and affect the religious and political landscapes of America and the broader world. This church is also important because contemporary Pentecostal scholarship has painted fresh portraits of the Azusa Revival in efforts to reclaim it from scholarly insignificance. In the past, much of religious scholarship treated early Pentecostalism as marginal and not a key shaper of American religious history. While I am not a historian and do not wish to enter those historical debates, what interests me is centering Azusa as a major religious movement in order to uncover the countercultural political practices this community embodied, particularly practices of resisting the white racial-capitalist order of the day. The subversive community this church cultivated compels me. That community defiantly refused the racist and market-driven momentum of early industrial capitalism. In this, Azusa was not just disregarding the racially divisive practices of society but was also a countercultural force and even a threat to how early American capitalism attempted to form American morality.

To claim that Azusa's religious life fought against bigotry and injustice is not to frame this church as solely combating social injustice—that would be a view of the Azusa community that goes against its own self-understanding. Rather, its religious life promoted and cultivated just and caring relationships, which included yet moved beyond quests for structural justice. This church's embodiment of intimacy, communion, tenderness, friendship, joy, belonging, *and* justice in the midst of white racism and a hypercapitalist society exemplifies how black churches contested the racist machinations of white Christianity and of the broader American capitalist project.

This book explores how Azusa's religious life embodied a critique of America's racial-capitalist order. Although the political economy in which the Azusa Revival was situated has received scant attention, Azusa was responsive to problems of racial capitalism in the United States. The community rejected the commodifying and exploitative practices of American industrial expansionism through its religious life. By foregrounding American economic expansionism and the racial logics that undergirded such economic practices at the turn of the twentieth century, I illuminate the countercultural forms of political agency that Azusa embodied in response to America's distorted ways of life. *Azusa Reimagined* turns to sermons, testimonials of Azusa participants, newspaper articles, historical records on the world fairs and expositions at the turn of the twentieth century, and religious pamphlets in order to reconstruct the American industrial world and its appropriation of religious language such as Pentecost to legitimate colonial worldviews and underwrite capitalist interventionism around the world. Through these diverse sources, one recognizes that the Azusa movement attacked and countered the distorted market and racist values that much of white Protestantism gladly embraced. It was suspicious of the American state and its gospels of segregation and material prosperity. It critiqued racialized conceptions of citizenship that guided American markets. Azusa confronted the erotic life of racial capitalism through its liturgical and sacramental forms of life.

The present book makes this history of racial capitalism more explicit and commends Azusa's religious life as a form of social *and* economic critique. Members of Azusa demanded a different vision of justice and belonging than the economic and racial fragmentation they witnessed everywhere around them. Only through uncovering the ecology of racial capitalism can one understand the transgressive agency the Azusa community embodied and why the political agency of religious communities (such as Christian churches) remains essential to imagining more radical democratic futures.

Apostolic Faith Mission

How did such a radically subversive religious community emerge? Apostolic Faith Mission was a church that started as a Bible study group in the home of Ruth and Richard Asberry on Bonnie Brae Street in Los Angeles. A small group of janitors and washerwomen, along with itinerant evangelist William Seymour, used to gather to pray and study the Bible in the kitchen and parlor of this home. Most spectacularly, they gathered on the porch of this home to sing, shout, and dance, often drawing crowds of people to view what was transpiring. Passersby stopped to catch a glimpse of and talk about this eccentric group of people who claimed to have a message from God.

In the beginning, it was a few black residents who gathered in the home and around the porch to witness the unusual yet intriguing activity transpiring. Eventually, whites and Mexicans began coming too, wanting to witness what was described by the media and onlookers as a curious spiritual movement. The crowds soon became too large for the Asberrys' home, a reality most acutely experienced when the porch collapsed after an evening of singing and dancing![1] The group of leaders decided to rent a small abandoned stable on nearby Azusa Street. In time, they converted it into a church, and called it the Apostolic Faith Mission, appointing Seymour as the pastor. In a few short years, this church and its message reached thousands of people and birthed a movement known as the Azusa Street Revival.[2]

Apostolic Faith Mission was a deeply symbolic name. Similar to the ancient church in the book of the Acts of the Apostles, this church community understood itself as reclaiming the acts of the Apostles of Christ that marked the early church. These acts included healing and deliverance from all kinds of illness, the gathering of different peoples and cultures in true peace, and evangelizing the message of Jesus Christ as Savior of all people.[3] Of particular interest to Apostolic Faith Mission was the story of Pentecost, which was the foundation of the early church's work. According to this biblical story in Acts 2, all the disciples of Jesus were gathered in the Upper Room in Jerusalem after Jesus' death and resurrection. He had instructed them to wait there to receive power for the mission that lay ahead of them. Acts 2 describes what happens. The Holy Spirit descended upon all those in the room and they began speaking in tongues so that all those gathered outside the room throughout the streets of Jerusalem could hear the message of salvation and healing in their own language.

This image of tongues being spoken as the evidence of God's power for Christian mission would be a defining feature for the Azusa community. Moreover, this divine encounter at Pentecost was about the miracle of radical community, groups previously divided now experiencing a desire to be with and for each other.[4] This faith community wanted to reclaim this Apostolic mandate for modern times and believed that what was needed in the church and nation more broadly was a contemporary experience of Pentecost. The renewed vision of Pentecost was what animated the Apostolic Faith Mission. It was what they believed would purify the personal and social sins of churches and initiate the end-times revival and the return of Jesus that would culminate history itself.

While Azusa was definitely a church marked by eschatological forms of spirituality, it *equally* embodied subversive forms of religious and political agency. This community understood Christian faith to be enacted and lived out through transgressing and subverting the racist, sexist, and classist *habitus* of American culture and economy at the dawn of the twentieth century. A number of religious and theological scholars such as Amos Yong, David Daniels, Cheryl Sanders, Gaston Espinosa, Cecil Robeck, Walter Hollenwager, Iain MacRoberts, Nimi Wariboko, and Estrelda Alexander have already captured how Azusa challenged the racism, sexism, and classism of churches and broader society.[5] In terms of Azusa's interracial vision, it was Seymour who pastored thousands of white Christians in a nationally segregated atmosphere within the first year of this revival. This revival was seen as subversive to the dominant racial reasoning of the day. One white Pentecostal minister, Charles Parham, said that he found white women in the arms of "salivating black men" at the altar when he arrived at Azusa a most disturbing scene for him. Black men could get lynched for even looking at a white woman, but Azusa was a context in which black men laid hands on white women in order to receive the Spirit, scandalous practices for this era.[6]

In terms of emancipatory gender norms, when the congregation organized itself, the twelve elders comprised five men and seven women.[7] The barriers of gender were very briefly overcome at Azusa, which contrasted to much of Baptist and Methodist tradition. Womanist scholar Cheryl Gilkes notes that many Baptist and Methodist women left their denominations and joined holiness and Pentecostal communities that participated or came out of the Azusa movement precisely because of Azusa's equal treatment of women as legitimate preachers and pastors.[8] To be fair in describing the founding of Azusa, I note that black women guided and birthed Seymour's religious experience of the Spirit, making them equal cofounders of Azusa with him, a womanist–black feminist interpretation I discuss in this text. Although the institutionalization of the Azusa Revival gave way to a number of Pentecostal denominations that over time reinscribed patriarchal logics (such as not ordaining women), the early Azusa congregation was more egalitarian in its approach to leadership, welcoming women to lead in record numbers.

Azusa was also a unique moment in the American religious landscape in terms of class, as most major religious movements (e.g., the Great Awakenings) in America certainly included black people but were not started and led by poor black people, as Azusa was. In its beginning years, this revival's embodiment of communion, longing, and belonging across racial, gender, and class loyalties can be contrasted to the dominant ecclesial and juridical institutions of the day that strictly upheld racial apartheid and class division.

Various biographers and testimonial narratives speak about Azusa "washing away the color line" in the "blood of Christ" through black, white, Latino/a, Irish, Italian, Armenian, Russian, African, and other people worshiping and living together in radical community.[9] For certain, the statement that Azusa washed the color line away in the blood of Christ is highly contested, even among those writing about the meaning(s) of Azusa in 1906. In this book, I do not seek to offer a hagiography of Azusa. Although it was deeply confrontational to American racist and capitalist culture through its religious and communal practices, moments of racial and gender strife nonetheless bubbled up within the life of this movement. Azusa was complex and deeply liberative within ecclesial and social spaces, *yet* as the revival continued it also unfortunately reinforced oppressive ways of being.[10]

I interpret this church community as deeply engaged in a form of political agency that is actualized in and through its religious life, which directly challenges modern American political and economic institutions because these institutions failed to provide democracy, equal citizenship, and equity. Although Azusa members did not formally try to overturn racist laws, those associated with the Azusa Revival did embody a religious agency that defied the white social, political, and cultural ethos and order of the era (e.g., through challenging formal and informal segregation laws as well as rejecting a lack of gender parity in church and society). However, some white scholars describe Azusa's religious life as primarily oriented toward otherworldly dimensions. They focus on its practices of speaking in tongues or healing to the exclusion of its embodiment of a subversive community that stands as an affront to the segregated cultural norms of that era.[11]

It is also rare for black religious scholars to view early Pentecostalism (as seen during the beginning days of Azusa) as a revolutionary example of black religion. They tend to regard Pentecostalism as a religious mechanism of coping and adaptation, not as a religious and political protest movement. This assumption is not always the case. As I will discuss throughout this book, Azusa's early religious life is grounded in and fashioned by slave religious practices. These slave religious practices not only provided spiritual transcendence for the enslaved but also protested and talked back to white Christian ideologies and practices that denied blacks their humanity. These practices would be defended and preserved by poor black leaders who founded Azusa, although white communities and educated black communities described these practices as pagan, primitive, and demonic. Through the spiritual practices of the enslaved, Azusa's religious life brought whites, blacks, Mexicans, Chinese, and other ethnic groups together, demonstrating a radical togetherness often not possible within the broader society. White supremacy and its racial capitalist apparatus no longer set the terms of community for blacks and other racial groups associated with the Apostolic Faith Mission. Instead, Azusa fashioned its own terms, and slave religious practices provided the *relational context* out of which various groups that were socialized to distrust and hate each other experienced radical communion and belonging. Black Marxist scholar Cedric Robinson is right that "the black radical tradition in its diversity insinuated itself quite unexpectantly" into many cultural, political and religious terrains "such as Pentecostalism in the early 20th century."[12]

Reading Azusa as a revolutionary example of black religion expands how we think about black revolutionary religious forms. Descriptions about what constitutes black revolutionary religion often rely too much on binary categories such as prophetic/priestly, radical/accommodationist, protest/adaptation. Such readings treat the Nation of Islam (NOI) under the influence of Malcolm X as exemplary of what black protest religion is and/or should be, for instance. They exalt its attention to the celebration of black power and its stinging indictment of white racist structures as being what black revolution requires. However, any study of NOI reveals it to be a complex and contradictory religion, embodying both radical and conservative elements of religiosity and social agency. The NOI was not exactly egalitarian on questions of gender parity but it attacked American racism without apology. While this religious group directly critiqued American racism, it did not actively address institutional injustices because it did not believe that the American state could ever act justly and remedy them (prior to the leadership of Malcolm X). Hence, the possibility of structural transformation was simply something many NOI leaders did not embrace. Even after Malcolm X left the NOI, he was aware that part of what made black religion revolutionary was a whole range of experiences such as black joy, celebration of black beauty, the possibility of solidarity between blacks and among different ethnic groups, justice, and more.

Black Christian traditions have upheld black liberation theology as the quintessential form of black protest religion. Certainly, liberationist scholars like James Cone were deeply concerned about questions of protest and justice. But Cone was equally concerned with questions of freedom, joy, communion, and transcendence.[13] Although black liberation theology has been exemplary in showing that racism is a theological problem that demands attention, it has failed, at particular historical moments, to think radically about questions of gender and sexual justice as well as to offer substantive critiques of American capitalism, which black womanist theology and black queer theology by contrast have made efforts to address.

I want Azusa to be read similarly—as a complex and at times contradictory religious movement that embodied forms of protest yet also remained preoccupied with other experiences of human transcendence. For like all black religions, Azusa's complex relationship to the black protest tradition invites exploration.

Azusa Reimagined: Why Racial Capitalism Matters

In discussing the Azusa Revival in this text, foregrounding racial capitalism as a primary analytic is central. I take my cue from black Marxist scholar Cedric Robinson and postcolonial scholar Gargi Bhattacharyya in discussing racial capitalism. For Robinson, racial capitalism is an acknowledgment that race has been capitalism's "epistemology, its ordering principle, its organizing structure, its moral authority, its economy of justice, commerce and power."[14] The development, organization, and eventual expansion of Western capitalism pursued essentially racial directions along with its cultural and social ideology (i.e., racial classifications and categories).[15] To this, Bhattacharyya adds that racial capitalism describes a "set of techniques and a formation, and in both registers the disciplining and ordering of bodies through gender and sexuality and dis/ability and age flow through what is happening."[16] When I speak of racial capitalism, I am referring to how modern capitalism bolsters itself through the logics of race, including how these logics are manifested in and through gendered and sexual identities. Racial capitalism, specifically in the United States, is the belief that American capitalist institutions arise from historical and contemporary practices of racialization, racial exclusion, and racist boundary marking in all of its gendered, sexual, and class dimensions.[17]

Moreover, racial capitalism "operates both through the exercise of coercive power and through the mobilization of desire."[18] As I will discuss, part of the story of racial capitalism in the United States is about the expropriation and exploitation of black labor and lives in the emergence and development of capitalism from slavery through the industrial period. The coercive power of race in the development of slave markets and industrial markets shaped how people of the African diaspora experienced modern capitalism: as a context of domination and oppression.

Yet another part of the story of racial capitalism in the United States is about how it deliberately cultivates "regimes of longing." These regimes of longing are not only about how people are forced to participate in racialized economic arrangements that place them on the social and economic margins of society; they are also about how people rush to be included in the cultural modes and ways of life (re)produced by racial capitalism.[19] In Chapter 4, I substantively describe the erotic life of racial capitalism, which seduced, not only elite and poor whites to participate in practices of whiteness, but also educated blacks to believe that their assimilation and acceptance into the white structures of society depended upon their ability to be productive capitalist subjects. Some black communities truly believed that their human worth could only be attained through their absorption into capitalist development, consumerism, and wealth. Unfortunately, racial capitalism operates both through coercion and desire.

Certainly arguing for the essential racial logic of modern capitalism challenges the common interpretation that the emergence of modern capitalism was a negation of early feudal and racial orders (in particular European mercantilism and American slavery) that depended on class and/or racial logics. Modern capitalism transcends these particular racial or class ideologies and practices in favor of color-blind and classless modes of production and exchange that are oriented toward economic efficiency and profit for all. However, this presumed objective description of modern capitalism ignores how Western capitalism was less a negation (destruction) of feudalist and slave orders than an extension of these social and racial relations into the larger tapestry of the modern world's political and capitalist contexts.[20]

Robinson invites us into a more critical and open way of thinking about the emergence of capitalism in Europe and the Americas. As early as the thirteenth century in Europe, he reminds us, there were already burgeoning ethnic divisions of economic activity, ethnic logics that would be used in the formation of modern racial capitalist institutions. Although Robinson acknowledges that race was not understood then in the scientific way it would be understood by the eighteenth century, the role played by imagined ethnic differences in developing economic and market resources would be present nonetheless. For instance, the social basis of European civilization formed between the Romans and what they referred to as barbarians who were beyond the reach of Roman law and morality. The vast majority of these barbarians were North Africans, Italians, and Poles who came to metropolitan France looking for work.[21] These people were assimilated into society as slave labor, which was a critical basis for production.[22] By the Middle Ages, forms of economic life differentiated and exaggerated these regional, sub-cultural, and dialectical differences into racial ones. The "Slavs" (Slavic-speaking Eastern Europeans) as well as North Africans became the "natural slaves," the ethnic (racial) inferiors who could be exploited for economic ends.[23] Medieval English religious devotees even recorded dreams in which the devil appeared as a "blacked moore," or an "Ethiope."[24] This was part of the theological vocabulary of the church in Europe during the Middle Ages. These groups were seen as the barbarians and their ethnic differences were later used to form the category of slave within expanding economic production. In short, the racialization (in a loose sense of the term) of migrant labor was already present in Europe, through the ethnic/racial marking of Africans and less desirable European immigrants. With capitalist expansionism by the sixteenth century onward, peoples of the Two-Thirds World began to fill this expanding "slave" category. Within Catholic and Protestant theological discourse, satanic representations of the African gained momentum, representations that portrayed the African as beastly, dumb, and essentially animal labor,[25] and it was this trend that eventually legitimated European and American slavery and shaped and cultivated early industrial capitalism. One can see that racial logic was not a modern production that simply emerged in the eighteenth century. Robinson shows how this racial-capitalist logic, whose antecedents go back to the Middle Ages, was appropriated at the dawn of industrialization in Europe and the Americas.

Robinson has a global understanding of racial capitalism and shows why modern capitalism is *not* a complete break with the racialized logic of slave or feudal orders but a reshaping of this logic for new capitalist ends in the modern era. What he doesn't do is help us to understand the deep *gendering* of racial capitalism. I argue that modes of reproductive labor (here reproductive labor refers to *everything* that is needed to remake human life) are often translated into racialized conceptions of economy.[26] For instance, the story of American capitalist development has been one about black women who have washed the dishes, made the beds, cooked the food, and raised their white master's children (and their own children) from slavery onward. Beginning with slave economies through early industrialization, racial capitalism has depended on the bodies and reproductive labor of black women to serve political and economic ends. As black women's reproductive labor was expropriated to make plantations increasingly profitable, black women's bodies were also monetized within the domestic sphere to make possible the reproduction of capital and profit in early industrial America. Black women's reproductive labor (washing, cleaning, nursing, etc.) was about the business of reproducing everyday life within the circuits of racial capitalism in the United States from slavery through industrialization.

The reality of gendered labor within a racialized economy helps one grasp more deeply capitalism's shadowy underside with respect to working-class black women. The violent expropriation of black women's bodies and labor reveals how racial capitalism moves in and through gendered and sexual identities. Most important, the vicious positioning of black women's reproductive activity within modern capitalism allows us to see how these women resisted capitalism's objectification and commodification of their very bodies. They were vocal about speaking out against early capitalist structures. As discussed in Chapter 3, I will show how racial capitalism appears in these gendered ways and how black women embodied resistance through their forms of religious agency.

One cannot discern the emancipatory political agency of Azusa without substantively attending to this racialized economic ecology in which this church-turned-movement resided. Most scholarship on this religious revival tends to undertheorize America's system of racial capitalism. This book intervenes and makes this context explicit, showing the diverse ways in which Azusa's religious life responded to the evils of racial capitalism. To highlight Azusa's religious and political agency is to critique what has been at the heart of American capitalist history: the racialization of labor exploitation, the unequal distribution of income and wealth based on racial classifications, the gendering of racial capitalism, and the racist theologies and practices of white Christianity. All of these elements are intertwined and have produced capitalist domination in the U.S. society out of which Azusa responds.

There is another reason why uncovering racial capitalism matters to exploring the religious and political agency of Azusa. Azusa's religious life can be read as a form of social criticism in relation to American democracy under racial capitalism, which generated states of cruel optimism. Drawing on philosopher Lauren Berlant's definition, a relation of cruel optimism "exists when something you desire is actually an obstacle to your flourishing. It might involve food, or a kind of love; it might be a fantasy of the good life, or a political project."[27] Most important, the object you desire "promises to induce in you an improved way of being."[28]

I will demonstrate how the American democratic project shaped by racial capitalism created such relations of cruel optimism. Although the United States promised equality and equity for blacks at the turn of the twentieth century, racial capitalism prevented blacks from democratic access to the good life. To them, American democracy often felt like a fantasy, offering things like upward mobility, job opportunity, and political and economic equality, but not delivering on them. Some black communities' uncritical embrace of industrial progress and rabid consumerism was actually an impediment to their flourishing because those very same industrial processes depended upon the dehumanization, expropriation, and unequal treatment of black labor and lives. The desire among educated black communities to participate in America's racial capitalist state reinforced the very conditions of black subjugation. Hence, the American democratic project so profoundly shaped by racial capitalism generated cruel optimism for blacks, demonstrating that their quest for American capitalist success (as savior) was often an impediment to their flourishing.

Azusa's religious life and political agency can be understood against this backdrop of cruel optimism. The life of the Azusa community gives us a different account of the political, rejecting the American democratic project fashioned by racial capitalism. Within relations of cruel optimism, many precarious communities "invent new rhythms of living, that can congeal into norms, forms, and institutions."[29] They manage, in creative and life-giving ways, the incoherence of their lives against the backdrop of how they imagine their lives might be. Most important, such vulnerable communities attempt to maintain their sense of identity, authenticity, and humanity within the uncertain, contradictory relations of cruel optimism. The community of Azusa fashioned new rhythms and ways of being through its religious life that challenged these relations, which also meant detaching from the capitalist "democratic" state as the optimistic object that so many vulnerable populations (such as black communities) believed would grant them justice and human fulfillment. Instead, Azusa was an intimate public "that organize[d] life without threading through dominant political institutions."[30] This community's project of democratic world-building was not in service to the political ends of the American state, shaped and funded by racial capitalism. Azusa knew that American democracy presented a cluster of promises that depended on the expropriation of black life, which impeded the flourishing of their communities.

Azusa therefore rejected the idea that the American democratic state could save them. We see this in the materials (sermons, articles in the Apostolic newsletter, etc.) of William Seymour, who was pastor of the Azusa church community, or by reviewing the economic practices of this early church community. Such materials and practices show clearly that this church community critiqued American-style democracy because the latter was deeply wedded to racialized capitalism. The community understood that early American capitalism depended upon racist classifications as a way to exploit labor, and that this impeded democratic flourishing among vulnerable groups like African Americans. Attention to this racialized economic ecology and Azusa's rejection of cruel optimism invites a transformed vision of democratic politics. Azusa offers a more radical vision of democratic politics, one not trapped in the existence of racial capitalism and its inability to foster communities of human belonging.

The Book's Flow

My argument—that Azusa's religious life was a form of critique of America's system of racial capitalism—unfolds in three parts. First, I investigate how the Azusa Revival of 1906 was not the only community employing the biblical language of Pentecost. There were many similar visions of Pentecost. Chapter 1 explores the American capitalist vision of Pentecost near the turn of the twentieth century. In particular, I retrieve the stories of two world fairs, the Philadelphia World Fair of 1876 and the Chicago Columbian Exposition of 1893, because of the religious vision of Pentecost they explicitly articulated in talking about America as a future cosmopolitan utopia. The American idea of Pentecost was married to a form of white nationalistic industrial capitalism. I therefore interpret the political character of the Azusa Revival within this broader white nationalist discourse on Pentecost that emerged near the turn of the twentieth century. Chapter 2 turns to how Azusa asserted its religio-political agency against this capitalist backdrop, primarily by contesting Evangelical and market orthodoxies. I describe what sits at the center of Azusa's experience: slave religious practices. Such practices at Azusa challenged white Evangelical orthodoxy, which described this kind of black religiosity as demonic, primitive, and savagely wild. Through slave religious practices, the Azusa community contested how white Evangelical orthodoxy participated in the American capitalist process of treating black bodies as commodified property and human excess. Moreover, Azusa challenged the market orthodoxies of early capitalism through its rejection of a consumeristic "moneyed" eschaton that guided white and educated black churches alike.

In this book's second part, I will delve deeper into *how* Azusa's religious life is a form of racial and economic critique. In Chapter 3, I explore how although black women domestic workers were treated as disposable within the matrices of American political economy, they became the figures that ignited and shaped the Azusa movement. It is important to highlight the religious leadership and cultural practices of black women domestic workers who were central to Azusa yet were treated as insignificant within American capitalist processes. Black women were not mere participants at Azusa; they were central to its founding and shaping, proving that they were subjects and not merely objects of the rich white elite or black patriarchal contexts. Chapter 4 explores how Azusa's liturgical and sacramental forms of religious life challenge the erotic life of racialized capitalism. Queer theorists have focused on how capitalist processes and practices produce and manufacture erotic desires. Within America's growing industrial economy, intimate and erotic lives were commodified, assigned value, commercialized, and packaged for consumption. American capitalism thrived (and thrives) off the erotic life of racism, as the nation's market machinery depended upon particular kinds of white racial bonding and belonging to thrive. However, Azusa's erotic patterns of intimacy and communion across racial, gender, and class differences—what I refer to as erotic fugitivity—challenged these patterns of white racial bonding and belonging that were in service to the market.

In the final part of this book I rethink Azusa's politics of hope. Azusa did not place hope in the state. For this community, the state could not save them. Azusa embodied a nonstatist idea of political agency, most notably seen through how these parishioners embodied citizenship as a radical practice of human belonging rather than a practice of racial or capitalist loyalty. Chapter 5 explores how Azusa embodied a sweeping critique of American democracy under racial capitalism, challenging how American political institutions ordered common life.

This chapter seeks not only a complex range of ways to understand the relationship between ecclesial and political life that exceeds the horizon of the state and American capitalism; it also shows how Azusa's apocalyptic sensibilities rethink the political within and beyond the American capitalist state.

The final chapter, Chapter 6, suggests how religious communities might rethink the modes and moods of democratic belonging for today in the wake of Azusa's legacy. Azusa's religious life not only offers a radical critique of early modern racial capitalism but also a way for contemporary religious communities to envision democratic practices of belonging against the backdrop of neoliberal capitalism's deep racial divisions and material inequalities. A large part of cultivating democratic practices of belonging involves embracing a *political moodiness* about current practices of American democracy. Azusa was moody about democratic life. It held with suspicion America's cluster of democratic promises. This chapter argues that we must practice "grave attending" (in the words of religious scholar Karen Bray) to those trapped within the demonic circuits of racial capitalism in order to cultivate political moodiness. Part of practicing grave attending is acknowledging the political moodiness of those who continue to suffer under racial capitalism and how such moodiness enables us to envisage new modes of democratic belonging not beholden to racialized structures of capital.

The pages ahead offer a creative interpretation of a church that fostered a radical movement, a movement that continues to shape religious life around the world today. This is a story about a group of people with subversive beginnings, who imagined an otherwise future of care, communion, justice, and belonging within the racist machinations of early American capitalism. It is a story that is long overdue.

1 CAPITALIST VISIONS
OF PENTECOST

THE *NEW YORK TIMES* CHRONICLED one man's reaction to the spectacular arrival of the Philadelphia World Fair of 1876: "He was a young man, evidently just fresh from some interior village. He was naturally no fool, but it could be plainly seen that he knew next to nothing of men or of the world, and that his visit to the world's fair was the crowning event in his quiet life."[1] The fair had a startling number of things to see: large scientific exhibitions; contraptions that demonstrated a global technological future; expositions on world peace through showcasing world religions; and educational booths that allowed one to meet people of different cultures from faraway lands. This fair was not like any other event. Its cultural, scientific, and commercial exhibits had the power to change minds, from youngest to oldest. It told a story about a new age of health and prosperity for the United States that was quickly emerging. One could sense the groundswell of excitement etched on the faces of each visitor. Yet, this fair was not an arbitrary emergence. Although this fair sought to commemorate the centennial of the Declaration of Independence, its arrival also coincided with economic and cultural turbulence in America.

The country was experiencing drastic flux and change. The industrial depression and class conflict in urban cities had compelled leaders to seek ways to foster economic certainty for everyday citizens. Cities were becoming urban areas of cultural diversity, as black migrants and immigrants moved North and

West seeking better opportunities to flourish. Yet because most of the United States was dominated by white Protestant values, whites interpreted this burgeoning cultural pluralism as a threat. Moreover, black protest over the failures of Reconstruction in the South following the Civil War led to a sense of racial fear, causing white leaders to ask how they could preserve the white racial order while appearing to affirm that slavery was a thing of the past.

Revivalists, novelists, business tycoons, and political leaders all had different ideas about what was needed to move America into a progressive future. The prophecies and speculations abounded. Some Christian revivalists predicted that Jesus would come again to establish his reign and bring all societal chaos to an end. Some novelists called the country back to its Puritanical roots of love for nation and neighbor above all else. Most white political and economic leaders began looking for ways to manage these various shifts by reasserting white Protestant morals and intensifying support for capitalist endeavors. At a time of major conflict, the country needed a moral blueprint that could offer material and cultural certainty for its citizens.

One way in which white political, religious, and business leaders attempted to offer cultural and economic certainty at such a time was through the creation of world fairs or expositions in major cities, like the one the *New York Times* described in Philadelphia. These expositions not only promised to create unprecedented profits for the American economy but also to inaugurate a cosmopolitan utopia. Of their number, I am interested in exploring two world fairs in particular—the Philadelphia Fair of 1876 and the Chicago Columbian Exposition of 1893—because they gesture toward a religious vision of Pentecost in talking about America as a future nation of multicultural belonging.

One might assume that Christian churches have been the only groups to employ the biblical language of Pentecost, but this is not so. Nor was the Azusa Revival of 1906 the only community employing the language of Pentecost in envisioning America's future. There were many visions of Pentecost. This chapter explores the American capitalist vision of Pentecost near the turn of the twentieth century. For one can only understand the subversive character of the Azusa Revival when one turns to America's national appropriation of "Pentecost" language in morally legitimating its racist, capitalist, and colonial projects. The American idea of Pentecost functioned as a form of white nationalism tied to industrial capitalism. To be read correctly, the Azusa Revival must be situated within this broader white nationalist discourse on Pentecost that emerged near the turn of the twentieth century.

The World Fairs and the New Pentecost

In response to the prevailing uncertainty, white political leaders decided to draw upon the biblical discourse of Pentecost in underwriting a new business venture—that of world fairs and expositions. These fairs would capture the capitalist dreams and moral order white middle-class citizens desperately desired. White leaders saw the creation of world fairs as a way to narrate what America's future could be through preserving and building upon its Protestant racial order and capitalist achievements. White leaders hoped these fairs would provide answers for the nation, especially urban cities, on how citizens should deal with cultural pluralism, the "Negro question," class division, and industrial disparities.

The Chicago Columbian Exposition of 1893, for instance, was partially responding to class tensions, most notably manifested in the Haymarket riot of 1886.[2] The Haymarket riot was one of the bloodiest labor riots that occurred toward the end of the nineteenth century in response to the corporate exploitation of workers, especially immigrant laborers. Ironically, investors were experiencing a golden decade of profits in 1886. It was reported that Chicago's "net value of goods produced by [its] leading industries multiplied twenty-seven times, ten times faster than the average yearly wage."[3] Unfortunately, workers who toiled in factories and railroads under poor working conditions and wages did not experience this gain in wealth. Beginning on May 1, workers went on strike, demanding eight-hour work days, among other humane conditions.[4] They would no longer accept their subjugated economic position. Tensions were high between owners and workers in Chicago. As railroad titan George Pullman remarked to his wife, anxieties intensified during the strike, which brought factories and railway stations almost to a standstill.[5]

Three days later, the strike was broken in the most confrontational way. The *Chicago Daily Tribune* captured this "night of terror."[6] On May 4, around fifteen hundred workers, mostly immigrant laborers, rallied in Haymarket Square to denounce the police for killing some strikers the previous day. Known for his charisma, August Spies, the nation's leading German socialist, called the meeting to order and introduced a renowned labor activist and agitator, Albert Parsons, who spoke for an hour.[7] Near the end of the rally, about six hundred people were left, primarily immigrants who publicly declared themselves to be at war with the government, especially police who were merciless with immigrant workers.[8] A police force of 176 marched into the square and demanded that rioters disperse.

As the first division of police moved toward the crowd, a bomb was detonated and the newspaper reported that "the anarchists and rioters poured a shower of bullets into the police."[9] The newspaper reported that at least fifty police officers had been wounded, several were near death, and one of them, Mathias Degan, died in the arms of his fellow officer.[10] A street station close to Haymarket Square was filled with wounded civilians as well. White affluent classes blamed this violent clash on the protestors, who were bent on disrupting social order and unleashing anarchist terror. The *Tribune* called for severe action against those who rallied in the square, and indeed later in the year several were found guilty and hanged. Moreover, European immigrants that had previously been welcomed were viewed with more suspicion, and this affected immigration policy.[11]

The labor activists themselves contested this account of the riot in the *Tribune*. They wanted to have their say. To the immigrant workers, those who fought police in the Haymarket square were heroic martyrs who were committed to working-class emancipation.[12] Immigrant protestors in Haymarket viewed their actions as self-defense, as police were the first ones to begin advancing on their peaceful assembly. Immigrant protestors also felt that the violence they (and their families) often incurred at the hands of patrolmen (for challenging labor practices) was inhumane. Many workers who assembled claimed that some fringe element had set off the bomb, although law enforcement and Chicago's white middle class blamed the protestors.[13] These conflicting accounts of what actually happened at Haymarket Square reveal the deep class warfare urban cities were experiencing in America's burgeoning industrial landscape.

These deepening divisions needed some kind of healing. In part, the Chicago World Fair would be an initial response to such conflict in order to shore up certainty that economic and political freedoms would be a reality for all, including immigrant workers. Thus the Chicago Fair tried to model a vision of wealth and abundance for all through industrial and technological progress. Leaders of the fair claimed that they wanted to restructure America by making everyday citizens feel part of this restructuring.[14] The *Chicago Tribune* wrote that a more equitable country would be accomplished "by the average citizen—the plain, sturdy, self-reliant, ambitious man, who is known as the typical American."[15] *Cosmopolitan* magazine likewise assured its readers that the fair was for "average people . . . not for the few at the top or the for the helpless lot in the gutter, but for the Average."[16] Everyday working citizens were told that they were the reason for such expositions. This fair would give working- and middle-class populations a vision of how they could better their own lives through industrial activity, thus fulfilling their own destinies. As I will discuss later in this chapter, although it was in fact the white economic elite who primarily benefited from these fairs, continual advertisement told the working-class masses that they were the primary benefactors of these important events.

Architects of these world fairs also imagined that these events would instruct citizens on how to engage the race question. The fact was that after the Civil War white leaders were unclear on the role of blacks in America. What would be the extent of their freedoms? How might white society maintain its racial order in light of slavery's abolition? Two decades after the Civil War, these fairs sought to reinscribe the racial hierarchy in a way that *appeared* to affirm black freedom. Although Reconstruction ultimately had been a failure for black communities in the South, the Reconstruction period did give black communities their first senators, congressional leaders, business owners, lawyers, and more. In light of the constitutional emancipation of blacks, white leaders found that erecting racist institutions was more complicated. The world fairs became a way to reshape America's racial institutions. The expositions modeled for blacks the kind of role they could play within America's revised racial pyramid. The fairs reinforced a particular kind of Negro who would be compliant with segregation, a point to which I will return.

White leaders who sponsored these fairs believed that white cultural renewal and capitalist reformation would make America a nation of spiritual renewal. In their marketing materials, these expositions described America as a "New Jerusalem," a spiritual center of moral and political reform. The term "fair" derives from the Latin *feria* or "holy day."[17] And indeed, America's world fairs were treated as religious celebrations and holy days. At the Philadelphia Fair of 1876, a local journalist referred to the crowd of visitors as a "modernized Babel without its guilt or folly."[18] The journalist invoked the biblical imagery of Babel, a mythical city with many primitive languages that descends into cultural confusion and moral chaos. Whereas this Babel is the city without order and civilization, the journalist calls the Philadelphia fair a *modern* Babel in the sense that the "familiar and vigorous Anglo-Saxon" language could be heard and distinguished from all the more inferior forms of human language such as the "guttural of the barbaric Aboriginese or the sing-sing jargon of the 'heathen Chinese.'"[19] In other words, this American exposition represented a "modern Babel" *cured* through American (Anglo-Saxon) culture and progress. The Philadelphia fair and its narration of European and American achievements in religion, technology, the arts, and economy situated American progress as the sign of civilization and the *spiritual* cure for cultural and moral confusion.

Describing the Philadelphia fair as representative of a modern Babel was important because it also implicitly invoked the biblical image of Pentecost. American cities were a Babel of cultures and customs that reeked of spiritual and moral disorder. While biblical imagery of Babel was marked by confusing languages that people could not understand, Pentecost was marked by languages that could be comprehended perfectly by native communities. Babel was interpreted as a narrative of cultural confusion and chaos while Pentecost was a narrative of cultural unity and order, bringing different people together across a Jewish (national) diaspora. Within Christian scriptures, Pentecost marked a new community of spiritual order, reversing the curse of Babel. Similar to the ancient Christian community of Pentecost, America (so this narrative went) would usher in its own Pentecost, fostering order and civilization out of cultural chaos. A new nation of unity, undergirded by wealth and abundance, is what the Philadelphia fair imagined itself as modeling.

The Chicago Columbian Exposition of 1893 speaks about America's future more explicitly through the language of Pentecost. Although the Chicago fair was partly in response to the Haymarket riot, it was also established to commemorate Columbus's "discovery" of the "New World." Investors, politicians, architects, and religious leaders framed Columbus's work as "discovery" rather than plunder, which justified all future American expansionism. The Columbian Exposition would become "an illustrated encyclopedia of civilization."[20] This fair brought together leading authorities to discuss religion, labor, women's rights, and other important social and cultural concerns of the day. It also demonstrated the power of capitalist markets in America's future. And it reinforced the creed of American progress through capitalist advancement as the key to American wealth and well-being.

The Columbian fair had a number of international congresses. One congress was the World Parliament of Religions. This World Parliament comprised the major faiths from around the world with the sole purpose of cultivating and sponsoring unity and peace among different religious traditions. This engagement among world religions some dubbed "The New Pentecost."[21] In part, its creators referred to the Columbian Exposition and its Parliament of World Religions as the New Pentecost because they imagined they would gather back together diverse tongues and tribes that were scattered throughout the world.[22] They imagined the Kingdom of God and a New Jerusalem in America happening through technological and scientific progress. Christian visitors saw the in-gathering of various nations and cultures and related this gathering to the ancient day of Pentecost.

The Parliament desired to develop a unified global faith that reflected the tenets of Western Christianity with a scientific and market twist. The elite leaders from European Christian countries were given a more direct role in this Parliament than non-Western religious leaders. As religious scholar Harvey Cox states, "American theologians have always been taught to look to Marburg or Tübingen for [their] inspiration in interpreting the Christian faith."[23] Even though world religions do not interpret history through Christian categories, the Parliament of Religions asserted its religious vision of a global society in White Protestant Christian terms. George Townsend, a columnist of *Chicago Tribune*, stated, "The motives and facts around this exposition are the confessions of faith of a new dispensation."[24] In part, Townsend was referring to the tenets of capitalist faith and the idea of evolution which fueled the fair. But there was also a new Christian dispensation being articulated, marked by cultural unity among diverse peoples. The symbol of Pentecost represented this cultural unity and was appropriated as a national narrative about who America could be in the midst of cultural pluralism and deep disagreement.

Similar to the Chicago fair, those who attended the Philadelphia exposition implicitly gestured toward the image of Pentecost. Episcopal Bishop William Bacon Stevens of Pennsylvania expressed his desire that "people from all parts of our recently divided country will meet around the old family hearthstone of Independence Hall and pledge anew heart and hand in a social and political brotherhood never to be broken."[25] Other Philadelphia leaders spoke of gathering together in peace the diverse nations and cultures represented in America.

The image of Pentecost, of gathering the nations, was especially seen at the opening ceremonies associated with these fairs. At the Philadelphia Fair, attendees were encouraged to open their hearts and take their shoes off, because they were standing on holy ground.[26] An opening remark reminded attendees that America was God's chosen nation, a New Jerusalem from which nations around the world would learn and by which they would be led. The orchestra and choir sang and American dignitaries took their places at the head of a procession of four thousand invited dignitaries, foreign and domestic. This image of the nations and cultures gathering together in a procession manifested this New Pentecost. It encouraged people to embrace the American faith in economic progress and white cultural order.

White Colonial Visions of Pentecost

Whatever scientific and technological benefits the Chicago Fair may have provided, its vision of the New Pentecost was a gross malformation of the ancient event of Pentecost. For this fair sought to reinscribe a white colonial vision of the world. In contrast to this exposition's understanding of Pentecost, the ancient experience of Pentecost was an event that happened in the underbelly of the Roman Empire, contra colonial occupation and religious persecution. It was an event initiated by dispossessed Jews who articulated a new egalitarian community not grounded in violent hierarchies that dehumanize. Ancient Pentecost was about fashioning patterns of intimacy and belonging within an imperial context of division, fear, hatred, and despair. Pentecost sought to reverse the oppressive status quo in Rome.

The Chicago Fair did not reflect this egalitarian spirit of ancient Pentecost. Instead, it thrived on racial hierarchies and racial fear. Consider how the exposition was ideologically structured through the "White City" and "Midway Plaisance" exhibitions. This world fair had a department of ethnology, made up of scientists from the Smithsonian who wanted to demonstrate the evolutionary idea of civilization and progress through racial classification and hierarchy. White City was a group of buildings, exhibitions, and displays that depicted modern American society.[27] This idea of the modern was thoroughly Anglo-Saxon. It depicted technological, religious, cultural, political, and industrial advancements as the achievements of white Americans (and some British and French). For example, as part of the exhibitions of White City, inscriptions from the Constitution and heroic statues of white American leaders could be seen throughout the exhibitions. As a visitor gazed upon White City, America could be seen at the center of quests for global political and economic development and advancement.

White City was founded upon the Anglo-Saxon Myth. Womanist theologian Kelly Brown Douglas describes this myth as having its roots in Germany through the Roman historian Tacitus, who portrayed ancient Germans as possessing a distinctive respect for individual rights as well as a love of freedom, desires he considered to be intuitive. Tacitus's ethnological descriptions of these German tribes generated the construction of the Anglo-Saxon myth about the intellectual and moral superiority of Anglo-Saxon people. This myth would eventually make its way over to early American shores through the English reformers. These reformers believed that they were descendants of the Germanic tribes about whom Tacitus had written. America, these reformers decided, would be defined by two traits: its Anglo-Saxon character and its chosen nature as a "New Israel." It was a racial-religious construction of a morally and intellectually superior nation chosen by God. Literally, Anglo-Saxon blood would be proof of being chosen by God.[28] Thus it was that White City was referred to as the "New Jerusalem," a beautiful, utopian depiction of where America and the rest of the world needed to go. This could only happen through America's Anglo-Saxon Christian leadership.

This myth associated with White City also showed up in the prayers, speeches, and consultations associated with this fair. American Presbyterian minister and missionary Henry Harris Jessup gave a rousing speech, proclaiming that "all nations are part of God's plan," but "no nobler service has been given to any people, no nobler mission awaits any nation than that which God has given to those who speak the English tongue."[29] He suggested that those who spoke English stood on a "vantage ground of influence," as its voice "sounds throughout the nations."[30] Even North America's geographical positioning had religious implications. He stated, "a map of the world with North America in the center shows at a glance the strategic position of Great Britain and the United States . . . their invigorating climate, matchless resources, world-wide commerce . . . gives these peoples the control of the world's future and the key to its moral and ethical problems."[31] The Anglo-Saxon people of Britain and the United States were held up as moral exemplars who had the ethical solution to social, cultural, and economic problems around the world. As a result, Jessup concluded that the "highly favored Northern races" were called by God to go aid "the less favored continents of the South."[32] For him, Christ had commissioned them to free the morally and spiritually enslaved people on other continents through evangelizing them.[33]

Similar to what White City communicated, Jessup believed that Anglo-Saxon nations had a divine mission to unenlightened lands. One would think that because he cautioned Britain and the United States against capitalist greed and unrestrained attempts to profit from exploring new lands he was more amenable to respecting the humanity of non-European people. Not so. Rather, he rhetorically affirmed that non-Europeans were made in the image of God, but he subscribed to a benevolent paternalism that sought to colonize and civilize these different people groups. Civilizing such peoples and lands was part of the Divine Plan, he thought. Anglo-Saxon people had a God-given responsibility to train the religious and moral character of other nations.

This Anglo-Saxon myth was further solidified at the fair through Midway Plaisance, which was a collection of exhibitions and buildings of non-Western cultures of the world that were depicted as barbaric, heathenish people in need of civilization. Ethnologists constructed Midway based on assumptions that non-Western people were childlike and in need of American intervention and salvation. Although *Plessy v. Ferguson* had not yet been decided (legally establishing formal segregation in the South),[34] Midway provided a scientific basis for racial classification and eventually legal segregation in America despite the burgeoning black freedom struggles and influx of immigrants two decades after the Civil War.[35] The vision of a White City as a celestial future and the "depiction of the non-white world as savage were two sides of the same coin—a coin minted in the tradition of American racism, in which forbidden desires of whites were projected onto dark-skinned peoples, who consequently had to be degraded so white purity could be maintained."[36]

Midway attempted to justify why the moral, religious, and cultural practices of black migrants and immigrants needed to be feared and prohibited. Tourists often remarked that they experienced Midway as one big anthropological revelation.[37] One first encountered the primitive handicrafts and artifacts of Native American tribes and saw how technologically backward they were and why they were in need of civilization. The ethnologists gathered artifacts that represented Native American life as savage, chaotic, rude, and homely. The point of including Native American tribes was to demonstrate that these "people belonged to the intermingled wasteland of humanity's dark and stormy beginnings."[38] The Native American exhibit was only useful as a counterpoint to American progress and Anglo-Saxon dominance. Through handicrafts and artifacts, it was easier to justify the exploitation of these people in the name of American progress. As a way to emphasize Native American savagery, a tourist's visit strategically began in Midway and ended in White City, replicating the linear, evolutionary idea of progress in which America is the answer to all global cultural and economic problems.

This kind of evolutionary thinking was also reflected in the African exhibits at the Chicago Fair. Midway housed a sprawling exhibit of the Dahomeyans, the people of a vast African kingdom eventually annexed and colonized by the French. Not only did the Chicago Fair depict the Dahomeyans as bestial, for example describing their participation in war dances and cannibalism, it also literally put some of them on display, as if part of a human zoo. One journalist reported that they were there in all their "barbaric ugliness" and that they were "blacker than buried midnight and as degraded as the animals which prowl the jungles of their dark land."[39] One woman was bewildered and regretful after seeing these Africans, compelling her to ponder "the gulf between them and Emerson."[40] In short, Midway was deliberately structured to push visitors to see the need to colonize and civilize a barbarous land. Moreover, it was constructed for blatantly economic reasons. It emphasized the vast natural resources that Africa possessed but allegedly could not properly steward. Midway influenced citizens and foreigners to regard colonization not as a violent exploitation of other people and lands but as a dutiful Christian response to help such people move towards salvation and civilization. In short, colonizing these lands was part of God's providence and beneficence.

This view of the African legitimized the racist American future that architects of the Fair projected. Some felt that one could easily detect the characteristics of the American Negro in the wild African. Despite formal freedoms granted after the Civil War, blacks had to be kept within a racial hierarchy because of their "savage" heritage. Racial order was necessary for the spiritual welfare of black Americans as well as the nation's well-being. In line with such portrayals, at Midway, there were no real depictions of black Americans' advancements or contributions to the nation's past, present, or future.

Of course this was a completely dishonest depiction of non-European communities. Fair organizers perceived Africans, Native Americans, Asians such as Chinese, and black Americans as warlike, cunning, and violent in contrast to whites whom they depicted as peaceable, rational, and civilized. Consider the popular image in the white American imagination of the Wild Wild West, which stereotyped this region as a brutal, primitive, adolescent space. The narrative is that America saves and civilizes this chaotic space, fulfilling the biblical duty to have "dominion over the earth" and care for the wealth of the land. This image of the Wild West showed up at both the Chicago and Philadelphia Fairs. But this is far from the truth. Places of the Wild West like Los Angeles are not simply civilized or saved by the United States but thrown into racial disorder and violence *after* being annexed into the nation. In the white popular cultural imagination, Los Angeles is seen as quintessentially American, a melting pot of many immigrant stories made possible through American democratic principles of freedom and liberty. But this is a false narrative. Prior to American annexation, early Los Angeles was an *aberration* to the racially restrictive social order that marked most of early colonial America. It was a different social space from most of North America.

Let's consider the history of early Los Angeles that is erased at these World Fairs, demonstrating the colonial order these fairs sought to propagate. Los Angeles has a complex history of interracial community that doesn't simply begin with American democracy and economic freedom. One might travel back to the eighteenth century to witness L.A.'s long history of interracial engagement. Los Angeles began as a Spanish colony, what scholars refer to as the Western *frontera* (frontier), which included the Pacific coastal areas of Sinaloa, Sonora, and Baja, California.[41] Because most Spaniards were not willing to relocate to this frontier, this colony was primarily constituted by a substantial free black population or a population of significant African ancestry. Of the original forty-six settlers, at least twenty-six of them were part African.[42] African and mulattos were greater than 25 percent of the overall population living in these regions during the eighteenth century. Spanish reports stated that most of the soldiers on this Western frontier were mulatto.[43]

Despite the mixed-race makeup of this settlement, it was nevertheless a colony. Spain invested military and financial resources to protect it from encroachment by the English and French. The lifestyle of the residents was controlled by the Spanish Empire through its military, local governing authorities, and the Catholic church. For instance, each *poblador* (settler) had to register to live in a settlement and could not leave their village without permission from local authorities. The job of the settlers was to grow crops and raise livestock to feed soldiers in the surrounding areas. In exchange, these settlers were provided materials and supplies to survive, eventually becoming self-sufficient and able to build villages into thriving centers.[44]

Americans tend to think of early pueblo L.A. as a remote, violent, lawless, unprofitable frontier village.[45] Certainly, this frontier dealt savagely with the indigenous Native Americans who occupied this land prior to it becoming a colony of Spain.[46] But this history must be held in tension with its rich diversity and the opportunity for people of African descent to lead in ways that the rest of early colonial America forbade. This original settlement of primarily African ancestry eventually morphed into a multicultural center, as retired soldiers moved into the settlement and the residents of the pueblo L.A. engaged, intermingled, and married other residents from surrounding pueblos (nearby villages of what now would be San Diego and Santa Barbara).[47] As the population grew, the frontier became a context of commerce and exchange, eventually opening up this frontier up to engagement with the young American nation, which unfortunately transformed this settlement forever.

Spain possessed a rigid system of racial classification, placing Africans and *Indios* (Spanish Indians) at the bottom of the ethnic hierarchy. Spain restricted how high non-Spanish individuals could rise in military, social, and political circles. Yet this system did not overdetermine the forms of social life that would sprout up on this Western frontier. African and other mixed-race individuals enjoyed greater social mobility on the Western frontier of early pueblo L.A. than they would have done in Spain. For example, there is evidence supporting the upward mobility of blacks in the settlement (of early Los Angeles) through the election of Francisco Reyes, a bi-racial man who was mayor in 1793.[48]

Leaders of African or mixed ancestry were common in this early Spanish colony, in contrast to the Anglo-dominated parts of North America.[49] Spanish imperial authorities allowed Africans and biracial persons from Spain to establish clergy networks and missions, army forts, and pueblos (villages) in order to develop this colony into a flourishing center.[50] Because such ethnic groups were leaders on this frontier, they were able to live with few racial or ethnic restrictions. Although early pueblo L.A. began as a Spanish colony, it nevertheless had more relaxed racial restrictions and possibilities for upward social mobility among people of African descent than the rest of the United States.

In 1822, after the struggle for independence from Spain, settlers of early pueblo L.A. were informed that they were now part of the new nation of Mexico. The political transition from Spain to Mexico did not produce any drastic shifts in their ways of life. However, one important prohibition was established: slavery was declared illegal by Mexico's new government. This prohibition may have felt egalitarian and have helped some of the residents (particularly those of African ancestry) feel safer and in better social standing. Compared to the United States' support of the slave trade and slavery, Mexico would have been seen as quite progressive and more racially welcoming.

This period in Mexico was a time when Mexicans with African ancestry held some of the most important positions in Californian society. At least two of Mexico's governors, Manuel Victoria and Pio Pico, had African ancestry. Some writers reported that Victoria was a "full-blooded Negro."[51] This is an important claim in a burgeoning Mexican nation, one that contrasts with most parts of the United States, where blacks were held in slavery. Records identify Pio Pico not only as the grandson of one of the earliest mulatta residents of the Los Angeles pueblo, but note that he "looked like a Negro."[52]

Interestingly, Pico is one of the most famous early Afro-Mexican residents of Los Angeles. His fame eventually led to the city naming a street after him, Pico Boulevard. Pico was highly successful in commercial and civic life in L.A. After being the owner of a dram shop or bar and tanning salon, he became involved in politics, playing a significant role as governor and then as a liaison to the United States as part of Mexico transitioned to becoming the state of California within the United States. Although he fled during the Mexican American war, he eventually returned to L.A. and built the famous Pico House Hotel—a building that remained until 2000 and was located in the heart of the original pueblo.[53]

This example of Pico offers some evidence that blacks were not as severely limited by race as they were in other parts of the United States. Instead, it seems that a multiracial society blossomed in early pueblo L.A. into the years of Mexico, as revealed in many stories of social mobility among residents of African descent. While social prejudice certainly existed and dark-hued settlers most likely experienced more personal discrimination because of their appearance than their lighter-hued counterparts, Mexican residents of African ancestry experienced fewer limitations in relation to social mobility than persons of African lineage in the United States. And any discrimination they experienced was not representative of the caste system that plagued the country. In much of the United States, racial hierarchy and discrimination retarded any economic and social mobility among blacks. Blacks were locked in an unending caste system, which provided no room for advancement of any kind. In contrast, while imperfect, early pueblo Los Angeles was sufficiently multiracial and lacking the strict racial order of America to enable some mobility. This more racially relaxed environment distinguished early pueblo L.A. from the rest of early America.

The Philadelphia and Chicago Fairs conceal this complex history in the White City and Midway exhibitions. They don't tell the truth about when L.A. became more racially restrictive—namely when the United States seized control of the early pueblo L.A. settlement in 1846. Even in 1846, most residents of Mexico considered themselves "Mexican." Mexican residents did not have as narrow an understanding of race as early colonial America did. Yet those Mexicans who looked more African in appearance and specifically were darker hued, began to experience structural racism and injustice similar to English-speaking blacks.[54]

One example captures the profound shift in the racial imagination of L.A. once it became part of the United States. Major Horace Bell, an early American resident of L.A. and a significant figure in California Democratic politics, told a story about the 1853 elections. One of his aides, a southerner, anxiously reported a black man attempting to vote at a polling place in Los Angeles. The aide asserted that he wanted to use violence against him because of the black man's overt attempt to vote. When Bell investigated this situation, he discovered that the black man spoke only Spanish and considered himself to be Mexican, not black or Negro. Through an interpreter, the man questioned why he was being harassed, as he had always voted prior to American rule. He wanted to continue voting. Although Los Angeles was not technically a slave state, most American blacks in L.A. knew not to push the boundaries of white supremacy, which meant not pressing their right to vote. Once Bell found out that the Mexican (black) man who attempted to vote was voting for a Democratic candidate, Bell allowed the man to cast his vote. Besides that detail, what's also important to note is that in order to let the Mexican man vote, Bell reassigned the Southern aide to another polling place, despite the Southern man's public anger.[55]

During the 1850s, the racial order in L.A. became more pronounced and more "American," reflecting the racial order of Jim Crow. Although California was a "free state," many Southerners who moved West decided to keep their slaves. As a result, the majority of blacks who lived in L.A. during this time period unfortunately retained their status as slaves. The majority of the Anglo population in the city was proslavery and was committed to cultivating L.A. as a slave-holding town. Slavery was outlawed in California, but its rural nature and geographical vastness made law enforcement impossible at the time. Black individuals, whether enslaved or free, felt the weight of this growing Jim Crow sentiment, which created racial practices and policies that previously had not been present or were not as severe.[56]

Despite greater aggression shown toward blacks, free black communities nevertheless worked tirelessly for their own rights, frequently challenging segregated laws eventually passed in L.A. In 1856, Biddy Mason, holding her own freedom papers, participated in a Colored Citizens Convention in Sacramento (the state capital of California) and testified against the White Witness Only Law.[57] She asserted, "This deprivation subjects us to many outrages and aggressions by wicked and unprincipled white men."[58] This convention and the courageous activism of people like Mason eventually led to some of these acts being overturned, including the Fugitive Slave Law and the White Witness Only Law.[59]

This history of America's national story is completely erased at world fairs such as the Chicago Columbian Exposition. The United States painted the nation as a savior of non-Anglo people. It depicted political and economic freedom as quintessentially American. The real story of early pueblo L.A. demonstrates how non-Anglo people such as Africans and Mexicans enacted more egalitarian visions of society, ways of life that America categorically rejected despite its claim to be a land of liberty and justice for all. Mexicans and Africans were not simply objects of history, waiting to be civilized: they were subjects and agents of history who fashioned ways of life in early L.A. that revealed the rest of white America to be violent, barbaric, and immature. Fairs that narrated colonial history instead of American history in all of its diversity silenced this more complex history. Instead of portraying diverse chronologies of American history they chose to depict ones that excluded all but white colonial power.

A New Dispensation of Market Faith

Industrial capitalists underwrote these fairs' white colonial vision of Pentecost because they stood to reap massive profit. It was no secret that the Chicago World Fair provided economic gains from which the financial elite would primarily benefit—although the fair deceptively advertised the masses of working-class people as its primary benefactors. It was financial titans like Elihu Root, William Rockefeller, and Cornelius Vanderbilt who underwrote the Chicago Fair, and did so easily and quickly: $5,407,350 of exposition stock had been amassed in less than a month. Even more unsettling, "948 people purchased 70 percent of the stock."[60]

In the beginning, investors rejected Chicago as the city where the Columbian Exposition would take place, opting for New York. The decision was placed in the hands of a congressional committee, which gave Lyman Gage, a businessman leading the Chicago effort, twenty-four hours to raise five million dollars as a guarantee. He immediately approached top financial and business leaders in Chicago for pledges of financial support. Within twenty-four hours, Gage said he "received a fully supporting telegram signed by thirty or more citizens whose aggregate wealth was known to be more than a hundred millions of dollars."[61] These investors in the Chicago Fair were the top 1 percent of society and they knew that any material gains from this fair would go straight to their pockets. This financial and business elite clearly controlled what was presented at this and other expositions and stood to reap the benefits of the fair's success. Fair officials' promise that the economic gains of this endeavor would go to the working poor was simply false.

The Chicago World Fair confirmed why immigrant, black migrant, and poor white workers were frustrated. The emergence of industrial capitalism in the United States was not leading to wealth and abundance for all. Instead, the urban masses were experiencing poverty, economic dislocation, and social alienation due to industrial processes. Even some white Christian ministers refused to acknowledge the inequitable realities of the urban poor. Though this fair claimed to be for the everyday citizen, the winners of this business venture were clearly corporate executives, business owners, and financial titans.

Nevertheless, this market faith persisted, especially surrounding the "Negro question." Ironically, educated black Christian ministers supported this colonial vision through markets. Among some black leaders, this market faith was seen as the answer to black disenfranchisement and oppression. Black leaders such as Booker T. Washington felt that black freedom was tied to African Americans' contribution to free markets. In his Atlanta Exposition speech that was eventually dubbed the "Atlanta Compromise," Washington remarked that "the wisest among the race understand that the agitation of questions of social equality is the extremest folly" when it comes through "artificial forcing."[62] He thought that their struggles for social equality would be unsuccessful. Instead, Washington suggested that blacks would no longer be ostracized when they are seen as contributors to capitalist markets.[63] As participants in economic development, the United States would be forced to engage black communities with respect, he opined.[64] Yet some black leaders like W. E. B. Du Bois felt that Washington was compromising, siding with the white segregationist leaders who wanted blacks to stay in their place, including by not critiquing how white supremacy and market exploitation produced the very conditions of black subjugation.

Washington's statements were part of a debate raging over the role of the South in industrial development and growth. The South was still largely an agricultural economy, adrift from the loss of slave labor. The Atlanta International Exposition of 1895 (along with other world fairs in New Orleans, South Carolina, and Tennessee) depicted the "New South" as a major contributor to the development of domestic and foreign markets. Architects of these southern fairs wanted to create an impression of racial harmony in the New South; they wanted to show how racial hierarchy could be in service to economic development and social order—an important goal for whites due to the racial unrest and uncertainty generated by the Civil War and Reconstruction period. For the South to be seen as progressive, said these business and financial leaders, it needed to expand America's agricultural and industrial productivity through the discovery of new markets, new supplies of natural resources, and creative ideas about labor.[65]

Washington knew that this kind of economic development would require a large industrial and agricultural labor force in the country, especially in the South. In response, Washington sought to offer a guarantee: that blacks would be best suited to be the industrial and agricultural labor force the country needed. Washington spoke to this in his fair address, not only reiterating why black laborers are central to economic progress, but also maintaining that this can be done within America's existing racial order. In short, Washington was seeking ways to expand black possibilities for economic activity without this activity being a threat to white society.

Many white business leaders took notice of Washington's argument. Atlanta officials were able to corroborate Washington's words by reporting that they had saved over a hundred thousand dollars by using chain-gang labor to "excavate about a million yards of earth during the early months of construction" for the fair.[66] One southern newspaper remarked about the labor situation in the South: "It is very noticeable that while strikes are the order of the day at the north and many sections of the west, they are comparatively unknown in the south."[67] The racist brutality and severe violence that blacks experienced in the South were well known. They typically didn't protest it or call a work strike knowing full well that a black person could get lynched or her entire family murdered simply for stating that the white social order was unjust. Unfortunately, this vicious reality was *celebrated as an economic incentive* for Northern financiers to invest in the development of the South. The South could keep blacks in their place, these financiers were told. This "strength" of the South (literally on the backs of Blacks) was advertised as a market incentive for investment purposes. The New South's vision of future economic development in America seemed to answer the (white's) Negro question, making these world fairs appealing to white investors around the nation.

This allowed educated black leaders to have a more direct role in the southern fairs like the Atlanta Exposition, although they could do this only by arguing that their contribution to economic development would also preserve the racial order. Black ministers and educators such as Bishop Wesley Gaines and Abram Grant testified before committees to get their approval of black exhibits at the Atlanta Fair. These ministers emphasized that blacks were more interested in the manufacture of cotton than all other products. They encouraged blacks to avoid all politics and aspire to industry and thrift in order to gain the respect of whites. They felt this fair would be a great showplace for blacks to model this behavior.[68]

Some white political leaders were persuaded by Gaines's and Grant's words. These white politicians believed that blacks would not be a hindrance but offer a great labor force to accomplish America's future of wealth and health. Black directors would be appointed to create black exhibits at this fair, something that had not been done at fairs in the North. Approved by Congress, the "only" restrictions for black exhibits at the Atlanta Fair was that they be displayed in a separate Negro Building.[69]

Not all black leaders agreed with black participation at these fairs. Renowned journalist and advocate Ida B. Wells thought that such fairs were forms of disciplinary power—a way of shaping the desires, yearnings, subjectivity, and agency of its black citizens without the use of coercive power. In a pamphlet entitled *The Reason Why the Colored American Is Not in the World's Columbian Exposition,*

Wells asserts that these fairs intended to pacify blacks and sought to create a "New Negro" that believed in capitalist progress as key to black freedom.[70] Wells wanted to publish and distribute this pamphlet in foreign languages to tell the world about the injustices, brutalities, and oppression that American blacks endured.[71] She felt that blacks should boycott these world fairs entirely. She was criticized by other black leaders like Washington for this approach, as some black leaders noted that this would increase white hostility and defeat the purpose of black advancement.

Black leaders like Frederick Douglass supported Wells by contributing to her pamphlet, but he disagreed with her that blacks should boycott the fair. Instead, Douglass believed that black participation would draw attention to the black freedom struggle as they told their story at these expositions.[72] But this perspective was a hard sell. The requirement of black exhibits at southern fairs was that they needed to be approved by all-white committees.[73] Blacks had no direct creative control over what they displayed at these fairs, and consequently whites used blacks' presence at these fairs in service to the larger goals of industrial profit. White domination and economic interest lay at the root of this entire discussion of the New South and New Negro. Wells knew this. To be fair to Washington, at stake for him were jobs and blacks having ways to survive economically away from sharecropping in the South. Washington did not realize that his hopes were things this nation could not deliver.

Leaders saw these fairs as inaugurating a new dispensation characterized by faith in the market to resolve class warfare, racial wounds and divides, and immigration violence that had long plagued the country. The South was headed into a new era, they insisted, one marked by unlimited economic growth and racial harmony. American world fairs were treated as religious celebrations and holy days. But front and center was worship of the market. The fairs presented modern industrial capitalism as a *transcendent* answer to questions about the future. Undergirding this faith in capitalist markets and progress was white nationalist fervor and colonial visions of society. They hijacked the Pentecost narrative to persuade people of how America could gather cultures and nations (within the United States and around the world) in peace and harmony. This was a gross malformation of the egalitarian ancient vision of Pentecost.

Winds of a New Pentecost in L.A. City

The winds of this colonial vision of a New Pentecost certainly blew through Los Angeles. I suggest that it is no coincidence that the Azusa Revival arose on the heels of these white capitalist visions of Pentecost. It would be mistaken to assume that Los Angeles' political economy had little to do with Chicago, Philadelphia, or Atlanta simply because the sites of these fairs were mostly industrial centers or in Jim Crow lands. The truth is that the entire country was asking how America could shape itself as an industrial leader in response to black migration and immigration. In order for Los Angeles to become a leader, its political leaders, business tycoons, and newspaper giants likewise promulgated white nationalist visions supported by language of cultural unity and economic prosperity.

Local leaders in Los Angeles saw this city as utopian and racially progressive, a model city of Babel reversed. Jefferson Edmonds perceived Los Angeles as a racial paradise. Being the editor of the *Los Angeles Liberator* (a black newspaper), Edmonds wrote in 1902 that "California is the greatest state for the Negro."[74] Moreover, the historian Josh Sides quoted Edmonds's 1911 article at length (on the greatness of California for the Negro):

> Only a few years ago, the bulk of our present colored population came here from the South without any money, in search of better things[—] and were not disappointed. The hospitable white people received them kindly, employed them at good wages, treated them as men and women, furnished their children with the best educational advantages offered anywhere. . . . They were treated absolutely fair in the courts. . . . Feeling perfectly safe, the colored population planted themselves.[75]

Edmonds describes L.A. as a utopian context for blacks, a place that was categorically different than the rest of the United States, particularly the Jim Crow South. This is what the readers would have heard. But was this true, especially when recalling the aforementioned laws and acts that made life difficult for both enslaved and free blacks in L.A. at the end of the nineteenth century?

For certain, black leaders like W. E. B. Du Bois tended to agree with Edmonds, referring to L.A. black communities as an "aggressive, hopeful group—with some wealth, large industrial opportunity and a buoyant spirit."[76] However, not all would have agreed with Edmonds and Du Bois. Consider Caleb Holden. Holden and a white associate walked into a bar one afternoon and ordered drinks. Holden was charged one dollar while his white companion was charged only a nickel.[77] When a group of black citizens subsequently advocated for equality on Holden's behalf, the city attorney, John Shenk, agreed that business owners had a right to discriminate. This was dubbed the "Shenk Rule."[78] How did the Shenk

rule support Edmonds and Du Bois's assertions about L.A. as "perfectly safe,"
"fair in treatment," and home to "hospitable white citizens"? There seems to be
a disconnect between these comments and some of the quotidian experiences of
black L.A. residents. Los Angeles was hardly a racial paradise or a modern-day
Jerusalem at Pentecost. It was a place of deep racist contradictions.

It was also a place of dubious employment prospects for blacks. Industrialization was on the horizon in L.A. when Azusa emerged, but Los Angeles was
still largely an agricultural economy and therefore one of the few employment
sectors available to blacks, along with domestic service, which ranked top. According to the 1930 census, "87% of employed black women and 40% of employed
black men in the city worked as household servants."[79] Another "22% of black
men worked in the manufacturing industries as janitors and laborers."[80] Even
though these figures reflect the situation twenty-four years after the 1906 revival
began, this is an important observation as among those present at the start of
the Azusa Revival was a group of black domestics and janitors, together with the
more well-known founder, William Seymour. In addition, 17 percent of black
men worked in the transportation industry as porters and waiters. And some
black men were hired as street sweepers, garbage collectors, and truck drivers.[81]

This narrow range of jobs and opportunities reflected how whites generally
thought about blacks—namely as "servants." That employment trend continued,
even when job opportunities for the population as a whole shifted somewhat with
the times. For example, although between 1900 and 1910 retail trade became the
largest source of employment in Los Angeles, and although in 1910 there were
6,177 store salespersons working in the city, only 8 of them were blacks.[82] By
1920, there were 11,341 salespersons but only 28 were black.[83] Because Mexican
and European immigrants were also growing in number, hiring management
often discriminated against blacks applying to these same jobs. Despite growing
opportunities in sectors such as retail trade and even manufacturing, most blacks
(particularly the uneducated) were pigeonholed into menial jobs.

To be fair, Edmonds's and Du Bois's claims must be read in relative rather
than absolute terms. As Josh Sides remarks, "Migrating from areas in the South,
where a black man was lynched, on average, every four days, deeply influenced
views about what constituted paradise."[84] In Los Angeles, black people could
avoid some of the most brutal experiences of racism that plagued the South,
such as political powerlessness, economic impotency, abject poverty, and more.
Their claims of L.A. as paradise should also be interpreted in ways readers during that time period would have heard: as a comparison between the "promised

lands" of the urban North and Los Angeles. Black migrants from the South truly believed that their migration to Northern cities would mark a new chapter of freedom in their lives. It did not. The segregation in housing and employment, the poor wages and working conditions associated with the factories, and the white terror that rained on them in the form of rape and beatings demonstrated that this promise was a myth. Black people who moved to urban centers like New York, Detroit, and Chicago experienced social and spatial isolation. While this was a disappointing experience, some did maintain that northern city life was better, in relative terms. As one satirist asserted, the difference between the South and North was being "gently lynched in Mississippi or beaten to death in New York."[85] Los Angeles was seen against this false promise of northern cities. Read this way, it makes a certain kind of sense by that Du Bois and Edmonds perceived L.A. to be fulfilling its promise because of the unprecedented opportunities that black communities possessed there that were virtually nonexistent in most of the South and much of the North. Comparatively speaking, L.A. had little antiblack violence at the time.

Yet, Los Angeles was a city of paradoxes. Take for example black homeownership in L.A. Although white supremacy persisted in this city, L.A. nevertheless had one of the highest proportions of black homeowners of any major American city. By 1910, almost 40 percent of African Americans in L.A. county owned their homes, compared to only 2.4 percent in New York and 8 percent in Chicago.[86] And L.A. residents themselves offered different reasons why blacks experienced a better standard of living in this city. A black real estate agent asserted in 1904 that "Negroes of this city have prudently refused to segregate themselves into any locality but have scattered and purchased homes in sections occupied by wealthy, cultured white people."[87] Notice that this agent suggests the reason for high rates of home ownership is due to blacks' refusal to segregate or to acquiesce to white hostility and injustice. This high rate is then seen as a result of black agency and individual will power as well as racial tolerance among whites.

This reasoning is overstated. One major reason why blacks were able to disperse themselves more easily throughout the city was due to the vast land in California and the small number of blacks. Space in L.A. created an illusion of tolerance that influenced how people described the operations of race in L.A.[88] The vast size of the city also kept the price of property relatively low, enabling property to be within reach of even poorly paid blacks, which diverged from the economic situation in other major cities such as New York and Chicago. Most urban dwellers (disproportionately blacks migrants and other immigrants) had to accept squalid housing conditions in many northern cities, packed in tiny quarters with astronomical rents. The vastness of available land kept prices down in L.A.

Another factor contributing to black home ownership in L.A. was the relatively small size of the black population. The small size of black communities, in some ways, minimized hostility to black dispersion. Northern cities often experienced a large influx of black migrants and immigrants into their cities, which caused white anxiety. White communities felt as if migrants and immigrants threatened their way of life, from economic security (black and immigrants were now competing for manufacturing jobs with white workers) to cultural practices (migrants and immigrants brought with them different religious and social sensibilities from white Americans). Because L.A. housed a very small black community, whites were not as threatened with blacks altering their ways of life. Blacks could be managed. This allowed blacks to do well during this time period (the 1870s to the 1920s). Blacks founded churches, businesses, and social organizations. This community even founded the largest black-owned insurance company in the western United States, Golden State Mutual Life Insurance.[89]

Yet, the paradoxical nature of L.A. persisted. Although L.A. allowed black homeowners who lived dispersed among white communities to flourish, the city nevertheless remained openly hostile to blacks (and other ethnic minorities such as Mexicans) in housing. Although there was a record number of black homeowners, L.A. eventually supported an extensive network of racially restrictive housing covenants which impeded the mobility of blacks in particular areas by the early 1900s. Though its neighborhoods were fairly multicultural and diverse (blacks lived alongside whites), racial segregation in the workplace was much more acute.[90] And so L.A. remained full of paradoxes in relation to black well-being.

Despite this discrimination at the turn of the twentieth century, black Los Angeles residents formed dynamic social organizations such as the "Negro Cooperative" in 1901. This cooperative was to be a "Stock Company organized to publish papers" and cultivate other social and business practices among black communities, which included an industrial training school and an employment agency.[91] In the early twentieth century, black residents sought to redefine their social standing in this changing city that was moving toward industrial aspirations and greater ethnic diversity. Consequently, community organizations like the Negro Cooperative also worked to attain access to higher levels of education for blacks.

Not surprisingly, white L.A. was ambivalent about the aspirations and gains black communities were trying to make. In 1903, a story about the first black lawyer in the city truly reflects the city's ongoing racism. The headline reads "First Negro to Practice" and the first sentence of the story reads: "Coon crap shooters of this town have found a triumphant Moses. He "is one little Baltimore negro as black as crow. He has come here to practice law."[92] What is jolting is how the defendants are described, as "coons" for shooting crap, and elsewhere as darkies. Such were the quotidian practices of racism. What is also shocking is how this attorney, Isador Blair is described: as "black as crow." This image of blackness invokes impurity, irrationality, and primitiveness. Those who read this article would have understood what was being signified: that "black" and "lawyer" together were oxymoronic. It was the white way of delegitimating him.

Blacks did fight back, particularly the black elite. We see black communities' resistance to this kind of racist discourse in a 1906 *Los Angeles Times* article entitled "Only 'African' Will Do," which complains that "Negroes" objected to being called "coon, darky, or even Negro."[93] There was a certain baffled and teasing tone to this article, as though the white journalist could not grasp why blacks were so angry and distrustful of media and other American institutions. This callous article revealed a central problem with white people: they did not understand (or perhaps understood but didn't care about) the mental pain and psychological assault black people constantly endured through these signifying racist logics.

The view of L.A. as racially progressive, even color-blind, concealed the paradoxes I have been discussing at length. This statement was complicit with a neat, uncomplicated reading of L.A.: as a social space that was comparatively better than the South and North. But L.A. still had its own strange Jim Crow life and attachment to capitalist values, which could only be captured through the stories and experiences of local black (and Mexican) residents.[94] It was not a new Jerusalem and nor did it reflect this New Pentecost.

Los Angeles is the space out of which the Azusa Street Revival emerged, a place that was buoyed by capitalist aspirations and mired in racist practices. Many whites *and* educated blacks in L.A. believed in the market faith that undergirded the New Pentecost. To understand the religious consciousness of Azusa, one must grasp this larger economic and cultural context that the New Pentecost represented. For the New Pentecost was *not* a justice-seeking and reconciling discourse but a white nationalist and capitalist discourse of American Empire and expansionism.

The world fairs, such as the Philadelphia Fair of 1876 and the Chicago Co-lumbian Exposition of 1893, and their racialized capitalist ecologies were an integral aspect of the context out of which Azusa came into voice as a religious movement. Los Angeles, the city where Azusa emerged, certainly felt the winds of this New Pentecost, and Azusa's religious life challenged the distorted market values and racial hierarchies associated with American industrial capitalism that white Protestantism and even many educated blacks gladly embraced. In the next chapter, I turn to Azusa's religious life.

2 TOPPLING WHITE EVANGELICAL AND MARKET ORTHODOXIES

AS THE WORLD FAIRS COMMENCED, white Evangelical voices believed that the nation's return to Christian orthodoxy was the answer to the threat of cultural pluralism and economic precariousness. However, black political and women's rights activist Fannie Williams offers a powerful indictment of one branch of Christianity—white Evangelicalism. She asserts, "It is a monstrous thing that nearly one-half of the so-called evangelical churches of this country repudiate and haughtily deny fellowship to every Christian lady and gentleman happening to be of African descent. It is a shameful thing to say of the Christian religion as practiced in one part of our country that a young colored man susceptible of spiritual enlightenment will find a readier welcome in a saloon or any other place than he will in any evangelical church."[1] Williams exposed its deep-seated racism that made it impossible for many blacks to feel a sense of belonging. Her observation appeared to much of white society to be counterintuitive, since they saw early American Evangelicalism, especially in New England, as progressive, cultivating many antislavery efforts and abolitionist causes. Fannie, however, knew this was not a complete picture of white Evangelicalism. As a black woman who spent her life advocating for the advancement of African Americans especially on questions of racial and economic justice, she knew the pain and trauma blacks endured within white spaces, especially white churches.[2] Her image of the saloon as a less dangerous space for blacks than white churches (particularly white Evangelical churches in the South) was meant to shock the public and communicate how hypocritical

41

white Evangelical churches were. For Williams, one could not assess American Christianity morally through tests of orthodoxy. What good is such orthodoxy when used in service to black death? Williams's words were an explicit indictment of many white churches' complicity with white supremacy. One cannot examine Christian orthodoxy apart from how it *functioned*, which included not only doing nothing to prevent but actually advancing black degradation and the socioeconomic disenfranchisement of racial others—both black migrants and Chinese and Mexican immigrants, for example.

Mirroring Williams's critique, this chapter explores how the Azusa community asserted its religious and political agency in response to the corrupt white Evangelical orthodoxy of the day and its commitments to economic racism and consumeristic culture. At a historical glance, it would be easy to interpret the Azusa Revival as another white Evangelical Christian movement that simply reflected dominant Christian ideas of the Holy Spirit. Instead, I ask what an orthodox Evangelical framing of Azusa represses, conceals, and hides. I offer an extensive description of what sits at the center of Azusa's experience: slave religious practices. It was slave religious practices at Azusa that challenged white Evangelical orthodoxy, which described this kind of black religiosity as demonic, primitive, and savagely wild. Moreover, it was through slave religious practices that blacks and immigrants asserted their subjectivity and agency, opposing how American capitalist processes treated black bodies as commodified property and chattel. Through these religious forms, blacks at Azusa reasserted themselves as human subjects within an economy that tried to commodify their existence, which was underwritten by white Christian orthodoxy. I conclude this chapter by discussing how this revival also resisted two primary market orthodoxies: the assumption that markets inherently sponsor freedom and equity, and the belief that constant consumerism would create wealth, happiness, and contentment for all people. Azusa strikingly rejected the moneyed eschaton that guided so many Evangelical churches in Los Angeles, white and black churches alike.

The Purity of White Evangelical Orthodoxy?

White Evangelical leaders believed that the nation's return to Christian orthodoxy was the spiritual solution to the moral and economic confusion generated by cultural pluralism. Some white Evangelical ministers wanted to preserve the Evangelical piety and values that had marked America since its inception as a nation. They believed that Evangelical faith had the kind of spiritual and moral purity needed to correct the cultural divisions and economic uncertainty. One such white Evangelical leader who spoke of America's future of moral purity and progress in white Evangelical terms was the renowned traveling evangelist Dwight Moody. Moody attracted thousands to his Christian revivals in the United States, revivals that emphasized individual repentance and conversion. His preaching was so popular in the United States that his fame spread abroad, garnering him invitations to lead revivals in other countries such as Great Britain and Sweden.[3]

Although Moody was known for his preaching, he was also a businessman. He began early in life as a shoe salesman—and a rather ambitious and aggressive one at that. He once remarked: "I can make money quicker than anyone except Marshall Field."[4] Of course, Marshall Field became one of America's pioneers in business, particularly through developing the department-store model. Moody was drawn to the world of business and eventually used his business acumen to institutionalize his evangelistic activities through the Chicago Bible Institute, later renamed the Moody Bible Institute.

Moody described his special calling as being to evangelize the industrial city, which led him to settle down in Chicago. When the Chicago World Fair started, Moody inevitably recognized it as another opportunity to fulfill his calling. To Moody, the Chicago Columbian Exposition held both possibilities and dangers for the nation. On the one hand, it attempted to offer secular answers to what Moody fundamentally interpreted as spiritual problems. So for example, to him industrial cities oozed cultural modernism—the dangerous growth of "theaters, Sunday newspapers, drinking, lust, worldly amusements, and threatening scientific ideas like Darwinism."[5] Fairs such as the Columbian Exposition, he felt, supported heterodox beliefs and therefore sowed religious confusion. Moody was concerned that the exposition's "promiscuous mixing" of competing religions and cultures could destroy the white Evangelical Christian foundation of the nation.[6]

It was not only the mixing that concerned him, but also specifically the *type* of Christianity that dominated the Parliament of World Religions at the Chicago Fair. It was not the Evangelical gospel to him. The parliament reminded attendees that "the narrow Christianity" characterizing the United States would "disappear, for its errors have become palpable."[7] The errors to which the parliament was referring were Christian ideas that denounced scientific and technological innovation and advancement. By contrast, the Parliament of Religions envisioned a global Christian faith that was grounded in the promises of scientific progress. Moody interpreted this view of Christianity as nothing more than secularism.[8]

Despite these flaws, Moody thought the fair could be an opportunity to evangelize sinful cities like Chicago and return them to Evangelical moral and social order, to sanctified cities. Specifically Moody worried about immigrants or "newcomers" to cities and their heterodox beliefs, imagining that these different beliefs and customs would adulterate the purity of the Evangelical Christian faith among Americans and inevitably incite moral, social, and political disorder and disobedience.[9] Moody was clear through his correspondence with a close friend and business partner, Turlington Harvey, that he wanted to expand his urban ministry toward Chicago because of the social disorder demonstrated in the Haymarket riot.[10] Moody and Harvey regarded protestors unilaterally as communists who needed to be converted from their sinful ways into peaceful, law-abiding citizens through the power of Christ. Moody warned that unless urban dwellers were converted by the gospel, the "leaven of communism and infidelity will assume such enormous proportions that it will break out in a reign of terror such as this country has never known."[11] Moody saw the answer to such disruptions as revivals that could turn people back to the true Evangelical faith.

And so the Fair became Moody's opportunity to reach sinners. To that end, he adapted his revival strategies to popular culture.[12] For example, he was known to create tickets for his Evangelical services that looked like theater tickets or entry passes into the Chicago Fair. This strategy was countercultural to Christians' sentiments of theaters, public halls, and saloons as corrupt and errant. Eventually Moody used this same strategy to claim popular culture for Evangelical Christianity. He hoped to create an Evangelical counterculture so that people could participate in popular culture—but with Christian content.[13] Of course these practices drew criticism. Some of his critics claimed that he preached for his own fame, to please people. Others commented that he preached for money.[14] No matter the particular criticism, Moody believed that his revival would usher in the true Pentecost, not the "New Pentecost" associated with the Parliament of World Religions. Moody's Pentecost would transform diverse urban areas into sanctified cities with citizens who would uphold Puritanical, Evangelical morality. This moral order included white Evangelical values and practices not tainted by immigrant or black migrant religious and cultural influences.[15]

Despite his accommodating and even creative strategies in relation to popular culture, Moody's Evangelicalism participated in the white racial order of the day. Moody was interested not only in how Evangelical faith could preserve the white cultural order but also in how Christian faith could support a modern capitalist vision of American society. He hoped to capitalize on the industrial boom in

Chicago when he arrived at the Chicago Exposition in 1893. As he wrote to one Chicago businessman a few years earlier, in 1889, there "can be no better invest-ment for the capitalists of Chicago than to put the saving salt of the gospel into those dark homes and desperate centers from which come the criminals."[16] In short, Moody saw Christianity as a natural ally to the industrial boom. Indus-trial capitalists possessed the "saving salt of the gospel" needed to redeem and regenerate impoverished contexts such as urban cities where black migrants and immigrants lived. Yet it seems that Moody blamed their economic and social ills not on new-fangled industrial processes but on the wayward character and indolence of city dwellers. The "natural" remedy for the circumstances of the urban masses he understood to be a return to white Evangelical values fueled by market opportunities for the urban poor to be industrious and self-sufficient.

Moody's unequivocal belief in modern capitalism was best seen in his collabo-ration with his renowned close friend and business partner Turlington Harvey. Moody's benefactor for many years, Harvey had launched a real estate venture prior to the Chicago World Fair. This venture was a new town that promised set-tlers a return to Protestant Victorian values and ways of life, free from immigrant and black migrant criminality such as drinking, gambling, and sexual promis-cuity. Leading Chicago philanthropists had purchased shares, as had Moody. Harvey, Illinois, was advertised as a redeemed town and celestial city.[17] Restrictive covenants were written into every contract forbidding future residents from any "offensive purpose or establishment" such as gambling or "lewd practices."[18] These restrictive covenants certainly gestured toward the unredeemed black migrant and immigrant masses. On the outskirts of Chicago, the small industrial town of Harvey would exist as a countercultural environment to the sinful dangers of urban life. This town was waiting to welcome permanent residents who desired to reclaim the white Evangelical moral order of the past.

The Chicago World Fair was the perfect opportunity for attendees to visit Harvey as their potential future home, and promotion capitalized on it. The height of the advertising campaign for Harvey transpired during the summer of 1893. Notices appeared in newspapers and magazines urging tourists to take a side trip and visit Harvey as part of their world fair trip.[19] Moody publicized the town in his services and revival meetings while in Chicago during the fair. Harvey, ever the businessman, even partnered with Temperance organizations to offer directions for how to get to Harvey from the world fair. As a result of such efforts, the town indeed attracted many visitors, to the glee of Moody and his partners, who stood to profit from this venture.[20]

Moody's wholesale belief in the salvific merits of the industrial process is an example of the kind of uncritical market faith that gripped the nation. For Turlington and Moody, investing in Harvey was not a crude economic calculation, solely oriented toward profit. They truly believed that investing in Harvey was an investment in the *saving of souls*. Capitalism, they thought, had soteriological benefits; it could save people from sin and destruction. Moody married Evangelical values with capitalist progress and the promise of Christian redemption. Yet, what Moody refused to acknowledge was that industrial capitalism was and is inextricably linked to racial exploitation and income inequality. The poor wages and inhumane working conditions that working-class people experienced completely escaped Moody when he praised America as the leader of global capitalist advancement. He was completely unwilling to concede that protests such as the Haymarket riot emerged from the deep disparities the urban poor continually experienced from participating in the American economy. Moody's Evangelicalism simply reinforced the white racial order (and class order) of the day that refused to grant blacks and immigrants basic human respect and worth.

Moody represents white Evangelicalism's refusal to acknowledge how industrial capitalism exploited black people (and immigrants). At the Chicago Columbian Exposition, black activist Fannie Williams questioned white Evangelical orthodoxy's moral regime. In her speech "Religious Duty to the Negro," she assessed how Christian religion has enabled *and* stifled the moral, spiritual, and economic progress of African Americans. Interestingly, in naming the crisis of American Christianity, Williams first drew attention to how white Christianity had treated black bodies as commodified property and had described blacks as morally reprobate. She identified the auction block as the primary site against which white Christian religion should be morally measured and judged, asserting, "All attempts to Christianize the Negro were limited by the important fact that he was property of a valuable and peculiar sort, and that the property value must not be disturbed, even if his soul were lost."[21] For Williams, this "pernicious and demoralizing Gospel" was grounded in the impurities of white Christianity, as black "mothers saw their babes sold by Christians on the auction block in order to raise money to send missionaries to foreign lands."[22] White Christianity funded and fueled racial capitalism, treating black bodies as commodities to purchase—and discard. Such Christian religion upheld racial hierarchies and treated blacks as utterly inferior. It was completely hypocritical.

Williams further maintained that Christian theology and its creeds provided the spiritual and moral framework to interpret blacks as morally reprobate, pagan, savage, and lazy, and therefore in need of salvation and civilization.[23] The assumed civilizing impulse of white Christianity in America involved the enslaved seeing their subordinate social and economic position as God-ordained, a way for them to work toward the saving of their souls. In the white Christian imagination, to work in the fields as a slave was literally to participate in God's redemptive plan. Many white ministers used Christian orthodoxy to justify the extraction and exploitation of black labor.

This was not lost on Fannie. She fully grasped the white Christian foundations of racial capitalism and that whites like Moody used it in service to cultural imperialism and economic hegemony. No wonder she questioned the purity of Christian orthodoxy, including white Evangelicalism. This legacy of plantation economics still structured America at the start of the twentieth century, an era in which blacks were still expected to remain in their place for these theological and economic reasons.

Fannie Williams indicts white Christian religion because it has been so clearly shaped by economic racism, ideologies and practices of treating African Americans as commodities to be sold and purchased rather than as human subjects to be respected and engaged. Womanist theologian Kelly Brown Douglass outs whites' conception of black bodies as chattel, a word typically associated with livestock, not humans, with those beings from whom one extracted free labor. Classifying blacks as property, as a source of labor, as less than human, made it easy for white owners to see them as other than persons like themselves. Classifying black bodies as chattel provided whites with moral justification for blacks' subjugated position in American society. Most important, if black people are *by nature* chattel, then it is an ontological impossibility for them ever to become fully human as subjects and agents.[24]

Thanks to the theological and economic justifications for the dehumanization of black people, white American Christianity lived and breathed this economic ecology of slavery. No wonder that Williams warned that less theology and more of human brotherhood, less declamation and more common sense and love for truth, must be the qualifications of the new ministry . . . the tendency of creeds and doctrine to obscure religion, to make complex that which is elemental and simple" must be challenged.[25]

This is why Fannie cautioned her readers about Christian orthodoxy, horrified that the white Evangelical church was indeed a more dangerous space for blacks than a saloon. Protestant reformers, Evangelical leaders, and especially members of temperance organizations saw the saloon as a bastion of drunkenness, sexual promiscuity, and lawlessness. However, for the urban poor the saloon was a much more democratic institution than other social and economic organizations.[26] For instance, potable water and milk were often inaccessible to the poor given the unsanitary conditions in cities like Chicago and Boston. As a result, working-class and poor families would purchase beer for their family from the saloon—a more sanitary option for them than water and milk. Besides, saloons were also sources of cheap food,[27] and were often more aware and accommodating of poor people's conditions and plight than churches. Most Evangelical churches stereotyped the working poor who patronized saloons as being sinful and wayward without acknowledging the unfair disparities that kept the poor in deprivation.

The saloon also addressed racial realities better than did most white Evangelical churches, an odd truth. While blacks were excluded from many white (and other ethnic) saloons, some nonblack saloons provided substantial employment opportunities for blacks. There were many different kinds of ethnocentric saloons with their own customs and cultural ways of life. While outsiders were not always welcomed, the owners made no special effort to reject or turn away other patrons, including black customers.[28] There would be a readier welcome in a saloon for a black person than most white churches, particularly in the South, a region of the country in which blacks were met with outright hostility and violence. Yet some saloons in Chicago, Boston, and even Los Angeles reflected the diversity of a city perhaps more than any other social institution.[29] Fannie knew this. And she wanted white Evangelical churches to repent and acknowledge that their forms of orthodoxy were tied to racist ideology and dehumanizing economic practices. Fannie's analysis of white Evangelicalism is significant because it allows one to grasp the distorted market and Christian ecclesial context out of which Azusa emerged and contested.

A Heterodox Movement?

The Azusa Revival's religious life can be seen as a *form of protest* against this racist, capitalist, white Evangelical backdrop. Many white Evangelical ministers regarded the Revival as a heterodox movement. At the center of Azusa's religious experience were what I earlier called *slave religious practices*. These practices with their oral music traditions and ecstatic praise expressions empowered black people to announce and affirm their humanity and agency. At Azusa, in contrast to the world fairs, black bodies were not sites of market exchange but sites at which divine presence lived and breathed. Black bodies were sacred sites of goodness, truth, and divine revelation which defied the market logic used to subjugate them. These religious practices allowed black members to assert themselves as human agents within a racial system that treated them like objects and commodities.

Certainly slave religious practices critiqued America's economic orthodoxies, but before turning to those, I want to explore how it challenged America's Christian orthodoxies. During early Christian plantation missions to the enslaved, white evangelists and ministers sought to purge the animism, polytheism, idolatry, and fetishism associated with slave religion. For them, slave religious expressions were nothing more than Africanisms that opposed the message of Christ.[30] Once white plantation masters overcame their reluctance to accept the Christianizing of blacks, missionaries were determined to destroy any vestiges of perceived heathen religions that might intrude upon or taint Christian worship.[31] Into the nineteenth and twentieth centuries, even elite blacks wanted to distance themselves from this "heathen" past. In the North, independent African Baptist and Methodist churches began patterning their worship services after white churches. For example, Richard Allen, the founder of African Methodist Episcopal Church, denounced emotional outbursts and displays in worship and made sure that emotive forms of worship were excluded from liturgy in his nascent denomination.[32]

Against this background, it becomes clearer that Azusa's religious life confronted the cultural condemnation of slave religious practices. Historian Cecil Robeck recounts that slave religious practices were rituals in which black people participated as they sought divine affirmation of their humanity amid and in spite of white plantation violence. For instance, Azusa featured "handclapping, foot stomping and ecstatic seizures similar to the southern plantation 'praise houses' of the slaves."[33] On southern plantations, the enslaved had often retreated into the woods at night, away from the watchful eyes of the overseer or slave master to perform the kind of shouts and dancing now seen at Azusa. This kind of religious worship invoked divine presence. Unfortunately, as whites began to missionize blacks on plantations in the eighteenth century, this plantation religious behavior was not welcomed and indeed strongly condemned, as whites considered these practices to be primitive and demonic.[34] Considered by some to be the father of North American Pentecostalism, white minister Charles Parham even retorted about Azusa that it was not Christian and nothing more than "a modification of the Negro chanting of the Southland."[35]

One primary slave religious practice seen at Azusa was praying over mate-rial objects such as prayer cloths as points of contact for those in distress. This practice likewise emerged out of slave religion in which artifacts were used for healing, both spiritual and physical.[36] Christian faith healing could be ascertained in and through the supernatural and material dimensions of the world. After such prayer, the prayer cloth, for example, was believed to contain and mediate supernatural power to overcome sickness and death. It was not simply a manu-factured piece of cloth but an object that mediated divine power. Believers thus gave material objects spiritual connotations and supernatural meanings.

Divining messages from objects of the natural world was also a slave religious practice associated with the Azusa Revival, especially among those leaders who established denominations after Azusa. Seymour was born in Louisiana where religious life among many slaves and former slaves was dominated by Catholi-cism and Voodoo. Many of the enslaved wedded these two religious traditions together, creating a variation known as "Hoodoo."[37] Hoodoo was a "slave cul-ture in which symbols, spells, incantations, sympathetic magic, and root work were a regular part of life."[38] Seymour, in particular, likewise believed in "special revelation"—divinely inspired visions and dreams, and invoking divine power. Slave culture also engaged root work and conjuring as ways to invoke divine power, healing, safety, and flourishing, all practices reminiscent of the religious culture in which he grew up in Louisiana. A mentee of Seymour, Charles Har-rison Mason visited Azusa in his first year and brought this practice of conjuring with him, although for Mason it was a distinctly Christian form of conjuring.

Robeck argues that Mason participated in what the enslaved would have understood as "conjuring culture." Mason believed that through the help of the Holy Spirit, he could discern the messages that God had placed in or mediated through a natural object, yielding what in terms of 1 Corinthians 12:8 are known as words of knowledge and words of wisdom.[39] In the late 1960s, Elder C. G. Brown, the first secretary of the Department of Home and Foreign Missions for the Church of God in Christ (COGIC), remembered Mason's "demonstrations from earthly signs." Brown remarked that Mason was able to "read the recesses of the object." He described how "Elder Mason would calmly pick up a stick, shaped in the exact likeness of a snake in its growth, or a potato shaped in the exact likeness of the head and ears of a pig in its growth, and demonstrate with such power that thousands of hearers are put in wonder."[40] Elder Brown noted that Mason's demonstrations met with skepticism, as blacks could hear "conjure" and "hoodoo" language in these practices. Brown countered that those who challenged Mason on this issue demonstrated "shortsightedness and a lack of spiritual vision."[41]

In form, Mason's divining of messages through natural objects certainly preserved something of the non-Christian "conjuring culture." However, his practices of reading natural objects he himself understood to be filled with Christian meaning, and he transformed this practice into a means of Christian communication about God, the world, sin, redemption, and more. Mason believed that it was the Holy Spirit of the Bible that revealed things to him through natural objects. In fact, Mason even preached at an Assemblies of God (then a mostly white denomination) convocation in 1914, and walked up to the pulpit with a sweet potato to discern God's message to those gathered before him.[42] Although Seymour never divined messages from natural objects, it is clear that he recognized the authority and value of Mason's ministry and practices. Indeed, through such religious practices the enslaved affirmed their humanity, and despite the commodification of their very bodies and labor, reminded others they were people with agency, creativity, history, and culture.

Slave religious practices were an expression of the cultural and religious creativity that involved African and European influences.[43] For instance, spirit possession was a major religious expression experienced within some West African societies. Spirit possession was also a central practice for slave religion in the United States. However, African practices of spirit possession were not equivalent to the spirit possession of the enslaved. For some West African societies, spirit possession was about the ancestor mounting the body of devotee, possessing the devotee in order to speak through this person.[44] Among the enslaved, by contrast, spirit possession was more about being overcome with divine awe, terror, and power as one experienced spiritual enrapture. It was a sign of oneness with the divine, a unity experienced only within the religious community. Despite such stark differences between African and African-American experiences of spirit possession, historian Albert Raboteau suggests that West African liturgical influences of spirit possession nonetheless shaped slave religious practices in the United States.[45]

The creativity of slave religious practices was evident also in it being a "danced religion." Many West African societies danced not only at social gatherings but also at worship, the latter as an offering of praise to the gods. The young and old participated together—and they participated with their entire being, not simply their feet and legs. No one merely observed. For dancing, besides invoking the divine presence, enacted the covenant between the members of the community who witnessed to the power of the Spirit in and through their collective beseeching and celebrations. Early forms of slave religion (including black Christianity) were shaped by these African expressions of the interrelationships between God, the Spirit, the ancestors, and the community.[46] It was such modified expressions of the power of the Spirit at Azusa that enslaved persons had performed in the hush harbors (a secluded informal gathering space, often built with tree branches, where the enslaved would gather away from their masters in order to worship as they desired, combining indigenous religious rituals with Christian expressions).

Scholars such as James Goff argue that it was sanctification and speaking in tongues as evident of the Spirit baptism that attracted people from Baptist and Methodist churches and to holiness movements and early Pentecostal movements like Azusa.[47] Yet for the black leaders who founded and led Azusa, their departure was much more complicated and nuanced than this explanation suggests. People also left black Baptist and Methodist denominations that did not approve of slave religion with its oral music traditions and its ecstatic praise practice precisely to protest whites' and many educated blacks' views that such practices were antiquated, primitive, and pagan.[48]

The children and grandchildren of the enslaved embraced these religious practices because they believed that God's truth and power were truly present in these ancestral forms. Black leaders of Azusa privileged and honored the religious legacy of their ancestors rather than acquiescing to white European evaluations of black worship. Their reclamation of such practices countered the power of the auction block, which saw black people as nothing more than objects for sale, commodities for purchase, and cheap labor to employ within the burgeoning industrial economy at the turn of the twentieth century.

I recognize that one might question just what was "African" about slave religious practices, as white ecstatic religious behavior in the United States is also well documented. Might these religious practices of the enslaved simply be derivatives of white ecstatic worship that blacks knew from ecstatic worship of the Great Awakenings? Some black scholars note distinctions between religious practices of the enslaved and white ecstatic worship. For example, the Great Awakenings and their camp meetings of the eighteenth and nineteenth centuries certainly chronicle how slaves tended to express excessive religious emotion in conjunction with dance and song that often continued through the entire evening after the revival came to a close (i.e., after whites left).[49] While slave religious expressions of music and dance show up in these camp meetings, much of this religious behavior was met with stinging disapproval from some white Evangelical ministers and missionaries. Raboteau states that "while white Evangelical missionaries prohibited dancing as sinful, they afforded the slaves a morally sanctioned context for a sacralizing type of dancing in the emotionally charged setting of the revival."[50] Note that *some white Evangelical missionaries and ministers at camp meetings distinguished* between "inappropriate," wild, and "sinful" African-influenced dancing in contrast to the "appropriate" and tame dancing of white liturgical expressions. So were slave religious practices really deeply shaped by African influences? Certainly historians of black religion like Raboteau maintain that even in the Great Awakening camp meetings, slaves danced in ways their African ancestors would have recognized.

Other white evangelists during the Great Awakenings wrote about how slave religious expression influenced the liturgical and religious behavior of white revivalists and members. In 1819, one white Christian evangelist, John Watson, wrote about the inappropriate musical and dance behavior of black revivalists at a Philadelphia conference that nevertheless influenced white revivalists. He recalls:

> Here ought to be considered too, a most exceptionable error, which has the tolerance at least of the rulers of our camp meetings. In the blacks quarters, the coloured people get together, and sing for hours together, short scraps of disjointed affirmations, pledges, or prayers. . . . With every word sung, they have a sinking of one or other leg of the body alternately; producing an audible sound of the feet at every step, and as manifest as the steps of actual negro dancing . . . the evil is only occasionally condemned and the example has already visibly affected the religious manner of some whites.[51]

Watson seems to suggest that black patterns of religious behavior influenced white revivalists at these camp meetings. Such religious behavior was popularly known to be a part of plantation services down South that were constituted of nothing more than heathenish habits. That many in the white Christian community disapproved of such religious behavior prompted black elites to reinforce white Christian views of slave religious practices as heathen, sinful, and uncivilized.

Many white Evangelical ministers are entirely incapable of fairly reflecting upon and explaining what happened at Azusa because they defined the "blackness" (i.e., slave religion) of Azusa as *not Christian*. Recounting his visit to the Azusa Revival, Parham reported finding disturbing the sight of white people freely associating with blacks and Latinos. He left the revival insisting that most of those claiming the Holy Spirit Baptism were subject to no more than "animal Spiritism."[52] As black scholar Ashon Crawley gestures, the way that white Christian leaders relegated black ecstatic behavior to the realm of the *animal* or termed it animal spiritism underscores how the animal and blackness were seen as equivalent categories in white Christian theological thought. For white leaders like Parham, Azusa was not only wild, excessive, and uncouth but even demonic. He located it outside of Christian Protestantism altogether. Others at Azusa believed that precisely such *excess* was the work of the Spirit. In doing so, they asserted themselves as subjects who could trust their own experiences of God and the broader world, and in so doing they challenged white Evangelical ideas of Christian orthodoxy.

Within, Against, and Beyond the Orthodoxy of White Evangelicalism

But there is more to how Azusa challenges white Evangelical orthodoxy. This is particularly important because this orthodoxy provided the theological rationale for the objectification and commodification of black bodies during slavery as well as projects of segregation and economic exploitation at the dawn of modern capitalism in the United States. Some scholars have ignored, downplayed, or dismissed the black origins of Azusa and how its slave religious practices collided with white Evangelical ideas of Christian orthodoxy. Historian James Goff discusses the problem that slave religious practices posed for Parham when he traveled to Los Angeles in order to visit the Azusa Street Revival. As Goff recalls in his book, Parham wrote a letter to Seymour stating that he was coming to "help him discern between that which was real and that which was false because spiritualistic manifestations, hypnotic forces, and fleshly contortions as known in the colored Camp Meetings in the south had broken loose in the meeting."[53] Parham is referring to slave rituals that he found unchristian. Parham claims that Seymour wrote to him about the "spiritual disorder" of Azusa, yet Goff concedes that there is no evidence that Seymour ever wrote such a letter (although Seymour did desire his teacher Parham to visit as Azusa was getting underway).[54] Though we do not know what precisely Seymour communicated to bring Parham to Azusa, what is clear is that Parham visited with the intention of enforcing doctrinal authority and restoring order.

Parham mentioned that when he arrived at the Apostolic Mission on Azusa Street, he saw people "practicing hypnotism at the altar over candidates seeking the Baptism [of the Holy Ghost]" and saw other "spiritualistic controls" that alarmed him to his core, such as identifying a couple of elders as hypnotists.

Now Parham's own Pentecostal revival in Topeka, Kansas, had been charged with emotionalism, so apparently there was something qualitatively different about what was going on at Azusa.[55] For him, this difference was the slave religious practices of the plantations in the South. He equated Azusa's religious rituals to hypnotism and spiritualism, pagan practices in contrast to the beliefs and practices of white Christian orthodoxy. Parham regarded Azusa's religious behavior as altogether *outside* of Christian Evangelicalism and holiness.

By contrast, elders such as Seymour interpreted the religious practices of Azusa *within* the bounds of orthodoxy, although Seymour did not understand orthodoxy in absolute terms as Parham did. Eventually Seymour would codify the beliefs and practices of the Apostolic Mission Church by publishing a ninety-five-page book entitled *The Doctrines and Discipline of the Azusa Street Apostolic Mission of Los Angeles*. Though Seymour spoke of doctrine, what he had in mind was a relatively open-ended concept—a way of talking about Christian instruction that functioned more as a revisable roadmap than a set of unbending laws or static truths unaffected by experience. For example, Goff argues that Parham equated Pentecostal identity with the doctrine of initial evidence, which was about the Pentecostal believer having an experience of speaking in tongues or foreign languages (xenolalia). Parham understood Pentecostals as needing the ability to speak in other languages (tongues) in order to evangelize people around the world before Jesus' second coming. This entire view and function of tongues were solidified in Parham's doctrine of initial evidence. Hence, for Parham speaking in tongues was a nonnegotiable doctrinal issue.[56]

By contrast, Seymour and other Azusa members understood speaking in tongues (glossolalia or unknown tongues) as a way to be present to the mediation of divine presence. In theologian Frank Macchia's essay "Sighs Too Deep for Words," he speaks of glossolalia as theophany rather doctrine.[57] He understands glossolalia as an encounter with divine presence that might be described as "theophanic." For him, glossolalia is characterized by God's spontaneous and dramatic self-disclosure. Azusa's Pentecostal experience did not hinge on actualizing the doctrinal function of glossolalia (or even xenolalia). Instead, the experience of tongues was more an intensification of divine presence, and tongues represented the pursuit of this intense encounter with divine presence. At Azusa, glossolalia was about experiences too deep for words, moments of divine encounter that escape linguistic grasp and categorization. Glossolalia enabled an encounter with a God who is ineffable, despite our attempts to capture God's essence through conceptual schemes. Although Seymour talked about the doctrine of tongues, he used this doctrinal language in a very loose sense, a way of talking about the general instructions and orientations to which the Apostolic Mission church subscribed, along with an understanding that the Spirit's work is always ongoing and often surprising. He even specifically remarked that the "gift of the Holy Ghost is more than speaking in the tongues."[58]

I therefore contest any reading of Azusa that interprets this religious movement as *simply* operating within the horizon of white Christian orthodoxy. Azusa can be seen as expanding and affirming yet also sometimes as collapsing Christian doctrinal categories altogether. Azusa is not properly "pneumatological" for Parham and other white ministers who visited. To such leaders, white Christian doctrine (here, the doctrine of the Spirit) is incommensurable with and even oppositional to "cultural forms" of blackness (understood as deriving from slave religious practices). Another example would be how the Apostolic "Oneness" denominations that emerged out of the Azusa Revival, such as the Pentecostal Assemblies of the World (PAW), break from Trinitarian formulations of God that have marked both white and black Christian churches in America (over 2 million in PAW today).[59] While many Pentecostal denominations affirmed the Trinity, other denominations forged at Azusa reject the doctrine of the Trinity. At Azusa, new doctrinal commitments were emerging and being forged, both affirming and imploding traditional Christian doctrinal categories altogether. This is the complexity of Azusa: it doesn't neatly follow the doctrine and orthodoxy that preceded it. Azusa truly is and was *contested theological space*. It operated from within, yet against and beyond orthodoxy in forging new religious understandings rooted in the power of black rituals and practices.

A number of black Pentecostal scholars have foregrounded slave religious practices of Azusa but nevertheless attempt to reconcile these practices with white Christian orthodox terms and worldviews. I think this is faulty. For instance, theologian Estrelda Alexander's cogent and compelling analysis shows how the *form* of African spirituality shaped the development of early slave religious practices. Her thick description of the similarities between African spirituality and some slave religious practices does not simply reduce these practices to African religions. However, that Alexander goes to great lengths to explain African traditional religious worldviews in monotheistic terms as a way to disprove the polytheistic character of African primal religions is, I think, a mistake. African traditional religions have their own internal sets of metaphors, rituals, and religious languages that cannot and should not be reframed within Judeo-Christian monotheistic categories. I agree with Alexander that perhaps resonances between them can be found, such as the idea of a Supreme God in some African spiritualities that may reflect Judeo-Christian ideas of a Supreme Divinity.[60] However, the comparative religious conversation between polytheistic and monotheistic religions is a Western enterprise grounded in racial logics.

Polytheistic religions are actually created (or named) in direct relationship to monotheistic religions as a way to configure religious and ultimately racial (and cultural) forms of hierarchy. The term monotheism was coined in 1660 by Henry More, a member of Cambridge Platonists.[61] These Platonists wanted to organize and categorize religions more straightforwardly on a continuum, progressing in an evolution from polytheistic and primitive religions (such as animism) to civilized and monotheistic religions such as Western Christianity. Because Europeans regarded monotheism as the most civilized religious worldview, they stationed it at the top of the religious hierarchy and used it to legitimate their colonial projects as "civilizing" the "primitive" religious lives of non-Europeans.

Theologian Willie Jennings offers a compelling account of how monotheistic European Christian ideas and practices theologically subjugated non-Europeans people and their religions, which led to violent colonial encounters. Jennings argues that four things were transpiring when European nations experienced "cultural contact" with non-European lands and people in the fifteenth century: (1) people were seized and stolen, (2) land was seized and stolen, (3) people were stripped from their space and place, and (4) Europeans described non-Europeans (such as Africans) and their cultural and religious practices through their Christian categories, which *distorted their meanings*.[62] European Christianity thus emerged as an interpretive marker of *non*-European cultures, providing the conceptual framework through which the dominant Europeans interpreted these new (to them) lands and people.

At the center of this interpretation was how non-European people related their religion to the land. Before Western colonialism, many non-European nations—such as African nations—conceived of their indigenous identity in relation to land, place, space, arrangement of days and nights, trees, animals, water, and more.[63] Such communities had a holistic religion that likewise related the land and environment to their spiritualities. The Christian West interpreted this way of understanding their spiritual identities as primitive, barbaric, and demonic. Many missionaries referred pejoratively to these indigenous religions as the worship of inanimate objects over the true God, often terming such religions in the language of polytheism (thus of worshiping multiple gods, for example).

The language of polytheism decentered how non-Europeans understood their own indigenous religious rituals and practices.

Monotheistic forms of European Christianity eventually became the framework through which the dominant West compared and evaluated all other religions. Although Jennings does not explicitly write with the "monotheism versus polytheism" debate in mind, I infer from his thesis that *religiously* naming non-European people in a particular way (as savage and demonic because their indigenous religious practices could not be explained through white Judeo-Christian logic) set the stage for the brutality and violence of colonial regimes. For me, Jennings's argument allows one to see how monotheistic presuppositions *function* in histories of colonization and conquest.

Estrelda Alexander, by contrast, moves (I think) prematurely toward an easy resolution of African spiritualities as partly (or essentially) monotheistic. Yet, arguments might be made against both monotheism and polytheism as appropriately describing African primal religions. Some scholars gesture toward African primal religions as henotheistic. Henotheism is the worship of a single god while not denying the existence or possible existence of other deities for a particular religion. Alexander asserts that the supreme God in African religions is served by "a host of lesser, immanent gods who function like the angelic realm in Western religious conceptions."[64] But is a Judeo-Christian comparison fair or accurate? There is robust debate on whether Afro-Asiatic religions out of which African traditional religions grew were *henotheistic*. Linguist Christopher Ehret argues that traditional religion among early Afro-Asiatic peoples was henotheistic in nature.[65] Each clan gave their allegiance to the community's own god while still accepting that other gods existed or could possibly exist.[66] Yet explaining African religious traditions within European monotheistic categories as a way to "save" these traditions from polytheism once again participates in the European project of racial and religious hierarchy and domination. African spiritualties have their own basic terms that do not necessarily need to be reconciled to Christian orthodoxy. Similarly, slave religious practices at Azusa are not *easily* reconcilable with white Christian orthodoxy at the turn of the twentieth century. Although the Azusa community was certainly Christocentric, they had a variety of doctrinal commitments that would eventually constitute mainline Pentecostal denominations. Strict doctrinal fidelity was simply not the test of Christian identity for this community.

What might it mean to speak about the black roots of Azusa in complex terms that resist too quickly reconciling it to Christian orthodoxy? In *Significations*, religious scholar Charles Long asks scholars of religion to deepen their understandings of what shapes different religious worlds or "those forms of meaning which lie between experience category."[67] Long reminds scholars that there are some religious forms that are fundamentally *irreducible to categories themselves.* Some religious expressions invoke an attentiveness to the unexpected, to excess, and to surprise beyond the systematization of ideas and their meanings. Moreover, such religious forms point to other ways of knowing beyond dominant doctrinal categories and dogmas. The slave religious practice of shouting and conjuring are different kinds of knowing that are ascertained in an embodied way rather than through abstract beliefs or doctrines.

Consider the work of anthropologist Michael Jackson. In his fascinating account of the initiation of girls into adulthood by the Kuranko people of northern Sierra Leone, instead of searching for and prioritizing overarching worldviews or dogmas, he attempts to demonstrate that the body praxis and actions of these girls do not stand for some abstraction or universal idea beyond itself, as their dances and movements produce adult subjectivity as well as their sense of orientation to space, time, and language.[68] The Kuranko people are far less interested in conceptual questions in relation to these cultural and religious rituals to adulthood (such as, "What constitutes particular actions that mark the initiator as an adult?"). For these people, this ritual is more about *practicing and performing* social wisdom and cultivating co-presence through dancing, greeting, working together, moving as one, and so forth.[69] It is an embodied ritual that does not point beyond itself to some pregiven epistemological formation. Jackson demonstrates that the Kuranko people's participation in these performances become an end in itself rather than a means to an end that can be observed and interpreted elsewhere after the event. The example of the Kuranko people points to a different way of knowing, a form of religious meaning that lies between experience and category/doctrine.

One might argue that the religious experiences of Azusa likewise lie between experience and category/doctrine.[70] Seymour's leadership demonstrates that Azusa was experimental territory. This movement and its spiritual experiences were radical, pressing the edges of orthodoxy. Robeck remarks that Seymour had "to provide safe space for his followers to experiment, setting them free to learn their own lessons."[71] Seymour was often tentative in his theological conclusions as "he had to provide a forum for various members of his congregation to make their case, without fear of recrimination."[72] For instance, the Azusa congregation experimented with "writing in tongues." Although there was no biblical or theological precedent for this practice, Seymour opened himself to the possibility. Within white Pentecostal doctrine (such as that which Parham espoused), tongues (xenolalia) was understood to be evidence and a sign of the third person of the Trinity, and specifically of the Holy Spirit empowering an individual for ministry during the end-times. Were tongues (glossolalia) something else altogether—perhaps a form of angelic speech? And could this speech be written and translated? If glossolalia was ultimately a kind of language that had a written form, why should one not be open to the possibility of *writing* in tongues? These inquiries allowed the Azusa movement to experiment with religious experience in ways that dominant Christian doctrine would not allow, although Seymour and other leaders also used doctrine to correct members if, in their opinion, such experimentation went too far. The truth is actually a bit more pointed: only after the newspaper press commented on the bizarre character of writing in tongues did Seymour no longer condone this practice.[73]

Doctrine still had a place, but a place *relative* to experience. Experience could always revise basic conceptual truths on any number of theological issues. In contrast, white Evangelical ministers like Parham go to great lengths to conceive and interpret doctrinally the experiences of Azusa. The rational and the doctrinal *were everything* for Parham; he notably stated that "very few of the [community] talk in real tongues."

What is at stake in this comparison between Parham and Seymour is that Parham's doctrinal turn could not make the slave religious practices of Azusa legible within the grammar of Christian orthodoxy. Deemed *doctrinally deviant*, they have no relevance for Pentecost. Parham interprets them as sinful and demonic, a result of fallen flesh. They are heterodox—having minimal orthodox elements (such as belief in Jesus Christ)—but are not in complete alignment with the true character and nature of Christian belief and practice. Sadly, white Evangelical leaders' interpretation of Azusa's religious life reveals the racist character of white Christian discourse at the turn of the twentieth century. I suggest that the Azusa Revival must be rethought as a radical intervention into the racist character of Christian orthodoxy.

Rejecting the Economic Racism of Market Orthodoxy

How might we think of the Revival as a radical intervention into economic orthodoxies as well? For one, Azusa challenged the market orthodoxies that many white Evangelical Christian churches embraced and celebrated. These market orthodoxies created a world which regarded markets as empowering societies to march towards unprecedented economic and social progress. These orthodoxies were bedrock for capitalists. They were orthodoxies such as the view that markets inherently sponsor freedom and equity, demonstrating a break from the inefficiency and backward ways of the old slave feudal order; that markets are colorblind, as markets assume rationale economic agents who are not swayed by nonrational racial reasons that could endanger profit; that markets will usher in an age of prosperity and peace; and that greater market consumerism could cultivate happiness and contentment among citizens. Unfortunately, the realities of capitalist markets contradicted the "truth" of these orthodoxies. Markets did not inherently sponsor political freedom and economic equity, for black people and immigrants endured gross forms of economic exploitation to make industrial capitalists even more wealthy. Markets were not colorblind, but in fact depended on the unequal labor of people of color, proving that economic racism was central to the American capitalist project. Markets did not inevitably usher in prosperity and peace, for one could see the ongoing systemic realities of racial, gender, and class injustice within the U.S. capitalist system. Expanding consumerism would not generate happiness and contentment if this constant need to accrue material things and financial wealth was the sole measure of one's human value and worth.

Specifically, the Azusa church community rejected the idea that markets secure greater political freedom and economic equity. Instead it was economic racism that was the foundation of early modern capitalism in the United States, and that capitalism merely repurposed structural racism for profitable ends. Unlike many white Evangelical churches, Azusa actually challenged this market assumption.

Consider how August 5, 1906, potentially sheds light on some Azusa members' rejection of economic racism on the question of labor, demonstrating that they were suspicious of viewing markets as essentially colorblind, and as securing freedom and equity for all citizens. On that day the police were called to Azusa Street for a different kind of disturbance than noisy religious services. According to the *Los Angeles Times*, a few Azusa participants had learned about a labor protest and threatened to join this organized march on the streets of L.A. Although ultimately no arrests were made, neighbors in the Azusa Street area reported this incident to police.[74] What made it so controversial? Perhaps, that Azusa participants would participate in what local neighbors (who lived near Azusa Street) called "communist" and "anarchist" behavior.

In fact the labor protest was being held in response to the arrest and trial of Charles Moyer, president of the Western Federation of Miners (WFM), a subversive and radical labor union that organized miners and smelter workers in the Rocky Mountain states.[75] This union was known for its advocacy of miners in response to the abuses they incurred at the hands of their industrial employers and governmental authorities. Having also played a central role in founding the Industrial Workers of the World in 1905, WFM was committed to industrial unionism and socialist ideals, not only objecting to how capitalism left mine owners with all the gold and the miners with nothing but also asserting that capitalism was inherently exploitative and oppressive.[76]

I am specifically interested in how this protest reveals the racial fault lines on the question of labor, an issue to which Azusa members would have been privy. On the one hand, the burgeoning labor movement in Los Angeles was deeply divided, often discriminating against blacks and some immigrants (notably Mexicans), refusing their participation in unions. On the other hand, white union leaders knew that employers often used (nonunion) black and Mexican labor as a way to break union control, a practice white workers resented.[77] The employers also used black and Mexican labor because these workers would often have no choice but to accept work under highly exploitative conditions in order to survive. While blue-collar white workers certainly experienced labor exploitation, black and Mexican workers were treated much worse. Compounded by many craft and trade unions that excluded African Americans, blacks (and at times, Mexican immigrants) remained doubly vulnerable to oppressive labor practices.[78]

In Los Angeles, black and white residents knew that union protests often affected black and immigrant well-being, even when white union leaders were not intentionally targeting these communities. For instance, the Union Labor Party in Los Angeles between 1901 and 1903 issued a list of demands to the municipal government which included an eight-hour work day, equal pay for men and women, weekly payment of wages for municipal employees, and more.[79] This list of demands would have directly affected black men who were municipal janitors and transportation workers.

As a result, one can imagine that protesting the objectification of labor in L.A. would have been to the benefit of members associated with the Azusa Revival, especially black and Mexican members. Perhaps they wanted to make a statement that black and immigrant labor, in particular, should not be treated as a tool within inequitable American markets, which was a practice that capitalist endeavors like the world fairs explicitly justified. Recall in the previous chapter that politicians and ministers supported the use of black labor in the South for America's burgeoning industrial economy precisely because of the South's stringent Jim Crow laws. If the South provided a large black labor force, then companies would not have to worry about protests and strikes due to the virulent racism meted out in the South for rebellious behavior. Black labor was an object in service to market ends. Unfortunately, early American industrialism depended on this kind of racialized capitalism.

These few Azusa members who protested surely would have seen this capitalist view of black bodies (and all workers) as erroneous and sinful. Black individuals at the revival saw their bodies as sacred sites of divine presence and activity. Through their religious practices and rituals, members were able to re-create themselves, to exercise their agency in ways that granted them meaning beyond American capitalism's instrumental usage of their bodies as labor. Even Azusa members' protest signaled their rejection of the white Evangelical vision of America, a vision that objectified black bodies in an effort to use blacks (and immigrants) as free or cheap labor.

Because Los Angeles was slowly becoming an important context for the growing labor movement due to its increasing number of black migrants and immigrants, it made sense that these members wanted to be part of this protest. According to *Los Angeles Times*, this protest would gather unionists and socialists not only to challenge the inhumane conditions that workers endured but also to contest the injustices associated with capitalism. This case potentially provided an easy opportunity for owners and governmental officials to shut down the labor movement, as the circumstances surrounding Charles Moyer's arrest were related to the murder of a former Idaho governor, Frank Steunenburg.[80] The *Times* reference to the protesters as anarchists and communists was intentional. It was meant to foster disapproval and animus toward workers who protested, many of them black migrants and immigrants. Union organizations and the workers they represented did not want this to happen. Therefore, union leaders in Los Angeles prepared for a night of march and protest throughout the streets of L.A. And some members of Azusa were described as threatening to join this protest in order to challenge the reigning market orthodoxy of the day on the question of exploitative labor.[81]

What was the general position of white churches on this issue of exploitative labor and union protest in L.A.? Many white churches were against any form of protest. In large part, the general white populace not only saw industrial activity as central to a prosperous future but also regarded protesting among immigrants and black migrants as a cultural threat to white Christian ways of life, of which capitalism was a central aspect of democracy. In other words, many white residents in L.A. saw protesters (specifically blacks and immigrants) as an exact representation of all that was morally and spiritually wrong with America. Immigrant and black migrant workers represented disorder to the cultural and moral fabric of white Protestant culture. They saw such protests not as a natural outgrowth of inequality and deprivation experienced among the masses of poor workers, but as a reflection of heretical religious and social beliefs among racial others.

The narrative of blacks and immigrants as morally and spiritually debased has an extended history in Los Angeles, and this impeded white residents of L.A. from seeing *why* such protests were essential to the flourishing of working-class and poor populations. I have already described at length about how whites in the country at large considered blacks to be morally and spiritually debased. By the end of the nineteenth century, Los Angeles would also possess these sentiments about immigrants. For example, Lexington (several miles from L.A.) had a settlement of Texas Baptists but they were known for their disgust toward Hispanics, believing that Spanish-speaking Catholics were hardened sinners who could not be reached.[82] Moreover, most of these Anglo settlers who were Baptist could not speak Spanish, so this further reinforced their racist bigotry. Presbyterians also held these xenophobic feelings, disliking Hispanic customs. In 1855, Reverend James Woods preached that like Sodom and Gomorrah, L.A. would be destroyed if it did not repent from its wayward religious beliefs associated with Catholicism. He referred to Catholicism as "idolatry, idolatry, idolatry."[83] He further remarked that the Catholic Hispanic aristocracy was "a dark-complexioned set with darker minds and morals."[84] White leaders like him, and their congregations, regarded Catholic Mexicans as heretics and sinners, with dark minds and hearts, who needed to embrace the white Protestant light.

Similarly, Chinese immigrants were also a large religious presence within the city of L.A., whom whites labeled as a threat to their Christian morals and values. Although the first Chinese person was recorded as a servant in early Spanish *pueblo* L.A., a number relocated in the 1870s in order to be agriculture workers. These Chinese immigrants followed the traditional folk religion of China, which white Evangelical leaders viewed as demonic and heathenistic.[85] These leaders called the Chinese pagan and heathens. Even local newspapers documented this white American feeling about the Chinese. A journalist wrote that L.A. residents had enough of the "substratum of the human family" without additional "outcasts from the Flowery Kingdom." This kind of racist ideology toward the Chinese eventually contributed to the Chinese Massacre of 1871 in which nineteen Chinese people were killed in what white L.A. residents referred to as "Nigger Alley" (a primarily black and Mexican residential area of town).[86] Unfortunately, white Protestant antipathy had been linked with this massacre, as Protestant Christian denominations in 1871 had begun a fervent campaign to evangelize and Americanize the Chinese.[87]

By 1880, white Protestant church leaders concluded that the religious solution to the heterodoxy of L.A. would be for the "right sort of people" to settle in this city. When white Americans moved from Missouri, Illinois, Ohio, Pennsylvania, New York, and other states in the 1870s, the city began to change quite drastically. These white American residents became more determined to promote white nationalist concepts of Christian religion, government, and society.[88] As discussed in the previous chapter, white Protestant Evangelical ideas of Christian faith joined itself to white supremacist ideology and unbridled free-market capitalism. It considered all other ethnic customs and religious expressions to be heathenistic and demonic. These white racist sensibilities arrived and were enacted with greater intensity in L.A. by the 1870s and 1880s. They became most pronounced when even more diverse immigrants moved into L.A. in the 1880s and 1890s, such as Chinese workers. White Evangelical anxiety was present in L.A. as the Azusa Revival was being birthed at the start of the twentieth century. White Evangelical leaders' denouncing of slave religious practices as heretical and pagan was a sign of such racist anxiety. And so they identified and labeled Azusa as deviant and heterodox, a direct challenge to the white Evangelical and market orthodoxy of the day.

Challenging the "Moneyed" Eschaton of Market Orthodoxy

Azusa also challenged the market orthodox view that possessing money and material wealth secures human happiness and contentment. This revival resists the moneyed eschaton that white *and* educated black Evangelical churches in Los Angeles championed. Why was it important for this community to reject the moneyed eschaton that guided so many Evangelical churches? When I speak of a moneyed eschaton, I am referring to the idea that money secures and inaugurates a new era of wealth, health, and well-being. It is the belief that financial wealth and expanded consumerism can secure meaning in one's life pursuits and endeavors. As discussed in Chapter 1, the world fairs promoted the notion that *the dawn of a new age of prosperity* could be secured through capital, money, and increasing consumerism. Likewise, many individual churches (white and black) believed that American capitalism was the key to human happiness. American capitalism's promise was that participation in the pursuit of money, capital, and consumerism would fulfill and achieve a state of future human flourishing and peace. This moneyed eschaton guided how some churches and the broader society conceptualized and practiced Christian faith.

Consider how this revival's building at 312 Azusa Street stood as a critique to the moneyed eschaton that guided many American organizations (including churches) in Los Angeles. Seymour stumbled upon an abandoned building on Azusa Street, which had previously been an AME church. Seriously damaged by fire, the "dilapidated forty-by-sixty foot, two storied whitewashed building had been converted into a horse stable and storage room on the first floor and tenement apartments on the second."[89] He decided to secure this unimposing edifice. In part, Seymour chose this building because he did not want to draw attention to the fact that a black man was helping to lead this multicultural congregation, knowing that it would have met with the local white community's disapproval and even ire. Seymour thought that choosing a building in a more disadvantaged working-class area would keep the congregation fairly hidden. (He was wrong. The press sought out the congregation despite its location and shabbiness.) This barn-turned-church had cobweb-lined ceilings, a sawdust-covered dirt floor, and handmade pews that made it feel as if the church were on a frontier.[90] Members often reported that the building smelled more like a barn than a church.[91] In addition, the church's immediate neighbors were a tombstone shop, a lumberyard, and a stockyard. It was into this barnlike building, one that attendees "compared to Jesus' humble manger in Bethlehem," that Seymour decided to move the growing community.[92]

Most intriguing, much of the contents of the church represented the *waste of capitalism*. For they used things that were considered to be of no value, outside the realm of commodification, commercialization, and packaging for profit. Pews were handmade, probably from thrown-away lumber they found in the industrial area in which the building was located. In the beginning, the Azusa congregation did not have musical instruments, but when they eventually integrated instruments into their service, most were handmade or donated.[93] In short, Azusa's building and its contents could not be monetized.

The humble, nonconsumerist character of the Azusa community stood as a formidable critique of moneyed churches in L.A., especially black churches. Black churches in L.A. appealed largely to the middle and upper classes of African

Americans whose families had roots in this city. For many black Azusa members, these elite black churches sought to achieve white respectability by embracing dominant white cultural values of American society, which included a preoccupation with the appearance of economic wealth. These black churches built imposing, multipurpose structures of brick and stained glass.[94] They invested in large pipe organs, purchased hymnals, and developed elaborate choirs and ensembles. They also rejected the primitive black religious practices of visions, dreams, dancing, and falling in the Spirit in favor of educated elaborations of scripture that privileged European critical methods of interpretation.[95] These churches emphasized titles and degrees as qualifications for higher cultural status within the community. It's not that these things, by themselves, are bad. The problem was that these middle- to upper-class blacks believed that being associated with churches marked by these consumerist trappings gave them superior cultural status than poorer black communities. They imagined themselves employing cultural sophistication around their activities and affiliations like their white counterparts in order to appear successful within a wealth-driven society. They believed that money and wealth could enable blacks to achieve happiness beyond the strictures of racial discrimination and exploitation.

By contrast, most members at Azusa did not have access to professions, degrees, or titles. In the Apostolic Mission church, there was no traditional middle-class pipe organ but a cappella singing often accompanied by hand-clapping and foot-stomping, creating rhythms and beats through spoons, washboards, and tambourines.[96] At Azusa, there were no hymnals. Instead, the whole congregation served as one large choir, often providing music in a call-and-response format. Interestingly, Frank Bartlemann himself noted that "hymnals today are too largely a commercial proposition,"[97] a statement which recognized that Christian hymnody in America participated in larger market, profit-oriented processes. No titles were really desired or necessary, as everyone just referred to each other as "Sister" or "Brother." The Azusa community did not accept that the consumerist trappings of the moneyed black churches in L.A. made middle- to upper-class blacks intrinsically happier, better, or more cultured.

Seymour personally rejects the moneyed eschaton and consumerist trappings that characterized these wealthy black churches in L.A. He doubted whether wealth and money would secure and inaugurate a new age of racial peace and overall prosperity. In his sermon "The Holy Spirit: Bishop of the Church," he notes that many people thought that churches needed "stone structures, brick structures, modern improvements, new choirs, trained singers right from the

conservatories, paying from seven to fifteen hundred dollars a year for singing, fine pews, fine chandeliers" in order to "attract the human heart to win
souls."[98] He further states that many people are glad to go to church "because
they have seen great wealth, they have seen people in the very latest styles, in
different costumes, and loaded down with jewelry, decorated from head to foot
with diamonds, gold and silver."[99] Seymour is directly critiquing historic black
congregations that mistook their wealth, money, and ability to participate in a
consumerist capitalist culture with divine favor and future happiness. Crude
materialism and endless consumerism would not be the means or ends of happiness and flourishing for this church community. Money would not be a symbol
of Christian fulfillment and progress.

Another sermon of Seymour entitled "Money Matters" further demonstrates
Azusa's resistance to this moneyed eschaton that many middle- to upper-class
churches in Los Angeles gladly embraced. In this sermon, Seymour tries to
locate the significance of money outside of a rabidly consumerist, profit-driven
economy, which values money for *money's sake*. This way of viewing money
teaches the individual primarily to concern herself with what she can accrue and
acquire rather than what she can give. Seymour suggests that God's economy is
not about how much the church can profit from others or through markets but
how churches participate in an economy of mutual giving and sharing. Having
money is not the problem; it's *what one does with money* that is. Within America,
money not only participated in the circuits of racial capitalism but also was seen
as securing a future age of cultural happiness and economic peace. Seymour
debunked this notion. In this sermon, he offers a vision of how the Azusa community might think about the significance of money away from primary values
of individual profit and rabid consumerism. This noncommodified perspective
of money is only possible by seeing money as instrumental within an economy
of mutual giving and sharing across racial, class, and gender differences.

Seymour makes it clear that giving is not framed as a demand or requirement in the Azusa church. Giving transpires out of knowledge and experience
of a gracious and giving God, and through remembering that the Holy Spirit
provides the production and distribution of endless gifts for the flourishing of
the church. He cites the "Acts church" as an example of how the Spirit inspired
some members to "participate in radical giving," here he is invoking Acts 4:32–
35, which describes many people in the early church as selling their possessions
and placing the monies from those sales at the feet of the apostles to distribute as
need arose among more deprived members of the community. The early church

understood the significance of possessions and material things within an economy of mutual giving and sharing. Yet Seymour tempers praise for such "selling out" by reminding people that they have families and their first responsibility is to care for their loved ones.[100] His overall point is that money is not simply a tool for unending profit. In Seymour's account, money can be used in creative and generative ways to create belonging, care, and connection within community.

In "Money Matters," Seymour also castigates preachers and teachers who try to pimp or exploit the masses through *monetizing* church services and other activities. Seymour offers a clear injunction: preachers and teachers must support their own ministries through their own labor, not through preaching and developing elaborate schemes to seduce people out of their money. Leaders must be responsible for the spiritual and material well-being of church communities, which means not acting in ways to promote one's own interest. This point would have been an important statement in light of the consumerist middle- and upper-class churches in L.A. Seymour knew how the masses of workers in Los Angeles were already being exploited. He intended the Azusa community to foster an alternative model of church and church leadership, one that did not treat the church as a capitalist enterprise and instead embraced the church as a context of mutual giving and receiving.

Seymour's words on private property are especially revealing regarding what motivates his discussion about an economy of mutual giving and sharing. He maintains that the Acts church's economy of giving is not the same as socialism. Seymour clearly supports private property, yet he doesn't have an individualistic, hypercapitalist view of property. He asserts in this sermon, "It is right for you to have property, but if the Lord says, take $200 or $500 or $1000 and distribute here and there, you do it."[101] The problem is not private property in itself, but *how private property often shapes our moral subjectivity*. Amassing wealth often leads the wealthy person to look down on others who do not share his economic status. Wealthy persons also tend to see their wealth as part of their own achievement rather than recognizing how economic and social structures—including people of a lower class than them—make their wealth possible, often through inequitable means. Money can change people for the worse and cause them to place material things above other human beings. Money can remake people into narcissists who are unable to see the humanity of others. Seymour wants to explore more generative forms of moral agency that allow people to handle money in humane ways that enrich entire communities. Seymour is not so much interested in modes of production as much as *modes of exchange*, how these modes shape us relationally and empower us to give with radical generosity, a way of life that was alien to modern capitalist arrangements. I recognize that a more structural emphasis on wealth creation by Seymour would have been helpful. While Seymour does not centralize this, he does gesture toward the systemic reasons why wealthy people should be more humble than they are: if unequal structures were not in place, they may not have their wealth at all.[102]

In "Money Matters," Seymour also maintains that this radical ethic of giving is not simply about the giving of things but the giving of *oneself*. Seymour talks about matters of money, deprivation, suffering, and destitution in order to specify how this community should be accountable—how each member should give themselves with and for others. He asserts, "It does not mean for you to have great real estate and money banked up while your brothers and sisters are suffering. He [Holy Spirit] means for you to turn [it] loose because all that money is soon going to be thrown to the moles and bats."[103] Seymour is clear about what marks God's economy: not just giving money but a radical giving of oneself, which includes one's material possessions, especially when one encounters suffering. This radical giving *of* oneself is not about giving *up* oneself. Rather it is about practices of mutual generosity and reciprocity, with special attention to those who suffer and are exploited. Individual flourishing is only truly possible when considered within the broader context of communal well-being, which means attending to those on the margins of society. Seymour gestures toward an economy of mutual giving that privileges those who suffer, a focus alien to American capitalist practices.

What is particularly interesting is that Seymour preached this sermon in November 1906—one month after some Azusa members had threatened to march with the labor protests mentioned early in this chapter. Was Seymour's sermon partly in response to the desires of these few participants to protest? We may never know. However, Seymour's conversation about God's economy helps one to understand more deeply the radical ethic of mutual giving and sharing that was commended, an ethic that took seriously both self-regard and regard of others. Despite their own impoverished status, he encouraged Azusa members to see radical giving of self and riches to each other (and the broader world) as central to their Christian witness.

This rejection of a moneyed eschaton (financial wealth securing a new age of prosperity and happiness) is further seen in the *Apostolic Faith Newsletter* that this church community established from 1906 to 1909. Much about the newsletter and how it ignited the global growth of Pentecostalism has already been documented (through Pentecostal scholars Gaston Espinosa and Cecil Robeck's writings) but little has been written about the ethics of the funding, production, and distribution of this newsletter. The newsletter provided firsthand accounts of the revival and its leadership through sermons, testimonials, and more. Seymour and his editorial team published thirteen editions from September 1906 to May 1908. The daily operations were performed mostly on a volunteer basis with a former news reporter named Glenn Cook at the helm (until Clara Lum replaced him after he moved on).[104] By 1907, the newsletter staff was receiving as many as fifty letters a day and the volunteer staff tried to answer each letter personally. This required two people to work full-time simply to keep up with the correspondence. Thus the production of this newsletter relied on volunteers who believed in the cause of this movement and who measured the value of their labor not in terms of money but in terms of the relationships they had with readers around the world who desired to participate in this revival.

How Azusa funded the newsletter was countercultural to the market strategies of the day as well. The Azusa church refused to charge its readers for the newsletter. They did not want to monetize it in the way other Christian organizations made money from ventures such as marketing Bibles, hymnals, and other Christian products and materials. In part, the Azusa leadership knew that charging their readers could create a *problem of access*, particularly for members around the world who were deeply impoverished. Besides, even in Los Angeles the vast majority of those who attended the revival were among the poor working classes. Being able to access and read about the activities of the revival was important for people who wanted to somehow join or support this church movement. Apostolic Mission church also never officially collected offerings, as leadership was deeply aware of the financial status of the people they were serving. However, readers were reminded of the needs associated with publishing a paper and the editor often suggested that some might like to make a contribution to the paper's ongoing efforts through cash or U.S. postage stamps.[105] The paper was self-supporting and the Azusa community imagined this newsletter participating in this economy of mutual giving, refusing to monetize the work of the church.

Azusa's distribution of this newsletter also directly challenged the rapid consumerism that other L.A. churches so easily embraced. Those who requested copies often received multiple copies—one for themselves plus some for further distribution.[106] The distribution of this paper operated against market logic. Market logic demands that products should be bought and consumed by individuals who will eventually move on to (i.e., purchase) the next great thing being advertised. This paper defied this market view. This paper was *recycled* and shared with and among communities. Money and profit margins would not regulate its circulation and consumption. Instead, a desire to share, over and over again, the stories and joy of this paper among different communities would be the end goal of this newsletter enterprise. The production, funding, and distribution of this newsletter challenged the practices of U.S. market capitalism because it did not treat the newsletter as a commodity in which the paper's meaning and significance was measured by its ability to make a profit. The value of the paper transcended market exchange and pointed toward a different economic vision, in which all are able to have access and share in the activities of this movement.

The Azusa community foregrounded alternate ways of structuring human worth beyond the values of early American capitalism. Azusa was not striving for human worth within the structures of value associated with early consumerist racial capitalism. It did not want to reproduce the fundamental values associated with industrial markets. Its members knew that they were more than labor units within American industrial processes. They also believed that securing joy, happiness, and worth could not be measured by what one bought or possessed. Wealth, they knew, was not a sign of divine favor or human prosperity. Members of Azusa refused the tragic market narrative which presumed the worth of black people (and other persons) through how they contributed to a white supremacist capitalist system. Azusa knew that their desires and becoming as human beings before God constituted their worth, not their participation in an evil and oppressive economic system.

So, Azusa reenvisioned wealth. Unlike larger society, this community modeled different experiences of wealth not married to the promise of money and its redemption. They could not be redeemed through capitalism. In fact, they were irredeemable within this market, profit-driven context. Wealth can serve as a source of freedom rather than entrapment but this means rethinking wealth as an abundance of joy, peace, and fulfillment secured in and through the quality of our relationships. This means conceiving of wealth in terms of human relationships and shared life in community. And this human community happens not through asserting our consumerist and moneyed capacities but through refusing to participate in racist systems of production associated with early market capitalism. Racial capitalism could not save. Azusa religious life captures this truth.

To use Oscar Garcia-Johnson's words, the Azusa community represented the "spirit outside the gates" of Christian orthodoxy.[107] I would add that Azusa also represents a way of life outside the gates of market orthodoxy. It was a church community-turned-movement that sought to break all rigid borders in order to imagine an alternative economy of mutual giving and sharing.

3 BLACK FEMALE GENIUS

BLACK WOMEN WERE NOT mere participants at Azusa; they were central to its founding and shaping. Neely Turner. Lucy Farrow. Julia Hutchins. These black women of Azusa were also black domestic workers. Black women domestics were treated as disposable within the matrices of American racial capitalism, but at Azusa they became the figures that ignited and shaped the movement. It is important to highlight the religious leadership and cultural practices of black women domestics who were central to Azusa yet dehumanized within American capitalist processes. Black women domestics and their leadership of Azusa's religious practices created the very conditions of radical relationality at Azusa, making possible practices of connection, care, joy, and intimacy within this religious community.

A number of scholars do regard women as leaders who contribute to Azusa, but not as *primary figures* who produced this movement. They are not seen as primary agents that make possible the founding of a series of events that we call Azusa and that change the course of American Christianity and global religiosity more broadly. What would it mean to write these black women back into the genealogies of early Pentecostalism as central to the founding events of Azusa? To be clear, this question is not about mere *inclusion* of women into the current masculinist scholarly framings of Azusa's founding. Rather, it is a question that radically revisits the conditions under which Azusa came into being and flourished. I propose "founding" as a process that names *the collective* (of women and men) as central to the founding events of this movement. For the individualiza-tion of "the founder" (whether Charles Parham or William Seymour) conceals an entire network of egalitarian relations that made this movement possible. The masculinist, individualist framing of the founder neglects the primary role black women domestics played in birthing and maintaining this movement.

This chapter will first turn to the history of trauma and resilience that has marked black women domestics within racial capitalism, before exploring these women's role at Azusa. Black women's cultivation and preservation of certain slave religious practices became instrumental to Azusa's countercultural forms of religious life. Black women's guardianship of these practices also challenged how America's racist economy imagined and treated these women—as lacking in reason, imagination, and genius. I conclude this chapter by examining how em-phasizing the collective disrupts current Pentecostal scholarship on *the* founder of Azusa, a discourse that is highly patriarchal and individualistic.

The Pained Resilience of Black Women Domestics

The black women who birthed Azusa were domestic workers. Throughout the history of the United States, black women have served as domestics, first as "house slaves" on plantations and then in wealthier white homes during the Jim Crow era. Even in the 1960s, 90 percent of black women in the South were still domestic workers.[1] These women held stories of abuse, exploitation, and grief around their time as domestics. The black woman domestic thus not only reveals the gendered forms of racism black women suffered but also points toward the objectification of these women in early industrial economies. Do-mestic workers were seen as merely free or cheap labor in service to America's racial-capitalist ends, although affluent white households depended utterly on their labor.

Black women's experience of domestic service at the start of the twentieth century is inextricably linked to the history of black women's servility within slave economies. Literary theorist and cultural historian Saidiya Hartman chronicles the story of black women migrants who moved from the South to northern cities such as New York City at the start of the twentieth century in search of work, fleeing the severity of racial apartheid in the South. Although Hartman charts the forms of resistance that these women created in the midst of harsh stigmatization and servitude in the North (what she refers to as "beautiful ex-periments" or creative, subversive ways of living that empowered black women to defy and disrupt the racist and hetero-patriarchal indignities they endured), she challenges the perception that black women's domestic work was a better or less harsh option. Hartman reminds the reader that during slavery, the house was no better than the oppressive heat and labor of the fields. Domestic work was merciless and unsparing inside the plantation house. It was about "shucking oysters and harvesting tobacco—the stench of fish, or hands sticky and yellow from nicotine, the headaches and nausea; or the unwanted touch, the pressing and grabbing under the dress. Submit or risk a beating. Ass, hands and capacities owned by mistress and sir."[2] No black woman could forget the indignities of the plantation house. Domestic service was absolutely tainted by slavery. The "kitchen was the field and the brothel" for black women.[3] Domestic service was black women's punishment simply for being a woman and black.

Even when these women migrated to northern cities trying to flee the grip of southern plantation racism, they were conscripted into domestic work. Institutes for black women educated them in domestic work. Consider Hampton Institute, where young black men and women received industrial and educational training, but where every girl received instruction in general housework and domestic chores, inculcating the very idea of servility deeply into young black women.[4] Black women were fixed in place as domestics, stuck doing laundry and chained to the ironing board, always cooking and cleaning for others.[5]

We could justifiably say that the black woman domestic was *sentenced* to manual labor. She labored within a home that was not her own, tackling duties that included cooking, washing, grooming children, cleaning, and tending to other chores dictated to her by the master and the mistress of the home, who of course never worked alongside her. Manual labor was an occupation in which a woman was treated as if she were owned, branded, invaded, not autonomous. Such labor separated her, marked her as different and servile compared to those who had agency to exercise their reason or imagination, particularly in their own spaces.[6] She was the representation of a tool or object of labor, "not a proposal for black female genius," in the words of Hartman, and hence a possession or property.[7] The domestic worker who performed manual labor signified nothing more than a mule of the world, to use Zora Neale Hurston's words, a possession in the hands of masters to grant the master pleasure and profit.[8]

Black women domestics were imagined in racist and commodifying ways. These women were handled—that word says it all—like a slave, a Jezebel, a wench, a bitch, a whore, and a nigger. Of those images and roles, the one of Jezebel has been treated particularly often by academics. For example, black feminist and cultural theorist Tamura Lomax talks at length about black women being imagined and interpreted by white capitalist society and even within black communities as a Jezebel. What did that mean? With its conceptual beginnings in Europe in the image of the Black Venus and as the biblical Jezebel in America,[9] the racial trope of Jezebel interpreted black women as wicked, immoral seductresses.[10] From the plantation house to the church house, this Jezebel image fueled how black women and girls' bodies were conceptualized and treated: as objects and tools made for capital, labor, and white male pleasure. Lomax describes in detail how the gendered representation of Jezebel aided in the construction of racial capitalism in America by distinguishing between white and black women for the purposes of labor.

Drawing on black feminist Angela Davis and black feminist and cultural theorist Hortense Spillers, Lomax demonstrates that this Jezebel trope enabled white capitalist society to imagine and treat black women and girls' bodies as "moveable property, bought and sold, seen in terms of nature and as workers, though not equal to men."[11] Lomax stresses an important point: that this Jezebel image sought to *naturalize* or make natural and normal the commodification of black women's bodies and, more specifically their wombs, for purposes of profit. She asserts, "Slaves were considered as quantities quantifiable by their ability to increase the owners' stock. Enslaved reproduction was especially crucial to plantation capital. . . . The commodification of black women and girls' wombs as simultaneously lucrative, imperfect, advantageous, grotesque, enticing, and wild/life distinguished them as quintessentially deviant."[12] The Jezebel image legitimated black women and girls' bodies as free labor, and in the process rendered them morally deviant, which created a vicious cycle of interpreting black women's economic and social status as a result of them being morally and sexually deviant (certainly a precursor to the "welfare queen" trope in the United States). This circular argument about the deviance of black women and girls was of course vicious and wrong. The enslaved woman's reproductive capacities were not her own but in service to economic output in a white racist plantation economy. These women lived and worked at the whim of their white masters and mistresses, used by them to achieve greater economic productivity and higher white cultural standing. Pejoratively deeming them to be Jezebels, then, in a twisted way justified the extraction and expropriation of their labor, including their reproductive labor—their very children.[13]

Even into the twentieth century, the black woman domestic continued to be framed through the Jezebel trope. The black domestic worker was never to be confused with *housewives* or *homemakers*. Only white women could be housewives. The Victorian cult of true womanhood which intensified during the industrial period was important for a few reasons. The narrative of white women reflecting Victorian values of domesticity and purity solidified patriarchal gender roles between white men and them, showing that women's domain was the domestic sphere while men's domain was the public square. Because the private/public split was less useful within an agricultural economy as the house was the site of both production and consumption, the cult of true womanhood was even more necessary to reinforce social and moral order (read: maintain white supremacy) as industrialization emerged. This narrative of white women embodying true womanhood was also to distinguish her from *other* women such black women. Whereas white middle-class women possessed virtue because of their commitment to a life of domesticity, to child rearing and homemaking (essentially cooking and cleaning, but home-making sounded so much more worthy!), black women were described as public and wayward women who violated such norms of purity, as it was unfairly presumed that they had a long history of sexual work in private and public spaces. These white Victorian values of women's domesticity distinguished between good wives and "nasty wenches," white women and black women respectively. This distinction certainly revealed anxious white patriarchs who needed to keep America's white social order intact for cultural and economic reasons.[14]

Unfortunately, the desires and emotions of the masses of black women domestics are without archive, as many were not literate and could leave no written record (although these women certainly left living records in other ways such as through songs, quilts, oral stories, paintings, and other cultural artifacts). However, among the ones who could read and write, they told stories of their experience. Harriet Jacobs and her book *Incidents in the Life of a Slave Girl* is perhaps one of the most well-known narratives of an enslaved girl who performed unpaid domestic duties, eventually escaping to freedom. She detailed her life as an enslaved woman and the sexual, physical, and emotional abuse she endured at the hands of her white masters. She also appealed to northern white women to expand their moral knowledge and intuitions surrounding slavery, and noted that many of these women failed to comprehend the horrors of this dehumanizing institution. Jacobs's direct engagement with race and gender issues, as well as the ways slavery colonized and exploited the reproductive life of black women, sheds light on how intimately connected racist culture and American economy were. Black women's oppression depended on gendered forms of racism that were in service to economic ends.

Whereas black women were totally unpaid in America's slaveocracy, these women were minimally paid as domestics after Reconstruction and during segregation. Dehumanizing treatment of black women domestics persisted in the early U.S. industrial economy. I have discussed at length about how the world fairs imagined black women, particularly in the Jim Crow South, as units of labor on which the fairs and their industrialist sponsors could depend to deliver unprecedented wealth in the bourgeoning modern capitalist context. As the industrial economy prospered, middle-class white women were relegated to the home and considered it a high privilege to employ black women as servants or domestics. In fact, to have such domestic servants was—and remains, in many contexts—a mark of the privileged and wealthy. Yet, this kind of employment was simply another form of *slavery.*

The context of domestic employment in cities during the 1920s and 1930s was jolting. Journalist Marvel Cooke became known for her courageous descriptions of black domestic work on 167th Street and Westchester Avenue in the Bronx, published in two black newspapers, the *New York Amsterdam News* and *The Crisis*. With the help of her friend and political activist Ella Baker, Cooke and Baker, disguised as domestics, described what it was like to seek employment as a worker on this street corner. Cooke wrote,

> Rain or shine, cold or hot, you will find them there—Negro women, old and young—sometimes bedraggled, sometimes neatly dressed—but with the invariable paper bundle [containing their work clothes], waiting expectantly for Bronx housewives to buy their strength and energy for an hour, two hours, or even for a day at the munificent rate of fifteen, twenty, or twenty-five, or if luck be with them, thirty cents an hour.[15]

Notice that Cooke (Cooke actually ended up writing the article by herself) invokes the image of the auction block when detailing how white housewives chose their domestics. It is not a humanizing process. Black women are waiting *on a street corner* in hopes that white housewives will *buy* their strength and energy, reminiscent of how black people were bought on the auction block, based on their strength, age, energy, or beauty to contribute to plantation profit and white pleasure. Cooke also describes the abysmal pay that these women received for their work. In her words above, Cooke reveals the market logic that operates over black women's bodies (and this included some poor immigrant women who were also seeking employment in the domestic sector).

Their bodies were treated as commodities for purchase. Small wonder that Cooke and Baker titled the controversial article "The Bronx Slave Market." They wrote that "human labor is bartered and sold for slave wage" and that the economic precarity these women endured "compels the sale."[16] For these women had no real choices other than such work, as political and economic disenfranchisement persisted. This was a different experience from the auction block, true, as domestics black women had some autonomy over their lives, but they were nevertheless sentenced to participating in such humiliating market exchanges because of the gendered racial hierarchy that still structured American life. Cooke assists in creating an archive on the ongoing objectification and commodification of black women's bodies and lives within the nexus of racial capitalism.

By the 1930s, due to the Great Depression, the exploitation of black women's labor was even more chronic in the Bronx slave markets and in other cities as well. Historian Alana Coble details how black domestic workers were faced with low wages, and those who lived with their employers faced additional charges for room and board, and even longer working hours in the throes of the Great Depression. While the average white maid earned at most only five-sixths of what she needed to sustain herself, African-American domestics earned markedly less than that. Domestic pay was so low for some black women in cities that they turned to prostitution in desperation, just to put food on their tables.[17]

The working conditions were also hazardous and debilitating in these domestic slave markets. Women worked extralong hours with no real time off, often rarely being able to see their children. Consider Tina Hill, who worked in Los Angeles in the 1930s, endured long hours, having only every other Sunday off.[18] She most likely worked twelve hours or more a day, was not given any annual vacation, and was often not paid for working overtime.[19] As in New York, cities like Los Angeles also ran domestic slave markets where black women's bodies were treated inhumanely. Black domestics spoke about sexual harassment but could do nothing to address it because they so desperately needed the money. Some black domestics even told stories about receiving work based on how exhausted and unhealthy their bodies looked. White housewives would inspect the knees of black women—much as one might inspect a horse's teeth. If they had crust on their knees, white women would hire the black domestic, as that indicated they had experience scrubbing many floors.[20]

One might think that black domestics had it easier than their black female counterparts working in urban industrial centers. But this was not necessarily the case. Women in factories worked forty-four- to fifty-five-hour weeks (albeit for about twice the wage of domestics) but in dehumanizing, unsafe, and equally laborious conditions. Yet, a black woman domestic employed by a laundry service would make only ten dollars a week for fifty hours of work under equally dehumanizing conditions. Simply because these women did not work in factories did not mean that their work was easier.[21] Whether as black domestics or factory workers, women were treated as expendable, a tool for white economic wellbeing and profit, humans who labored in jobs that spared whites the indignity and grueling conditions of such work.

I do not want to limit my discussion of black women domestics to their negative environment within the context of racial capitalism. Although I have tried to tell a brief story about the dehumanizing maltreatment of black domestics from plantation economics to early industrialism, I do not want to make the mistake of silencing their agency. Their lives also disrupt capitalist narratives of what black domestics lives have meant within broader cultural and economic structures. At the site of black domesticity, black women defied and resisted. For instance, they countered the low wages by planting gardens near their residences and either sold their produce at open-air markets or supplemented their family's diet that way.[22] Black women domestics did not simply occupy a place of subservience. They did not simply acquiesce. They were trailblazers and progenitors of liberating projects aimed at their own flourishing as well as the wellbeing of their communities.

For instance, Hartman offers a portrait of a young black woman, Mabel, who migrated from the South to Jersey City, and who resisted domestic service sentencing her to a menial existence. She was weary of domestic service, of working for the Parker family and taking care of their sons.[23] She ached for something better, a way to unleash her potential in *another arena than the kitchen or bedroom.* So Mabel took singing and dancing lessons, hoping to secure a better life than the sentence of domestic work. She eventually had a chance to be part of a chorus of a musical revue at Coney Island. All the young women and girls Mabel knew worked in a kitchen, factory, or brothel. She decided on something more, and worked toward getting out of such service by taking this opportunity to dance and sing.

One could say that despite Mabel's opportunity to perform, she nonetheless remained materially destitute without any real way out of intense poverty. So how could she be any freer dancing and singing than in domestic service? As Hartman notes, the stage was "free territory" for Mabel. Consider Hartman's words on what this experience meant for Mabel:

Joining the chorus encompassed much more than the sequence of steps or the arrangement of dances on stage of a music hall or the floor of a cabaret. Like the flight from the plantation, the escape from slavery, the migration from the south, the rush into the city, or the stroll down Lenox avenue, choreography was an art, a practice of moving when there was nowhere else to go, no place left to run. It was an arrangement of the body to elude capture, an effort to make the uninhabitable livable, to escape the confinement of a four-cornered world, a tight, airless room.[24]

Hartman describes how Mabel thought about her opportunity to dance and sing as a creative experiment in living on her own terms, refusing the terms of racial capitalism that sought to keep her "in her place" through domestic servility. Her creative agency through her art brought her pleasure and meaning, and allowed her to signal to white society that she was not intrinsically a servant, *their* servant.[25] Through performance, she refused the racist and capitalist meanings society attempted to place on her body by refusing them this power. Although the cabaret was a "meeting place for cocaine fiends, street walkers, sissies and pimps,"[26] this would be the context out of which she would dream of other possibilities, of new worlds waiting to be inhabited in which black women could be authors and agents of their lives. Mabel was in search of self-agency and pleasure, away from the strictures of domesticity.

Other black women domestics employed their creative agency to build entire communities, also refusing how white capitalist society treated their bodies and lives. Think about how washerwoman-turned-holiness-preacher Amanda Berry Smith used funds from being a black domestic (and eventually an evangelist) to finance her organizational efforts to help other young black children, particularly black orphans. Smith was a domestic in New York, cleaning and washing the clothes of wealthy families to keep herself and her daughter afloat.[27] After losing a child, she encountered the holiness movement and had a religious encounter of sanctification in which she asserted that if she were given a platform she would "be willing to get on it and walk and tell everybody of this sanctifying power of God!"[28] She became a traveling evangelist who preached holiness and eventually had an impact on Charles Harrison Mason, who would be transformed by the Azusa Street Revival when he visited Los Angeles and become the founder of the Holiness-Pentecostal denomination the Church of God in Christ.[29]

Smith also became a businesswoman, opening up an orphanage for abandoned black children in Harvey, Illinois. Recall Turlington Harvey and Dwight Moody's venture in establishing the town of Harvey (alongside other investors) in 1893, which would be a town to escape the moral excesses of urban life. Smith made a decision that it would be beneficial to build an orphanage in this town. Her desire was to "rescue destitute, needy children, especially those of colored parentage," and provide them with "care, education, and industrial training."[30] She wanted an orphan school that would also protect children from exploitation. Historian Adrienne Israel observes that in the early twentieth century, vulnerable orphans were often exploited by families to whom they were sent, often working under slavelike conditions.[31] So it was that on June 28, 1899, Smith opened the Amanda Smith Industrial Orphan home and remarked that while the school would teach these children manual skills (cooking, cleaning, gardening) and literary abilities, nothing was more important than Christian ethics, which for her meant living a character-building life.[32]

Smith was an effective fundraiser, having built networks among black and white denominations, particularly Methodist churches. She was known in the white Methodist circles for her speaking tours, and often joined various camp meetings around the nation.[33] Besides monetary gifts from friends and family, she relied on donations for her speaking tours as well proceeds from the autobiography she had written. These activities helped raise money for the orphan home and eventually allowed her to buy sixteens lots and another cottage, ultimately owning the entire city block of 147th Street in the city of Harvey.[34]

Mabel and Amanda Smith are examples of how black domestics resisted and cultivated subversive visions of change and transformation. These women were not mere objects and units of labor as white capitalist systems treated them. Rather, they imagined themselves as subjects and as agents of change.

The Leadership of Black Domestics at Azusa: Beyond Plantation Patriarchy

The black women domestics at Azusa stand in this tradition of pained resilience. These women were the ones who ignited the Azusa Revival, a revival that had long-lasting effects. Azusa was made possible by women whom the white capitalist world regarded as lacking reason, imagination, and genius. The leadership of black women domestics also directly challenged the plantation patriarchy that shaped and guided black churches and black communities more broadly.

Black feminist and cultural critic bell hooks's discussion of the history of plantation patriarchy casts light on under just what oppressive terms such women worked and existed. Plantation patriarchy was about the ways in which previously enslaved black men were taught by white men to become patriarchs, namely to exercise their power to attain political and economic freedom *through the sub-ordination of previously enslaved black women.*[35] Because black men had been radically locked out of the roles of primary providers and protectors for their families during slavery, plantation patriarchy was a way for many black men to regain their place of importance within black families. This plantation patriar-chy produced a toxic masculinity in which black men could only self-actualize through exercising power *over* black women in unilateral ways. Through patriar-chal masculinity, black men could be *men* by being "heads" of their home, which meant making all social and economic decisions related to the family, often at the expense of black women. After slavery, plantation patriarchy and its white supremacist patriarchal masculinity would become the accepted ideal for many black men as they sought both political and economic self-determination within a burgeoning white capitalist society. Because black churches were so deeply shaped by this plantation patriarchy, black women often also could not operate as black pastors, preachers, or primary leaders within congregations.

Yet Azusa's vision and practices of gender inclusion challenge and defy this plantation patriarchy. To speak of Seymour's leadership at Azusa is to foreground the women who made his experience possible. Seymour's religious leadership and the visibility of Azusa come into being in and through a collective largely constituted by a community of black women preachers and pastors.[36] So, for example, Estrelda Alexander notes that Seymour's Bible study at Richard and Ruth Asberry's home on Bonnie Brae was not the first. During the winter of 1905, Julia Hutchins—a woman pastor that first sent for Seymour to come help copastor her church in Los Angeles—needed another venue to have church other than the tent they were occupying. Hutchins turned to the Asberrys and used their home as a temporary place for services. On Monday evenings, the group held regular evangelistic services. The first part of the service was held on the front porch where the singers drew people from the community (similar to the early days of Azusa). Eventually Hutchins's group outgrew the home and moved to another facility. What is important about this historical fact is that this neighborhood was known for exuberant worship that drew crowds, an experience similar to that which Seymour's Bible study would encounter at the Asberrys' home. While I am not attempting to assert Hutchins's Bible study as some an-tecedent to Seymour's services at this home (Hutchins was a holiness preacher and did not subscribe until much later to the Pentecostal brand of Christianity that included speaking in tongues), I do think that the visibility and receptivity of Seymour's group on Bonnie Brae is directly related to the religious activity that many people had witnessed just a year earlier through Hutchins's ministry at this home. In short, seasoned black women pastors were already cultivating a climate of revival in this part of Los Angeles, a context into which Seymour steps and in which he flourishes.

The black women domestics of Azusa were the foundation on which Seymour was able to do his ministry. They provided fertile ground for his work. They paved the way. While there were women that shaped Azusa, such as Neely Terry and Julia Hutchins (who brought Seymour to Los Angeles), Pastor Lucy Farrow was most critical to the Azusa ministry and movement that Seymour would help ignite. To *understand Seymour, one must understand Lucy Farrow*. Pastor Lucy Farrow was referred to as "the central prophet igniting the Holy Ghost fires in Southern California."[37] She was also called the first prayer warrior, "key networker," and "major personality" in the black Pentecostal movement.[38] Alongside Seymour, she was seen as instrumental to the first "outpouring of the Spirit" through the initial evidence of tongues on Bonnie Brae Street in Los Angeles.

The Pentecostal experience into which Seymour was initiated was led by Pastor Lucy Farrow. The niece of the famed abolitionist Frederick Douglass, Farrow was born a slave or later sold into slavery before gaining her freedom. Prior to leaving for Los Angeles, Seymour arrived in Houston and became a member at Pastor Farrow's church, even preaching when she was away. While Seymour was at her church, Farrow met Charles Parham in Houston. In spending time with Parham, she began to learn about this new understanding of "baptism" or the doctrine of initial evidence (the initial evidence of the Holy Spirit being speaking in tongues). She decided to travel with Parham and his wife to Topeka, Kansas, as their domestic servant. Upon her return to Houston, she attended an evening service where Parham preached this new doctrine. Incidentally, Parham taught this doctrine during the day but this class was a "whites only" seminar. However, the evening worship included both whites and a few blacks. It was at this racially mixed evening service that she received her Pentecostal experience—the first recorded by a black person.[39] Farrow subsequently returned to her church and introduced Seymour to this new understanding of baptism. She also introduced Seymour to Parham. In short, Pastor Farrow can be credited for moving Seymour from being a holiness preacher to being a Pentecostal preacher.

Farrow, not Seymour, is also credited as being the first to lay hands on people at Bonnie Brae, leading to them having the experience of tongues. However, this observation is disputed, and there are two accounts of what happened. In the first account, Farrow arrived after Seymour's group had moved from the Asberrys' house on Bonnie Brae to the building on Azusa Street. The second narrative, supported by eyewitness accounts, placed Farrow at the earlier Bonnie Brae meeting.[40] This narrative notes that after several days of Seymour and his group unsuccessfully seeking the experience of tongues, he wired Parham in Houston to send pastors who could help. Parham sent Lucy Farrow and Joseph Warren. Lucy, Seymour's former pastor, arrived . . . and revival broke out. She was known for her spiritual ability to lay hands and impart the gift of tongues to others.[41]

Eyewitness accounts, such as the writings of Emma Cotton, therefore identify Lucy Farrow as the catalyst of this revival. Brother Lee was the first person in Seymour's meeting on Bonnie Brae to receive the gift of tongues. According to Cotton and Brother Lee himself, Farrow was responsible for his religious experience. She laid hands on him and facilitated this experience. According to Cotton's account, Farrow and Seymour were eating dinner at the Lee home when "Sister Farrow rose from her seat, walked over to Brother Lee and said, 'The Lord tells me to lay hands on you for the Holy Ghost.' And when she laid hands on him, he fell out of his chair as though dead, and began to speak with other tongues."[42]

Women like Pastor Farrow may have been catalysts in starting the revival that then spread around the world. This remains an important *genealogical* intervention—how these contradictions in accounts are often neutralized and silenced in broader Pentecostal scholarship on Azusa. In making this claim, I am not suggesting that the account that identifies Farrow as the catalyst for the revival is the indisputable truth. Instead, I am concerned with the complete *absence* of this alternative account in the narrative of Azusa's founding. By speaking about *the* "founder" of Azusa, this alternate narrative of founding, in which many persons——a collective of women and men—start and maintain a movement is underemphasized, and largely underarticulated in Pentecostal scholarship. For example, Pentecostal scholar Vinson Synan talks about Seymour as the pioneer and messenger of Azusa that speaks to our hearts today.[43] From him, one gets the sense that Seymour sparked the revival and all others played secondary roles to his leadership. Similarly, in offering a historical picture of Azusa's early days, both Cecil Robeck and Gaston Espinosa first draw attention to Seymour's pastoral leadership and only then explore who surrounded Seymour.[44] Consequently, one gets the sense that the movement is primarily tied to its chief agent—Seymour— although there are "supporters" who make the revival possible. To be fair, Robeck does describe at length the slave religious practices that show up at Azusa, and this inclusion allows one to interpret Azusa through its religious rituals as well.

However, Robeck nevertheless frames these slave religious practices in relation to Seymour's origins rather than the broader social spaces out of which these slave religious practices emerged—namely the plantation religious rituals and black women leaders who preserved and maintained these practices that Seymour would perform. So I set the record straight: black women domestics, along with other working-class black men on Bonnie Brae, were central to the founding events of Azusa.

Discussing these women's initiation of Seymour into early Pentecostalism is critical, as it also sheds light on conversations about black masculinity. Seymour might be interpreted as wrestling with the toxic masculinities of American racist capitalism and black hetero-patriarchy, which formed black men in ways that devalued black women and dismissed the benefits of a truly egalitarian community. As industrialization was emerging after slavery, the "strong black man" was the archetypal black man who could only establish his own male prowess and power through participating in the patriarchal political and economic spheres of American society. In order to inhabit this role, black men needed to assert their primacy in the family by being benevolent patriarchs, providing economically for their families as other white men attempted to do in the United States. To be a man meant to participate in American market structures for the good of black women and children. In other words, strong black men knew *best* what black women (and children) needed; in short, they knew this better than black women did. The strong black male ideal was articulated as a form of benevolent patriarchy by many black men seeking to reclaim their primary place in the black family through industrial capitalist institutions. The strong black man attempted to claim his voice in and through modern capitalist processes.

Yet this benevolence and provision tended to translate into the subjugation and oppression of black women who constantly endured the costs of strong black men regulating and controlling their lives. In order to succeed, strong black men were told to be invulnerable, dictatorial, and inflexible. This required them to use physical, psychological, and emotional violence and domination against black women to retain their place of primacy. Unfortunately, the strong black man is an extension of white supremacist patriarchal masculinity, as black men employed essentially the same hegemonic tools used by white plantation masters within black communities.[45]

However, there has also been a tradition of black male feminists who attempted to embody a progressive masculinity, believing in the need to practice mutuality and reciprocity among black women. Some black men have modeled a historical legacy of pro–women's liberation upon which other black men can draw.[46] Black male feminist and cultural critic Mark Anthony Neal posits that such progressive black masculinity is "fluid and malleable, a masculinity that challenges the rigid and truncated versions of black masculinity that masquerade in the bodies of the proverbial 'strong black man.'"[47] Taking my cue from Neal, I suggest that progressive black masculinity challenges the inflexible and violent proclivities and urges associated with the strong black man ideal. Yet progressive masculinity is hardly about embracing some positive or triumphant narrative of black masculinity in solidarity with black women. Rather, this progressive masculinity merely "acknowledges the many complex aspects, often contradictory, that make up a progressive and meaningful black masculinity."[48] Embracing healthier forms of masculinity for black men is about those "willing to embrace the fuzzy edges of a black masculinity that in reality is still under construction."[49] In Neal's words, progressive black masculinity allows black men to "dance with [the] contradictions" that come with attempting to practice feminist solidarity while divesting oneself from hetero-patriarchal power and privilege. To speak about Frederick Douglas or W. E. B. Du Bois is to acknowledge that although they advocated for the political and economic equality of women and men, they themselves nevertheless held contradictory positions on black women's ability and worth—such as Du Bois's proclivity to dismiss black women as intellectual equals to black men (think of his masculinist concept of the Talented Tenth) or Douglas's reiteration of black manhood through hetero-patriarchal images (he specifies that a physical fight with his white plantation master marked his manhood). As Neal reminds us, black men claiming to stand in black feminist traditions is about acknowledging the contradictions of claiming and investing in progressive black masculinity while being constantly shaped and influenced by hetero-patriarchy.[50]

Seymour might usefully be considered in this tradition of progressive black masculinity, *if* we understand that this masculinity is filled with contradictions as black men wrestle to advocate for black women's equality. Although imperfectly, what we see with Seymour and the men of Azusa is them wrestling with plantation patriarchy and trying to dance with the contradictions in terms of their own black patriarchal power as they attempt to model equal leadership beside the black and white women leaders of Azusa. For example, Seymour's performances of healthy masculinity talk back to sexist religious and capitalist structures that devalued women, especially black women domestics. We must remember that the Azusa Revival was not just an event—a series of services for a week or two. It was a congregation that hosted and strategically planned this revival and activities for three years. It was a movement. Seymour planned and led the revival alongside Sister Prince, Florence Crawford, and Clara Lum, even appointing Crawford as the state overseer of the entire Azusa work in California, one of the highest positions in the ministry.[51] He also supported many women in ministry who attended the revival, encouraging them to preach and pastor as they moved out into the world. He often sought the counsel of women in his ministry before making major decisions, and depended upon them to advance the work of the ministry. Most importantly, Seymour truly believed that black women in his ministry and those influenced by Azusa (but serving other communities) were agents and subjects who needed to be listened to as a community lived into its spiritual and social practices of flourishing after having been revived. This spoke directly against the way other black churches and the broader American political economy treated black women: in objectifying and commodifying ways.

Although Seymour led alongside women at Azusa, he nevertheless fell short with these egalitarian commitments when feeling pressure from outside socio-cultural forces. For instance, some of the husbands of women leaders at Azusa complained that these women had abandoned their domestic responsibilities to do the work of ministry.[52] They preferred their wives to stay "in their place" and felt that the Azusa church compromised these core values of feminine domesticity. This was a major complaint of Florence Crawford's husband, and it eventually led him to threaten divorce if she did not stop her religious activities.[53] Florence and her husband eventually did divorce. As a result of such interactions, Seymour became concerned about ensuring that "his" revival was not seen as condoning impropriety around norms of marriage. He decided to double down on this patriarchal view of women's domesticity by attempting to place limits on Florence in ministry, even threatening to demote her in ministry if she divorced.[54] Seymour's actions toward Florence reinforced the very sexist norms that the revival rejected. His actions also sought to regulate Florence's sexuality in ways that were deeply oppressive, a point to which I will return in the next chapter. Indeed, Seymour embodied all kinds of contradictions about gender equality even as he sought to embody a progressive black masculinity that was countercultural to the dominant gendered norms of the day. And yet it is also true that he wrestled with creating an egalitarian religious community where black women could truly be seen. Seymour insisted on listening to and being shaped by women, including black women domestics. And yet he was full of outright contradictions and ambiguities, too.

Black women at Azusa helped shape male leaders who sought to embody more progressive forms of black masculinity in hopes of nurturing a truly egalitarian community. They helped black men think beyond the plantation patriarchy that affected so many of them at the turn of the twentieth century. While black male leaders like Seymour embodied a more progressive example of masculinity, they nevertheless struggled to advocate and share leadership with women at Azusa in a consistent way. Black women's leadership at Azusa empowered these men to wrestle with toxic masculinities and confront their own contradictions as they attempted to live into healthier, more progressive gendered identities.

Beautiful Experiments: Guardians of Slave Religious Practices

Centering these women domestics shows that they are a "proposal of black women's genius," in Saidiya Hartman's words. Alongside being black women domestics who empowered black men to embody healthier forms of masculinity, these women also were primary agents in cultivating, preserving, and guarding slave religious practices (discussed in the previous chapter), as well as engaging in beautiful experiments of cultivating these "wayward" black religious expressions and rituals.

Harriet Jacobs called slave religious practices "the religion of the South," a religion often mediated by enslaved women. Enslaved women functioned as spiritualists, conjurers, and healers, and had an essential role among enslaved communities. Healers and conjurers were "entrusted with the knowledge and responsibility for maintaining the spiritual traditions of the enslaved," serving as "mediators between slaves and the spirit world."[55] In particular, women practitioners "made their mark in significant numbers."[56] Yvonne Chireau asserts that black women used conjuring and other supernatural traditions not only because they saw them as valuable resources for resistance, but also because they believed that the supernatural world provided diverse forms of empowerment for the enslaved community.[57]

In addition to being a gatekeeper between the natural and spiritual worlds within the enslaved community, these women were "at the nexus between two worlds, the material world and the spiritual realm."[58] For instance, enslaved women performed root work in relation to women's obstetric and gynecological issues, whether their root work was to preserve a pregnancy in order to deliver a healthy baby into the world or to terminate life for the sake of the mother and larger community. These women's mediation of such religious practices spanned the supernatural and material world, pointing to their essential religious role within the slave community.[59]

Such collective religious practices also sponsored experiences of empowerment, transcendence, and meaning-making within the dehumanizing vortex of slavery. For example, on southern plantations during slavery, the Pray's houses and their practices of "seekin' the Lord," would find its way to Azusa, empowering practices of which enslaved women were the gatekeepers. Religious historian Alonzo Johnson notes that Pray's houses were central to the institutional structure of folk religion among the African-American enslaved.[60] They were places where one went to pray and seek God. Yet, such "seekin'" of God was never simply about individual contemplation. Rather, this seekin' practice was a collective, fleshly practice of prayer enacted through dancing and singing: the black body prayed and black flesh mediated divine presence. Pray's houses can be seen as a successor of the brush arbors where the enslaved often met to practice folk traditions. After plantation missions became more accepted among white southern society, the enslaved were allowed to meet in a particular slave's house for further religious instruction. The enslaved community would often merge religious instruction with times of seekin' the Lord (mostly in the evening), allowing them to integrate their own folk traditions with the forms of Christian religious instruction they received.

This seekin' the Lord at the Pray's house was often where the ring shout and other slave religious practices were enacted. The women could be seen midwifing the conversion experiences of the enslaved through such practices. Imagine this: one might enter the Pray's house in order to seek the Lord. In fact, many slaves and blacks (postslavery) would not be seen as a member of a black church unless they had a religious experience at the Pray's house, which meant that the Pray's house often functioned to help one secure membership at a black Baptist or Methodist church. After the person entered the Pray's house, they would participate in the folk practice of singing, praying, and so forth. This person could then over the time of being in the Pray's house with others report on their experiences of dreams and visions, which served as their conversion experience. It was only after this experience that one would be ready as a candidate for church membership. Enslaved women often ran the Pray's houses (whereas many enslaved men served as preachers for the enslaved communities). This process was facilitated by black women in slavery and by black women during the postbellum period.[61]

In the words of white ministers, Azusa's religious rituals and practices hearkened back to these "plantation Africanisms" and "crude negroisms" that were pagan. Whenever one went to Azusa, one would at some point see enacted *the practices of the Pray's houses*, that is, black women providing leadership in mid-wifing the spiritual experiences of potential converts. Even secular newspapers reported observers finding black washerwomen and domestic servants praying at the altar with new converts to receive the Holy Spirit baptism, serving as midwives for men and women across racial and class categories. White men kneeled as black women facilitated these men's experiences. This revival and in particular this action drew the public's attention because black women were at the forefront, even leading white men, some of them prominent clergy or public figures, into this process of baptism.[62]

In bringing to light this history of black women, I am not merely attempting to acknowledge these women who led and participated in the Azusa movement. I want to reset the terms of discourse on Azusa by asking how we should talk about the conditions under which Azusa was possible. *These women's guardianship and preservation of these practices fostered a radical relationality at Azusa, into which Seymour is initiated.* The actual origins of his vision of radical relationality and just relationships lie in the religious practices that black domestic women not only cultivated, preserved, and guarded, but which they headed. This is not to say that black men did not also preserve and guard these practices. They did, and we encounter these men at Azusa. However, black women played a primary role in preserving these practices.

I have talked at length about the Pray's house and black women's role in relation to these religious practices. But there is another notable practice that eventually found its way to Azusa: tarrying. Black women stood at the center of this tarrying tradition. Tarrying was a key marker of religious experience at Azusa. Although its roots are in early nineteenth-century African-American spirituality,[63] tarrying was also an African-American spiritual practice within early Pentecostalism wherein a person repeatedly recited specific phrases at the altar. The person could only pray in this way with prayer leaders who stood nearby encouraging the person in this spiritual exercise. Tarrying lasted from one to two hours in the middle or after a service. This practice included praying, songs, supplications, special invocations and specific rules and expectations.[64] Specifically, tarrying was a spiritual practice that made the ground ready for someone to receive spiritual gifts of the Holy Spirit such as speaking in tongues.

What is most important about tarrying is that the person could only have a conversion or encounter with God *through the community*. Communal leaders midwifed personal experiences of Spirit. Consider this image: A young woman decides that she wants to receive the Holy Spirit and speaking in tongues as evidence at the Azusa Revival. She is invited to come to the altar so that the church mothers can lay hands on her and lead her into a spiritual encounter through tarrying. She is instructed mainly by the church mothers to stretch her hands up to heaven and repeat certain phrases such as "Have your way, God" and "Yes Lord" and "Glory." She is asked to clap her hands and center her mind on Jesus. The church mothers and elders stand around her, mirroring her actions, invoking the presence of the Spirit. The tarrying leaders tell her to pray hard and to repeat these phrases over and over again. She might stand or kneel to continue tarrying. There might also be other persons tarrying at the altar with her as the church mothers circle and facilitate this experience. It is an experience that can continue for hours until the person has received the Holy Spirit. That means all those surrounding the young woman stay too! For she is not able to have this encounter alone. It is not an individual ritual; it "is not a private experience of an individual directing him—or herself; it is a communal event with the encouragement of altar workers and a prayerful congregation."[65]

The collective nature of tarrying finds its roots in the ring shout, an early slave religious practice. During a ring shout, a ring is formed around a group of people who sing and clap. This ring moves in a counterclockwise direction. Through the ring shout, the Spirit is invoked and conversion cannot occur unless the Spirit is encouraged to come among the community through this practice. In the ring, participants raise their voices and encourage those who are encircled. It is a practice marked by dancing and singing in unison, all while people are moving their bodies together.[66] Historian of Christianity David Daniels notes that the ring shout could also be "a prayer resembling the rehearsal of God's acts in an enacted prayer; these liturgical re-enactments of biblical events included the Jericho March, a re-enactment of Joshua's army marching around the walls of Jericho or the Exodus march, the marching of Israel out of Egypt."[67] In short, the ring shout was about *communal* prayer and *communal* power ushering new religious adherents into conversion and transformation.

Interestingly tarrying was a ritual practiced at Azusa (and other early Pentecostal communities) to avoid charges of African paganism often ascribed to the ring shout. As discussed in the Chapter 2, the castigation of crude, pagan "Africanisms" such as the ring shout persisted among white and educated black communities. The rejection of the ring shout as heathenistic and theologically unsound led to its stigmatization as unchristian. During this period of intense debate about the ring shout, the "structure of the ring shout was transposed into tarrying."[68] Proponents of tarrying believed that this practice would be seen as more biblical, as biblical texts valued contemplation, prayer, jubilance, dance, and bodily demonstrativeness. It was also the case that tarrying allowed for biblical texts to support folk sensibilities.[69] This shift from the ring shout with its repetition of hand-clapping, singing, praying, and bodily engagement to tarrying with these same elements (although in different form) enabled the continuation of a particular practice of slave religious expression. Some imagined that tarrying was the more respectable early Pentecostal ritual, concealing its slave religious antecedents. Ironically, it seems that white ministers who visit Azusa nevertheless decry this kind of religious practice, despite the fact that tarrying was an attempt to remedy the nonrespectable character of other slave religious expressions such as the ring shout.[70]

At Azusa, black women were guardians of these diverse religious rituals and practices found in both the Pray's houses and in the building on Azusa Street where revival flourished. They were cultivating beautiful experiments with these presumed deviant and wayward religious expressions. Their experiments affirmed them as subjects and challenged how American racial capitalism and capitalists treated them: as objects and tools for profit and pleasure.

Open Rebellion: Subversive Practices

I would argue that these religious rituals and practices that black women domestics guarded were defiant. For instance, tarrying had profound subversive implications. It was open rebellion. Tarrying as communal prayer at Azusa was about acknowledging the sovereignty of God rather than the sovereignty of the state or market (or any other secular ruler or power). In the face of a segregationist nation, tarrying between black and whites (and among other ethnicities and nationalities) at Azusa created a counterallegiance. Their embodiment of the collective through tarrying gestured toward the rejection of the American segregationist state and the market's sovereignty over their lives as citizens. Azusa members would only be governed by God's sovereignty, which involved enacting a different vision of human relationality grounded in a radical respect and mutuality, a way of being that countered the social customs, laws, and market expectations of racial capitalism in the United States.

Such countering of white dominant norms through its religious life was commonplace at Azusa. Let me paint you another picture: A white woman wants to experience the baptism of the Holy Spirit at Azusa. Down at the altar, three black leaders of the congregation await her. A black male leader lays his hands upon her to receive the Spirit. She has a powerful religious experience. Notice that Azusa's ritual practice of "laying on of hands" is also a law-breaking practice, for the black man laying hands on the white woman is a law-breaking touch. It was illegal in the American South and socially inappropriate in the American North and West for black men to look at or touch white women. Young black boys could and did get lynched for merely staring at a white woman. Yet the Azusa movement was countercultural. It did not recognize or submit to the sovereignty of the state and its segregated social order. It ritually enacted a different kind of community, one grounded in human vulnerability, mutuality, and reciprocity. This community was law-breaking in and through its ritual agency. This inevitably led white ministers to describe the Azusa community as both sinful and *criminal*—breaking the law of the land and the laws of God through racial mixing. Azusa represented a "criminal existence" to religious and social authorities in Los Angeles. Through its religious practices, Azusa sought to inaugurate "a new heaven and new earth" or a more egalitarian order, a point on Azusa's apocalyptic sensibilities to which I will return in Chapter 5.

Azusa might be interpreted as a rebellious, countercultural social space where general antagonisms and differences aren't suppressed, punished, or excluded but *experimented* with. For while Azusa undoubtedly is a religious space, it simultaneously functions as a social space in which members experimented in creating alternative relational contexts. Differences are endemic to human communities. Segregated orders seek to build social spaces around uniformed conformity, as differences are not seen as natural but deviant and therefore a threat. In this case, community means homogeneity. If community means homogeneity, then alternative or otherwise practices and identities that enter this community must be converted or banished.

However, the countercultural social space that Azusa exemplified might be seen through how it experimented with fostering social and cultural bonds *across difference and privilege*, bonds that were actively created and imperfectly sustained. There has always been debate within contemporary society over whether privileged communities (such as white communities) can come into solidarity with marginalized groups (like blacks) and if so, how they might practice solidarity. The idea of collective power at Azusa is met with these questions: How did whites at Azusa wrestle with their forms of white privilege? How were questions of racial solidarity actually addressed within this movement, especially when the revival was racially embattled within its first year?

Consider that in the first year of the revival, 1906, Seymour experienced a massive exodus of the white members of Azusa. In part, this was due to white clergy and evangelists (white men and women) who visited Azusa deeming this revival to be vile and spiritually demonic. For instance, late in 1906, Nettie Hardwood, a disciple of holiness preacher Alma White, visited the Azusa mission and was incensed when she saw blacks and whites kissing each other and "a black woman with her arms around a white man's neck praying for him."[71] Charles Parham (similar to Hardwood) visited the Azusa Street Revival but determined that what is going on is nothing more than demonic gesticulations and unethical "race mixing." Although Parham introduced Seymour in Houston to the Pentecostal doctrine of tongues speaking as the initial evidence, Seymour eventually had to ban Parham from the revival in order to diminish Parham's potential influence over the congregation. Unfortunately, Parham's influence had already taken root.

After Parham's visit, Elmer Fisher precipitated the first mass exodus of whites from Azusa. During the first year of the revival, Fisher was left in charge at Azusa for four months while Seymour evangelized in the South. Fisher ended up leaving the mission and starting the Upper Room Mission in Los Angeles with three hundred in attendance during the first service, mostly whites from Azusa. There is a lot of debate surrounding what led to Fisher's split from Seymour at Azusa. Some scholars maintain that it was more for doctrinal than racial reasons. Cecil Robeck points out that Seymour initially established Azusa on the Pentecostal doctrinal commitment that speaking in tongues was the biblical evidence of the Spirit's baptism. After Parham's condemnation of the Azusa movement, Seymour found himself revising his former position on "initial evidence." Seymour broadened his understanding of Spirit baptism to include ethical dimensions such as racial love whites must have for blacks.[72] Seymour believed that if a white person spoke in tongues but did not have love in her or his heart for black people, they could not claim the Spirit baptism. Fisher suggested that Seymour backed away from the truth that those who receive the Spirit will *always* speak in tongues—a way in which Fisher tried to silence Seymour's revisionism. For Fisher, speaking in tongues is *the* biblical evidence of the Spirit, despite human weakness such as racism.[73]

It might seem as if doctrinal issues alone split Fisher from Seymour. However, racism played a profound role in this split as well. When Seymour banned Parham from the Azusa mission, Fisher allowed Parham to hold noon meetings at his Upper Room Mission. Parham was a known segregationist and preached a racialized theology in which whites were created apart from nonwhites during the biblical account of Creation. His Anglo-Saxon theological posture overtly declared nonwhites as ontologically inferior to whites. Yet, Fisher supported Parham's ministry. How can one argue that racial reasons did not fuel and fund Fisher's spilt from Seymour, taking a sizable population of whites along with him? Might one argue that despite Seymour's vocal preaching against racial inferiority, Parham's racialized gospel resonates with the *habitus* of many white members *within* the Azusa mission, along with their embedded cultural views that ultimately *preserve* the color line? The racial undertones during the first year of Azusa question whether the color line really had been "washed away" in the blood of Christ, as Frank Bartlemann maintained.

Alongside white ministers and evangelists, the pressure placed on whites at Azusa through the racist remarks of the local Los Angeles newspapers was ever present. One reporter labeled events at Azusa as "disgusting scenes." Another reporter mocked people at Azusa, announcing that "Holy Kickers Carry on Mad Orgies." Such headlines were designed to stoke the racial imagination, titillating the casual reader with sexual innuendo as well as the threat of black sensuality.[74] Before long, some whites were leaving the work of Azusa Street to join other churches and Pentecostal missions. Within the first two years, other splits occurred between white ministers and Seymour at Azusa, which led Seymour to make a move that people would not have anticipated during the first year of the revival.

By 1915, Seymour had revised the doctrine, disciplines, and constitution of his Apostolic Faith Mission to recognize himself as "Bishop," guaranteeing that his successor would always be a "man of color." In particular, his revision of the constitution required that the bishop, vice-bishop, and all trustees be "people of color."[75] What led to what seems to be a reversal of the hopes Seymour had in relation to this mission and movement? For sure, certain moments in the life of this revival disrupted and challenged the racial status quo of the day. However, the constant racial agitation from within the movement beginning in its first year points to a color line that many white members apparently wanted to preserve. Thus although Azusa confronted the racial *habitus* of day, it cannot be said to have washed away the color line, a line that, even if at times merely a glimmer, remained throughout the Azusa Street Revival.

With this complicated history of Azusa in mind, how can we be sure that Azusa really was a subversive, countercultural social space from the beginning? Or, if it was, does it matter that such radical relationality was fleeting and episodic, off and on, lasting only a few years? Can one argue that Azusa really embodied a radical community across differences and privilege? I think a case can be made for Azusa embodying a subversive space, if by that we mean a community that experimented with countercultural, defiant ways of creating social togetherness—even if these experiments against the dominant racial and capitalist order were episodic. Here, I find historian Margaret Nash's idea of "flashpoints" in history helpful. For Nash, flashpoints in history are moments at which the impact of a sudden transformation illuminates everything around it, good and bad, so that in those moments, the fullness of such transformation seems possible.[76] The focus is not on whether such sudden transformation can be sustained or has longevity but how it inspires future visions of change. A flashpoint creates an opening to see something new, a new way of living and being with and for others in community. Flashpoints offer up an alternative moral vision of what is possible because moments of transformation are already being experienced.

Azusa's religious life contained such flashpoints. By turning to moments inside of its religious life (tarrying, laying on of hands, worshiping together, etc.), one sees that Azusa did not settle for the normalized racial and market grammar of American society. It did not accept the notion that black bodies were nothing more than objects and commodities for market exchange. This community did not follow prescribed rules that kept whites, blacks, and other immigrants apart from each other as a matter of law. Azusa refused the segregated order and experimented with communal solidarity across privilege and differences. Recall that whites who attended the Apostolic Faith Mission were initiated into religious conversion through slave religious practices. It was one thing for blacks to participate in these practices. It was far more shocking and scandalous that whites gave up their racial power by engaging in such practices. Whites were led in religious experiences that could *only* be midwifed by blacks. White members of Azusa who followed the lead of black domestics and janitors were seen by broader white society as debasing themselves. The religious life of Azusa was scandalous precisely because it exercised power over white supremacy. It sought to remake whites away from the psychology of American racism. Azusa did, throughout *moments* of its life, re-create communities across difference and privilege that are an affront to the existing racial-capitalist order, however short lived those moments were. And this embodiment of countercultural community revealed, if even in a fleeting and episodic manner, what was possible.

The disruptive quality of Azusa, these flashpoints, are made possible through slave religious rituals and practices, which tended to be cultivated and preserved by black women domestics. To speak of Azusa's subversive religious life is to make a claim about the centrality of black women within this movement's founding. Acknowledging black women domestics at the center of this movement is about acknowledging the religious practices these women would guard and preserve, which formed the foundation of Seymour's leadership and the overall subversive character of Azusa's religious life.

A Proposal for Black Women's Genius: Rethinking the Founder's Debate

Simply bringing into view the role of black women domestics in Azusa's founding is not to make a claim that they are now *the* founders. To the contrary, I want to resist the urge to search for an individual woman founder or argue that these women were *the* founders. Instead, I want to express the idea of "founding" as a process that names *the collective* as central to the formation of Azusa's founding events, a process which centers these women's contributions alongside men such as Seymour. Moreover, centering the collective matters to how we interpret Azusa more broadly: as a church community and eventually a religious movement that defied how black women domestics were imagined and treated within America's racial capitalist order—as lacking reason, imagination, and genius. Without these women and the practices they helped guard and preserve, Azusa would not have been possible.

Centering the subversive agency of black women domestics helps in rethinking the debate surrounding the founder of early Pentecostalism.[77] Thus far, much of Pentecostal scholarship has argued over whether it is Parham or Seymour who was the founder of early Pentecostalism in the United States. To be fair, this is an important debate, for the question of who is the founder of early Pentecostalism functions to ground authority. If Parham is cited as the founder, it means early Pentecostalism and its religious significance should mainly be framed through the doctrine of initial evidence (that is, speaking in tongues) alongside acts of healing. In going with Parham, the origins of early Pentecostalism are grounded in a doctrinal distinction that I have already discussed at length in the previous chapter. If Seymour is noted as a primary founder of early Pentecostalism, the religious significance of this movement is much more than this doctrinal distinction. Early Pentecostalism and its significance is equally about embodying countercultural relations across dividing lines such as racial, gender, and class differences. In this case, Pentecostalism is not simply about Christian identity as assent to "right principles" on any number of doctrinal topics such as tongues, healing, the Trinity, and so forth, but more about how one actualizes a community of care, love, friendship, and justice in the midst of racially segregated orders and commodifying logics.

I want to affirm why scholarship has identified Seymour as the founder or pioneer of Azusa: as a way to avoid the erasure of this movement's black presence as well as the black roots of early Pentecostalism. Yet, the scholarly debate surrounding *the* founder of early Pentecostalism (Parham or Seymour) produces a series of constraints. The Parham-versus-Seymour debate does not allow one to see that how Azusa's founding has been described is often overdetermined by patriarchal investments. This debate causes one to interpret the origins of Pentecostalism in masculinist terms without asking how women change the conversation. In making this claim, I am not denying the importance of Seymour as a central figure in discussing the development of Azusa and early Pentecostalism. Instead, I am worried that the current debate ignores and/or dismisses the idea of "founding" as a process that names *the collective of women and men* as primary to the formation of Azusa and by extension early Pentecostalism. It leaves out certain narratives (even if those narratives are disputed) about the *central* role of black women domestics at Azusa. In addition, attempting to understand Azusa through Seymour's origins alone doesn't fully grasp the collective of black women out of which Seymour's religious experience and leadership were birthed.

Founding is often a collective enterprise, never simply about the lone superhero or charismatic leader. Contemporary ideas of founding rely too much on a heroic, mythical individual.[78] One might argue that without this person, the movement would not have occurred. Yet, this kind of argument overstates and even ignores the communities and network of relations that made possible particular events out of which this heroic individual emerges. I am not arguing that we should reject the "founder" language altogether. Rather, I want to suggest that instead of primarily reading certain events or movements (such as Azusa) through the figure of the founder, we might benefit from understanding founding as a process of community praxis, a set of events, and an ongoing movement saturated in the diverse work of courageous collectivities. In the case of Azusa, the reclamation of founding away from the "figure of the founder" privileges new agents: the collective of women and the subversive practices they preserved. The rejection of the singular founding figure of Azusa can reveal the collective which black women domestics helped to lead and guide. The *collective speaks.* Speaking of founding as a history of collective praxis provides epistemological alternatives to how we think about Azusa's founding. Thus, I advance a historical description of Azusa that is not limited to the *figure* of the founder (such as Seymour) but one that takes into account the collective process of founding, the collective process of creativity, and the collective process of talking back to America's deleterious forms of racialized capitalism. I think turning to the *collective shape of founding* allows one to see the multiple founding events and sets of religious practices that come to shape and give rise to Azusa.

There were historical conditions that gave rise to Azusa, and everyday conditions were largely grounded in the collective shape of rituals, religious practices, and habits, which emerged in and through enslaved communities, especially through black women. By putting the collective at the center of the Azusa movement, we are able to see black women domestics' role as guardians of these collective practices. We are also able to see how their leadership of Azusa is a direct critique of America's racial capitalist formation that saw black women as mere commodities and objects.

Most importantly, we recognize that these women were creating beautiful experiments at Azusa. They were defying the cultural and market status quo at Azusa. They were talking back in defiance of how white institutions attempted to assign them commercial value and meaning. They would not accept this fate. They wanted to be free. As Hartman notes, so many black women who migrated from the South at the start of the twentieth century found themselves wanting to "elude the hold of the plantation and the police," to pry open "an endless stretch of possibility."[79] Each day, these women "struggled to acquire a bit more breathing room in a world becoming more and more restricted by the color line, more and more defined by the routine brutalities of racism."[80] These women wanted to clasp a better way of life, a way of experiencing the joys of their own humanity and agency. Although Hartman writes about the sexual agency and freedom many black women employed against the enclosure of America's racist, heteropatriarchal worlds, I want to affirm that these women at Azusa were equally asserting their right to be free within America's white capitalist enclosure. They asserted their right to be free through these wayward religious practices, through these enslaved rituals that were seen as grotesque and demonic, even queer and erotic (a theme I explore in the next chapter). These women represented wayward lives to the white religious order. And yet they forged ahead.

The women that lead Azusa are a proposal for black women's genius. They were part of Azusa's founding and were central to the collective praxis that would contest the racial and market norms that grossly misinterpreted black women's bodies and lives. They fostered a religious community *on their own terms*. They decided to be free.

4 AZUSA'S EROTIC LIFE

MANY REPORTERS WROTE ABOUT the Azusa Revival as a social space that was erotically charged and queer. A reporter for the *Los Angeles Times*, for instance, described Azusa as a "queer mixture" of rich and poor, black and whites who "behave lustfully" toward each other.[1] Queer. Erotic. Deviant. Against the norm. Erotic desire has supported and reinforced racist and capitalist structures of domination in America, although some scholars underemphasize this relationship.

The capitalist event of the world fairs at the end of the nineteenth century quite deliberately fostered erotic desires. For the capitalist order is a *felt* experience and depends on racist desires and intimacies. Black feminist Jennifer Nash is right to say that "one of the tremendous insights of affect theory has been its invitation to consider how structures of domination feel, and to suggest that simply naming structures fails to do justice to how they move against (and inside of) our bodies."[2] Racial capitalism is an unequal system based on white, hetero-patriarchal domination but it is also a *scene* and *event* that is grounded in a set of affective energies and erotic desires that move through and between bodies.

This chapter examines how the emergence of early Pentecostalism at Azusa Street challenged the erotic life of racism associated with industrial capitalism in the United States. I first discuss what I mean by the erotic life of racism. I then turn to specific erotic scenes of racist desire used in service to capitalist ends at the Chicago and Philadelphia world fairs I discussed earlier in this text. Erotic connections and intimacies among white people were forged at these world fairs. Azusa resisted these erotic scenes of racist desire through its liturgical life. I ask: how does Azusa's liturgical life contest and subvert the erotic life of racist industrial capitalism that is cultivated and leveraged toward unchecked market profit? Azusa created emancipatory moments in response to the white racial bonding early capitalist practices depended upon. I conclude this chapter by foregrounding how Azusa embodied erotic fugitivity.

The Erotic Life of Racism

You may be asking what the erotic and racism have to do with each other. In my previous book *Religious Resistance to Neoliberalism: Black Feminist and Womanist Perspectives*, I reclaimed the category of the erotic as important to subversive political and social action. Drawing upon black feminist Audre Lorde, I showed that the erotic is more than what we do and desire sexually: it is how we as sexual and sensual beings foster connection, intimacy, and belonging with ourselves and others through various endeavors in private and public spaces and how that makes us *feel*. I agree with Lorde that the erotic is "in the way my body stretches to music and opens into response, hearkening to its deepest rhythms, so every level upon which I sense also opens to the erotically satisfying experience, whether it is dancing, having sex, building a bookcase, writing a poem, [or] examining an idea."[3] The erotic cannot—must not—be relegated to the bedroom. For the erotic is also about our deep desire and pull to connect and be intimate with our own self and others in all of our life projects. We can reclaim the erotic as we share those physical, emotional, sensual, psychic, and passionate expressions of what is deepest, strongest, and richest within each of us.[4] It is this consuming passion in many of our endeavors that can be shared not only within our romantic lives but also within other areas of our lives—in our eating together, dancing together, working together, and living together with and for others.

Yet, as Lorde suggests, the erotic can be corrupted and plasticized, emptied of its life-giving power. In the past, I took my lead from Lorde in identifying the corruption of the erotic as the pornographic. For Lorde, pornographic desire disconnects and produces forms of social alienation, disconnection, and despair. By contrast, erotic desire generates live-giving possibilities of intimacy and radical belonging. My mind has changed about this strict distinction between the erotic and the pornographic.[5]

Instead of maintaining the erotic as a separate, purer moment of desire than the pornographic, what might it mean to speak about the erotic as simply desire in all of its contradictory, ambiguous, and grotesque forms? What if the erotic *itself* can be corrupted? What if the erotic itself can be used in ways that foster certain intimacies among homogenous groups, intimacies that provide the psychosocial energy to fuel inhumane practices such as racism? People can feel intense desire for and connection over racist ideas and projects. What if racism enlivens erotic desire in corrupt and grotesque ways?

This conversation about the erotic is important for larger questions of racism. Much of liberationist, feminist, womanist, postcolonial, and critical race discourse describes racism primarily in systemic and structural terms. Certainly this has been an important intellectual intervention, for previously dominant groups referred to racism as an individual feeling or prejudice, rather than a network of relations and systems that (re)produce practices of disenfranchisement and material violence. The idea of racism simply as individual feeling and personal prejudice denied how racism is embedded in the structural formations of society, proving that to speak of racism is to speak of social, political, and economic formations that affect entire populations. This structuralist argument attempted to subvert psychosocial accounts of racism that singularly rooted racial oppression in individual agents.

Certainly a structural approach is central to explaining diverse racisms—their systemic character and the ways in which racial injustices shape the life-chances and opportunities of entire groups. However, such structural explanations do not capture racism as *events* and *encounters* in which *intimacies* and *connections* are forged in order to sustain filial bonds within groups. We know that structural resistance can be antiracist work. But can work on "desire" also be antiracist work? Can antiracist scholarship think about desire in its multiple and ambiguous forms that support racist bonding and belonging?[6] As scholar of American studies and black feminism Sharon Holland has asked: "What would happen if we opened up the erotic to a scene of racist welcoming?"[7]

Structural racism gains its sustenance, in part, from intense desires for white forms of belonging. As Holland notes, projects of racial belonging have two moments. Through discursive and material practices, the first moment produces presumed "real" biological connections at the level of blood (i.e., blue blood or the "one drop rule").[8] The second moment uses such discursive and material practices to establish racial identity and social relations that are reciprocal and mutual, forming a "community" or "nation." This racial community or "peoplehood" (such as the Anglo-Saxon myth I discussed in Chapter 2) requires exclusive patterns of intimacy and belonging, which materializes in separate and often racist relations and structures.[9] These two moments are worked out in quotidian ways, such as next to whom one chooses to sit on the bus, whom one chooses as a mate, whom one chooses to hire, or assumptions one makes about the kinds of people who show higher intellectual promise.[10] Racism, in this sense, can be described as "the emotional lifeblood of race; it is the 'feeling' that articulates and keeps the flawed logic of race in its place."[11] In this way, racism is an everyday practice. It is an erotic practice that maintains white intimacies within unequal structures and institutions.

We tend to focus on race and racisms through structural analysis associated with systemic sets of inequalities, but rarely do we focus on the everyday emotional systems of terror, pain, and pleasure that makes race so *desirable* as a useful category of difference.[12] For instance, why do poor whites participate with white capitalist supremacy when it may work against their own economic interests? Poor whites might find themselves supporting white supremacy even when it's against their material interests because the idea and practice of whiteness as a community and nation provides them with psychosocial intimacy, connection, and belonging. We tend to overlook the erotic life of everyday racism and certain kinds of intimacies it fosters that sustain community, making race a desirable and useful category for poor whites. This quotidian dimension of racist practice has a bonding and binding power for whites, quite apart from one's class status. It is important to attend to this ordinary felt experience of racist practice in order to offer an account of the feelings and intimacies that are released when bodies collide in pleasure or pain.[13]

The scene of everyday racist practice does not disavow the structural dimensions that make racist formations and systems possible. Rather it demonstrates that erotic desires and affective energies are tied to and fuel racist practices. Racism reveals a series of dependencies and intimacies that sustain structural racism. It is this series of dependencies and intimacies that continue to be unexplored and unexplained.[14] I want to reframe racist practice as affective encounters and events among bodies driven by erotic desires. We tend to describe racism as grounded in political and economic relations, which is not untrue. However, we fail to see how these relations shape and determine the procreative possibilities of our erotic lives. Such erotic relations generate daily encounters and events among people that continue to make race matter. A focus on the language of desire, then, does not personalize racism as prejudice but discloses how structural racism orders and is reinforced by the psychosocial life of racist practice.

It is important not to separate racism from who we are as desiring subjects and agents. What does it mean to think about desire in relation to systemic racist practice? On the one hand, desire can reinforce and reproduce an existing order that is fraught with racial, gendered, and class inequalities. On the other hand, counterhegemonic forms of desire can subvert the mimetic structures of racist desire itself, disrupting and rupturing the world of meaning making that racist practice guarantees. Racism can order desire but desire can also disrupt this order. Erotic desire is thus marked by ambiguity; it can be used in service to or against quotidian racist practice.[15] This is why I mentioned earlier my issue with bracketing the erotic from the pornographic. The erotic is not a transparent category, pointing to *pure* desire for healthy connection and belonging. The erotic itself is marked by messy entanglements. There is a polymorphous character to all human desire. Desire is a generative space but this space is not without complexity. To speak about the erotic is already to speak of a space that is *Dionysian*.[16] It can offer up intimate relations, energies, and connections that reinscribe the established racist order, and it can also sponsor revolutionary practice within a space of racist mimetic desire.

Desire makes worlds. The conversation about the erotic violence of American racial capitalism is important for understanding what Azusa was challenging: the erotic life of racism that marked white supremacy and its capitalist practices at the dawn of the twentieth century. It is to this erotic life of racism that I now turn.

Pleasure, Pain, Profit: Erotic Scenes of Racist Desire at the World Fairs

The erotic life of racism has been a technique that modern capitalism has used to accumulate profit. Queer theorists have focused on how capitalist processes and practices (re)produce and manufacture erotic desires.[17] Within America's early industrial economy, intimate and erotic lives were commodified, assigned value, commercialized, and packaged for consumption. As Azusa was emerging, industrial capitalism relied on and continually manufactured, commodified, and commercialized ways of knowing and feeling that employed racist forms of human desire and connection required for the accumulation of profit. Accumulating profit at the world fairs involved the manufacturing and manipulation of racist desires that rendered ethical and *profitable* white forms of intimacy and belonging (such as paying to view the "barbaric and primitive" exhibitions of non-European cultures from around the world in order to affirm and solidify the desire for a civilizing, benevolent paternalism among white

Americans). American capitalism thrived off the erotic life of racism, as the nation's market machinery depended upon particular kinds of white racial welcoming, bonding, and belonging.

The erotic life of the world fairs and business expositions was about a particular kind of racial welcoming and intimacy. Let us revisit for a moment the Columbian Exposition of 1893 to see how the erotic life of racism was in service to market ends, which was the context out of which Azusa emerged. The language of the New Pentecost that this exposition employed was undergirded by a desire for white racial bonding. To actualize the Anglo-Saxon vision of capitalist progress and cultural purity, a set of white racial intimacies, desires, and dependencies had to bind the nation together, and these intimacies needed to be felt experiences that appeared natural and given. For whites, this world fair participated in erotic economies of whiteness that fostered intense desire and passion for white purity and belonging through the sexual objectification and degradation of blacks, Native Americans, Chinese, and others. And whites experienced such white racial bonding as both painful *and* pleasurable.

Consider this erotic scene of racist desire in service to capitalist ends. Recall Midway Plaisance at the Chicago Columbian Exposition of 1893, a narrow strip of land at the fair that showcased ethnological villages from different nations and cultures. These villages often actually housed people from different parts of the world and their artifacts, and highlighted their customs and traditions. One village introduced the Dahomeyans to visitors. Dahomeyan people lived on the Gulf of Guinea. Roughly sixty-seven were in the Dahomeyan delegation, and when they arrived they generated great interest among white Americans.[18] Among visitors, these Africans were seen as having a "striking degree of barbarianism and seen as part of the lowest order" of the human family.[19] Dahomeyan men and women were discussed in books and at the fairs as hypersexual and culturally dangerous, the very symbols of moral impurity. European explorers remarked that these African people wore no clothes in their natural habitat in Africa, which, they insisted, gestured towards their morally barbaric and sexually lewd ways.[20] One could hear the erotic overtones in how these people were discussed and represented.

Ponder how Dahomeyan men and women were culturally represented. One American journalist described that these men could "balance a truck on their heads."[21] Notice that the Dahomeyan men are described through American cultural representations that long characterized African-American men. For instance, African-American men were portrayed as "violent bucks" who had supernatural physical strength that had to be tamed and kept under control.[22] Because these men were characterized as unusually strong and therefore given to passionate violence of all kinds (emotional, physical, and sexual), whites rationalized and justified racist laws and practices that kept them in "their place." One particular aspect of the violent buck was how he used his sexual strength and prowess to rape white women. As black female activist Ida B. Wells-Barnett demonstrated through her own investigative journalism, the raping of white women by black men colored the white American imagination, although this picture of black men was untrue.[23] No matter how domesticated these men might appear, they were "nothing more than violent, passionate beasts of prey" to whites.[24] The American journalist who wrote about how the Dahomeyan men are able to balance trucks on their heads participates in this entire economy of significations about black men. Similar to African-American men, these exotic Dahomeyan men were violent bucks. And this image of the unusually strong, violent buck had deep sexual connotations.

The journalist also stated that although the Dahomeyans were heavily clothed at the Chicago World Fair, it was hard to "keep any clothing whatever on them."[25] While the journalist admitted that the warm weather in Africa made this difficult for them, he also implied that white explorers (who were able to visit Africa's hot climate and clothe themselves) preferred the Dahomeyans to be clothed, much to the Africans' chagrin. In other words, this statement implicitly paints these African people as bawdy and vulgar. And this vulgarity also had sexual connotations. Dohomeyan women (and their children by extension) were read as unwilling to be clothed, which portrayed these women as inherently wanton, perverse, and morally deviant. These women also were seen in hypersexual terms, and this interpretation depended upon erotic notions about black bodies.

This erotic scene did not arouse just pain but also pleasure. White intimacy and connection were forged when whites encountered these morally and sexually deviant Dahomeyan people. Many white Americans felt an intense pleasure to reclaim the need for white purity and paternalism in light of their experiences of a hypersexualized people who were essentially licentious and debased by nature. This experience created deep emotional ties among whites. One correspondent viewing the village remarked that "in these wild people we easily detect many characteristics of the American Negro."[26] Through experiencing this African village, white Americans were forming intimate bonds among each other over the question of African-American humanity. Pleasure could be seen in white affirmation that they indeed were responsible for civilizing a primitive and savage world. For whites, racial hierarchy in the United States was a moral necessity to safeguard the future of America and the broader world. This erotic scene certainly reproduced and intensified patterns of white racial intimacy and belonging.

One liberal Boston woman who decided to visit the Dahomeyan village at the fair left a written record of her response. She expressed regret at encountering these Africans, as it forced her to reflect on the "gulf between them and Emerson."[27] Not all whites attending saw African people as animals or inherently debased. Some imagined themselves embracing a more liberal position in relation to blacks. The position went something like this: African people were not evil or animals but childlike and in need of civilizing. They had intellectual and moral potential, not on par with whites, but enough to be contributing members of American society. It seems that this Boston woman had imagined herself as a white liberal until she encountered this village.

For her, the white philosopher Ralph Waldo Emerson represented and embodied the best of the North American liberal intellectual tradition. Emersonian philosophy stressed a democratic society of free and equal individuals.[28] For Emerson, the purpose of stressing individuals as free agents was to allow individuals to self-actualize through self-reliance. Individuals could not actualize their humanity if they were in bondage, unable to be self-reliant. Slavery impeded Africans' ability to be self-reliant and so Emerson deeply supported the abolitionist cause to end slavery, although he still ranked African potential below white capacities and abilities. What we find in this woman's statement is a questioning of this Emersonian assumption—that blacks had the *basic* human capacity to self-actualize through self-reliance. She thought that perhaps they could not due to their inherently savage and bestial nature, demonstrated through the Dahomeyan people. She reflects on such a wide, unbridgeable gulf between what she saw at the village and Emerson's assumption about blacks having *some* ability to act morally and intellectually. This affective encounter caused her to question whether slavery was even an absolute evil given the debased nature of these people. She walked away regretful, invoking the racist order of desire that marked America's erotic economies of whiteness. She experienced pain and pleasure simultaneously—pain that her Emersonian assumption has been proven wrong, and pleasure that white dominance in America stood on morally high ground.

These ethnological villages were commercialized and packaged for white consumption. Whites experienced this World Fair and its ethnological "villages" as one big anthropological revelation, stirring their deepest and strongest feelings and desires about race, sex, and nonwhite bodies. After purchasing their tickets to the fairs and encountering these villages and their temporary inhabitants, middle-class and working whites felt affirmation that America's racial order was necessary and even moral. What they had seen stirred particular emotions, desires, and affects. These images and emotions (re)produced and intensified erotic desires of white racial connection and belonging against the backdrop of what whites perceived as primitive, dark realities about non-European peoples. As whites flocked and bought entrance into these fairs, they renewed their confidence in and moral commitment to justifying racial segregation and white paternalism. For so many white consumers of the fairs, the village experience of non-European people affirmed why white purity and capitalist institutions were necessary, enabling white Americans to experience pleasure and intimacy through being the historical redeemers of such childlike, hypersexual cultures. Visitors such as this liberal Boston woman realized that America was indeed the New Jerusalem that needed to lead other people (such as the Dahomeyans) into the divine light of white moral and social order.

At the Chicago fair, erotic scenes of racist desire also *monetized* and capitalized upon Christian notions of truth as well as the ideal of America as the New Jerusalem. A visitor would enter through the great central arch that marked the lakeside entrance and gaze upward at the words of Jesus Christ inscribed along its cornice, "You Shall Know the Truth and the Truth Shall Make You Free."[29] This inscription was not gesturing toward any truths Jesus spoke during his lifetime about loving human relations or virtues needed for an egalitarian society. Instead, this caption affirmed the perceived truth of capitalist expansionism, that capitalism was the redeeming truth to cure the world's ills and problems. These fairs sought to free people's minds to the redeeming character of capitalist institutions for American society and the broader globe. The Dahomeyan village participated in this "truth" of capitalist redemption. One could simply turn to these people and see why they had to be reformed. If America and cultures around the world were to experience progress, capitalism had to be treated like an absolute truth; people had to believe that the spiritual answer to poverty, sickness, and even war was the expansion of wealth through capitalistic market practices. Notice how the Christian idea of truth is married to a capitalist moral vision of progress. Jesus' words are monetized in order to legitimate the increasing accumulation of profit and material gain.

One also immediately noticed the biblical imagery that described the Chicago fair as the "New Jerusalem." Organizers and leaders claimed that this New

Jerusalem "had enabled the millions of visitors who came to Chicago for this massive commemoration of the arrival of Columbus to catch a glimpse of the Heavenly City the Apostle John had beheld in his vision on the isle of Patmos."[30] As one entered the fair, one was reminded of the vision that America would be a "New Jerusalem," a place of return and spiritual reflection for the weary traveler of life. This business event promised a glorious Christian America, and sought to extend this glory to the far corners of the world through unprecedented wealth creation. It proclaimed millennial hopes in which America's national glory would allow a new world of liberty, equality, and material abundance to break forth across all lands and cultures. Business leaders monetized this biblical image of New Jerusalem at the fairs, promising visitors that the nation's investment in market institutions would reap high economic, social, and *spiritual* dividends for its citizens. America as a New Jerusalem was about promising a "new heaven and new earth" that only racial-capitalist markets could effectuate.

This idea of New Jerusalem evoked all kinds of shared desires and intimacies among white Americans. It was already written into America's national narrative and political identity, familiar rhetoric in celebrating the founding and future of the United States. Anglo-Saxon Christians always believed that the British colonial settlers were on a mission for God when they landed and established the early colonies. Fleeing religious persecution and wanting to establish their own Protestant world that could be the biblical "city on a hill," Puritan colonists wanted to form a political and social community that embodied a pure Christianity and fostered civil liberty. Consider John Winthrop, the first governor of Massachusetts Bay colony, and his "City on a Hill" speech in 1630, which presents the Puritan settlers as a New Israel which has entered into a covenant with God. Using biblical references and imagery of the Jew's covenant with God to attain the promised land, Winthrop reminds the colonists that they have received a commission to make this new land a haven of Protestant faith, which means they need to practice God's moral commands and convert Native Americans and other non-Anglo Saxons to the faith, for only then could the colony receive God's favor and blessings.[31]

This covenant depended upon all kinds of racist affectivities, desires, and intimacies. Cultivating racist practices toward Native Americans and African slaves was not only about conquest such as wealth building through land and profits, but also about cultivating and affirming modes of white racial bonding and belonging. Whites would be taught *primarily* to desire the friendship, companionship, and moral partnership *of other whites*. Feelings of good will, compassion, and empathy needed to be shared among early white Protestant colonists. Affects such as disgust, fear, and sometimes a "benevolent paternalism" shaped white Protestants socially when engaging Africans, Native Americans, and even Asians such as the Chinese and Japanese. Talking about Christian covenant among white Protestants was also about their desiring lives—*whom* they desired and felt intimacy toward contrasted *with whom* they loathed or *for whom* they felt disgust (especially if the racial pagan did not convert to their Christian ways). This desire for white purity and belonging had to be intense and passionate in order to legitimate and maintain racial hierarchy.

Anglo-Saxon Christian leaders would eventually refer to this white American Christian covenant and its desires for white racial belonging as Manifest Destiny. John O'Sullivan coined this phrase in 1845 in an editorial arguing in favor of Texas's annexation to the United States. He said that those people opposed to Texas's annexation were "thwarting our policy and hampering our power, limiting our greatness and checking the fulfillment of our Manifest Destiny to overspread the continent allotted by Providence for the free development of our yearly multiplying millions."[32] The United States was chosen by God as the Jews had been, he said. It was the destiny of Anglo-Saxon Americans to desire greatness through empire building because this was the will of God. America had to remain focused on her special mission. And this special mission involved an entire set of desires and intimacies shared among white Americans. This desire for white racial bonding and belonging shaped the Columbian Exposition and its vision of capitalist expansion. The Chicago exhibitions and the activities of the Parliament of World Religions cultivated erotic economies of white intimacy and connection. And these erotic economies were in service to the massive profit business leaders and politicians stood to gain from such fairs.

Consider another scene that demonstrates the erotic life of racism and how it legitimated the untamed profit of the world fairs. In Chapter 1, I discussed Episcopal Bishop William Bacon Stevens's address to the Philadelphia World Fair of 1876. He encouraged people around the country who were divided to gather back "around the old family hearthstone of Independence Hall" and recommit "heart and hand" to a social and political brotherhood.[33] Stevens invokes the healing of intimate relations among divided groups across racial, class, and national lines. His plea gestures toward citizens desiring each other, passionately craving for the healing and renewal of intimate bonds. And that intimacy, connection, and belonging among American citizens he described in familial terms, people gathering together to recommit to an unbroken brotherhood, language which invokes blood ties, some of the most intimate relations of connection and belonging one can have.

Might such intimate encounters have solved the cultural and social problems of the nation?[34] Given the racial, class, and immigrant tensions in the United States, Stevens might have imagined black and white citizens gathering to look into each other's eyes, recognizing their mutual humanity. He might have imagined people touching by hugs, locking arms, and holding hands. Perhaps divided groups would then be in a position to hear the stories and narratives of each other and open their hearts to their neighbors. He might have imagined them forming fellowships across tables of food and drink. In any case, Stevens attempted to conjure a deep yearning for intimacy and communion in private and public spaces among divided people. His comments also suggest that he believed this kind of erotic connection among divided groups would heal the cultural confusion and economic precarity, as if the sources of economic trouble were grounded in racial misunderstanding rather than intentional institutional practices of segregation, inequality, and inequity.

Stevens's vision of multicultural communion was complicated by one problem: the Philadelphia exposition itself still operated within patterns of white nationalistic belonging. African Americans were not allowed to create exhibits that truthfully told their own histories and of their own contributions to America's landscape. Segregation of African and black American exhibits at this fair (created and approved by whites) persisted. Also notice the space where Stevens called for the fashioning of this new multicultural intimacy and communion: around sentimental national symbols such as Independence Hall. For many blacks, immigrants, and the poor, Independence Hall was a symbol of American triumphalism, Manifest Destiny, and white Christian nationalism. In Independence Hall, the African enslaved were once counted as three-fifths a person for reasons of representation, which was a way to expand northern slavery to the South in efforts to create wealth for the nation through free labor.[35] While independence was an ideal to which all marginalized groups appealed, they nevertheless believed and had seen that most white Americans used Independence Hall (as well as words from the Constitution) as a political instrument to advance white American cultural, political, and economic interests. What motivation would blacks have to gather around the hearthstone of Independence Hall with white citizens while sharecropping, lynching, rape, and a form of neoslavery (segregation) persisted? Why does Stevens use the language of renewal when already from the founding of this nation blacks were not desired as equal humans alongside whites? Why should the working class and poor commit their hearts and hands to capitalist owners when early industrialism depended on the unfreedoms and poverty of the masses? Why would blacks be moved by this plea when Stevens's idea of desire and intimacy was locked within white patterns of connection and belonging?

The Philadelphia exposition reflected *a certain kind of racial welcoming* that sought to reinscribe white racial intimacy and connection in the name of Christian unity and capitalist progress. It reminds us that the political project of American racism is not just structural but also affective, fostering erotic ties that sustain racist forms of bonding. The Columbian and Philadelphia expositions disclose structural racism and they expose racism as an encounter and event grounded in erotic patterns of white racial bonding.

Even more unfortunate, some African Americans were nonetheless shaped inside these erotic economies of whiteness. Some blacks resolved to find religious identity and meaning within the context of white racial belonging, believing that it would usher in equality for them alongside white people. For instance, many bourgeois black churches rejected religious patterns of intimacy and belonging shared by blacks, such as demonstrative and danced religion (witnessed at the Azusa Revival), as it represented (to whites, and therefore to some of them) an uncouth, uncultured, and demonic form of African-ness. White Protestant churches described the danced religion of plantation churches as lustful and fundamentally non-Christian. In order to appear educated, respectable elite black Christians truly believed that they needed to leave the primitive nature of slave religion behind. In this case, the erotic life of racism shaped the idea of belonging even within black communities. This is the contradiction. The ambiguity. The grotesque nature of America's erotic life. These world fairs operated with these racist assumptions about the primitiveness of other cultures and their religions, which meant that intimacy and cultural belonging could only be achieved through American ideas of white desire.

American relations of intimacy and belonging were couched in terms of whiteness and capitalist progress. The erotic, in these expositions, was used in service to capitalism and white cultural hegemony. For these fairs, gathering people from around the world was not for the purpose of facilitating cultural exchange among diverse communities but for reinforcing racist practices of conquest, thanks to which America and other European countries could experience capitalist gain. Foregrounding the erotic life of racism within the Columbian and Philadelphia expositions is important in order to understand the kind of erotic project of white intimacy and belonging that Azusa directly challenged.

The Erotic Life of Azusa

These world fairs appeared to endorse a liberating vision for people around the world, purporting to foster connection and belonging across racial, gender, national, and class lines. But this was not the case. At these expositions, erotic desire was employed toward white cultural expansion married to the eschatological promise of industrial progress and material abundance. The erotic landscape of the fairs was in service to American racial capitalism and its myth of progress.

The fairs' engagement of the erotic treated nonwhite persons as *objects*. They engaged racial and religious "others" in objectifying ways with an assumption that their responsibility was simply to contribute and affirm the larger American project of economic and cultural expansionism. Religious and racial others had only one option at this exposition: to convert and be subsumed into the broader white American project by being workers contributing to the growing wealth of the nation. As a result, the erotic energy present at the expositions corrupted practices of actual belonging and connection. This persistence of white belonging and intimacy was grounded in relations of white economic and cultural domination. This kind of erotic desire was an appetite rather than a generosity.[36] The erotic life of racism is fundamentally violent in its vision of "reciprocity"; the expositions demonstrated this critical insight.

In contrast to the Chicago Columbian and Philadelphia Expositions, Azusa's liturgical life disrupted the erotic landscape of racism associated with the American capitalist system. Azusa's liturgical practices of the erotic fostered a deep opening up to blacks and immigrants as *subjects*. In Chapter 2, I discussed at length how the religious rituals of Azusa were deeply *enfleshed*, involving the sensing, touching, and celebration of bodies that had been socialized to be repulsed by each other's flesh. The Spirit could only move when hands were laid on each other, when bodies danced in ecstatic praise together, when people hugged as prayers of power were offered. Even more transgressive, in an era in which black men could be lynched merely for looking at a white woman or a black woman raped for walking past a white man, black men laid hands on white women and black women led white men in conversion experiences.

Azusa's worship life might be described as a set of erotic events and encounters that open one up to the other, a welcoming and desire for intimacy and connection not grounded in the erotic worlds of white racial bonding and belonging. Black studies scholar Ashon Crawley asserts that Azusa reflected an *otherwise* world of intimacy and connection from the world of white racial violence. He refers to Azusa as an example of "Blackpentecostalism." Black-pentecostalism is not a denominational label or ethnic marker but "a critical sociality of intense feeling" that is in "service of the other."[37] Through aesthetic practices, Blackpentecostalism sponsors forms of intense connection, intimacy, and social organization that challenge racist modes of desire, bonding, and belonging. Crawley notes that aesthetic practices such as dancing, singing, noise making, whooping, tarrying, and talking in tongues enable religious communities such as Azusa to resist hegemonic modes of community and connection. Azusa members used these various aesthetic practices on the wooden floors of 312 Azusa Street to become a disruptive force.[38] Azusa's liturgical life disrupts the forms of white racial bonding that capitalist rhythms and ways of life encouraged. Azusa refuses the erotic rhythms and white intimacies that hypermarket practices demanded.

For example, Azusa's religious ritual of praying and tarrying at a desegregated altar opened people up to each other in ways that the erotic worlds of American racial capitalism would not allow. During the nineteenth and twentieth centuries, the altar was a site of white racial bonding and belonging for white Christians. Praying at the altar was a practice that reinforced racial superiority for white communities. Throughout the history of slavery in the United States, altars were highly segregated. In many churches, African Americans could not kneel at the same altar as whites, and if they did come to mixed altars, only whites could occupy those altars.[39] In fact, early holiness and Pentecostal leaders such as Charles Parham and Alma White supported altar segregation.

At this sacred site, white Christians' racist understanding of the world were affirmed, encouraging them to embrace white superiority as a religious virtue. At Christian altars, whites experienced erotic affirmations of belonging and intense connection. White Christians gathered around altars to reaffirm liturgically God's favor toward them, allowing them also to reenact their desires to be with and for each other as they carried out the will of God. In regard to the race question, the will of God involved saving the nonwhite heathen, which meant emotionally affirming slavery and Jim Crow as righteous institutions. One might see the altar as a site where intimacy and pleasure are experienced among whites as they expressed their racial identities and patterns of belonging in Christian terms. *They* belonged to each other and to the American project of democracy. The altar facilitated erotic encounters among white Christians, fueling their own emotional bonds in relation to racist and capitalist practices.

Azusa's liturgical life challenges white erotic connection and desire at altars. Recall the Asberry's home on Bonnie Brae, where the revival began. In opposition to Parham's Pentecostal practice (and the broader white church), Seymour and other white and black leaders made a makeshift altar in the Asberry's living room.[40] After a long night of tarrying, they *together* received the baptism. When they moved into the larger Azusa Street building, there were no segregated altars. At Azusa's altar, white and black bodies knelt side by side, skin to skin, flesh to flesh. Tears from a black man could find their home on the shoulder of a white man or white woman. White arms could flail and find themselves on the back of a black person. The breath of a black woman could be felt on the face of a white man, breath and breathing becoming one sound. The aroma of odors fused together as they cried out at the altar, sweating and moving their bodies in anticipation of some powerful outbreak of the Spirit. Praying and tarrying at the altar was most definitely an erotic encounter. As one knelt, one often felt the body of another against one's own skin. Being at the altar and praying was a collective practice, a practice of desiring and longing for each other. The transformation of erotic desire disrupted the white project of racial bonding and belonging fostered by segregated altar practices. Racial boundaries were being crossed through fleshly encounters, as bodies of white and blacks, Mexicans and Irish, Africans and Armenians joined each other in forging an otherwise community based on a practice of belonging not tethered to racist hierarchy.

Also consider how Azusa's erotic life was seen through the aesthetic practice of "laying on of hands." People across racial, gender, and class lines laid hands on each other to receive the holy baptism and divine healing. As I discussed earlier, at Azusa black men laid hands on white women and black women laid hands on white men, including some white men who were wealthy. This was in stark contrast to the economy of touch in American society, which was deeply racialized. Touch was deeply connected to intimacy, equality, and safety. Many white Americans (and Christians) would not touch the bodies of blacks, whose bodies whites interpreted as ugly, dirty, and morally tainted (although this is quite untrue when one considers the history of sexualized violence done to black women at the hands of white men). Black men were described as bestial and violent and black women as lewd and sexually promiscuous. Black men could not even look at a white woman for fear of being lynched. The practice of the laying on of hands overturns these cultural representations of black subjects and asserts the humanity of such subjects. White participants at Azusa challenged the erotic life of racism through touching, hugging, kissing, and desiring black congregants as human beings with equal dignity and worth. Moreover, the humanity of black people at Azusa becomes the "home" out of which white members experience intimacy and belonging. Whites could not experience their humanity in all of its fullness when engaging black people as objects, only as subjects.

For outsiders, the erotic life of Azusa created a socially transgressive space. As Gaston Espinosa intimates, it is one in which people engaged in behavior and practices that were deemed socially inappropriate and even lewd.[41] Inappropriate, because of the unaccustomed closeness of white and black bodies. Heretical too, because those bodies were out of place and out of order. This disorder was not simply a social problem; it was a theological problem, one that disordered the racial order of the world which whites regarded as a benevolent expression of divine providence. Yet Azusa's erotic practices confronted this so-called divinely ordained order of race and called *it* heresy. Azusa indicts the erotic life of racism and how it was supported by theological postulates. This new announcement of human intimacy and belonging was not based on racial hierarchy but on an intense desire for people across race, class, and gender to be in communion with each other. Azusa's erotic practices did not preach the gospel of racial subordination and capitalist expansionism associated with the "New Pentecost" of the Columbian and Philadelphia expositions. Instead, Azusa invoked the Pentecost of ancient days in which an otherwise community of persons fostered a more liberative practice of care and connection.

Many critics labeled Azusa's liturgical practices as *sexually* charged and repulsive. For instance, reporters of this revival wrote sensational stories about men and women from different races, nationalities and classes that knelt alongside each other at the altar, touching each other in suggestive ways.[42] Holiness leader Alma White stated that Azusa was a context of demon possession. She described it as a horrible revival in the slums of Los Angeles where witchcraft, wild kissing, and shocking "familiarity between the sexes" went on.[43] These kinds of fleshly contortions were seen as upsetting the natural order of things. White's words certainly evoke natural law claims in the early twentieth century, laws that depended on the preservation of white racial purity. The policing of sexual norms were at the heart of white racial purity. After all, "familiarity" between the sexes could eventually lead to "miscegenation," which supposedly tainted the genetic and intellectual make-up of the white race. If true faith and civilization came from the white race, then the preservation of the purity of this race was essential and Azusa could be nothing more than a teenage orgy.

Similar to White, Parham described Azusa as a bastion of "free love," hearkening back to how interracial mixing was seen as promiscuous and sexually deviant. Parham remarked that one could frequently witness a white woman of wealth being "thrown back in the arms of a big buck nigger."[44] He described such white women as being held tightly by these men, shaking "in freak imitation of Pentecost." He lamented that Azusa was nothing more than a "hotbed of wildfire," of "religious orgies outrivaling scenes in devil or fetish worship."[45] Parham believed that Azusa's magnetism was less about Christian purity and more about sexual lust and free love.

This theme of free love was central to how Parham and other critics measured other mission churches that came out of the Azusa Street Revival. Parham wrote about how a particular "woman leader" of a congregation in Oakland described the deep love ties that blacks and whites had in her congregation and at Azusa. She described how much she loved blacks and how black and whites stayed in the same house together, enacting this loving community.[46] Parham questioned the "lovey-dovey" nature of these congregations and commented that this kind of talk was "sickening." The hypersexualization of Azusa demonstrated that Azusa was seen as a transgressive space in erotic (explicitly sexual) ways.

The charge that Azusa was a bastion of free love is important. Although outsiders feared the erotic urges of this revival, participants at Azusa were likewise unsure and even afraid of its erotic energies. Specifically, I am interested in the silences surrounding the erotic desires and sexual choices among participants of this revival. Most notably, the departure of Clara Lum makes one wonder what exactly transpired between William Seymour and Clara Lum. Lum was Seymour's assistant and the newspaper's coeditor. They were seen as a great team that led and guided Azusa administratively. Together, they printed over 405,000 copies of the Apostolic Faith newspaper used to spread Seymour's vision of the Azusa Revival.[47] When Seymour unexpectedly and retrospectively announced that he and Jennie Evans Moore (a young black woman leader at Azusa) had been married on May 13, 1908—a ceremony witnessed by all the black leaders but none of the white leaders and members of the church[48]—among those most upset by the news was Lum, a white woman. Not only had Lum been the staff person with whom Seymour had spent the most time, she and others were shocked at a theological level, questioning Seymour's virtue and wondering why he had undermined the end-times theology that they preached, which often involved self-imposed celibacy and self-denial. He had betrayed the holiness call to "sanctification." The suddenness of their marriage and their age difference—Seymour was thirty-eight and Moore twenty-five years old—led people to assume a loss of virtue through sexual encounter.

In response to Seymour's marriage, Lum, often described as acting like a "jilted lover," opposed Seymour and left the mission.[49] She left the mission in protest and took Azusa's newspaper along with the only national and international mailing list Seymour had, bringing them to Florence Crawford's mission in Portland, Oregon. Although Seymour demanded and then more humbly asked that she return the mailing list, she never did.[50] Ithiel Clemmons argues that C. H. Mason believed Clara Lum wanted to marry Seymour. Seymour had sought counsel from Mason prior to marrying Moore about Lum's prospects after Lum had revealed to Seymour that she wanted him to propose.[51] Interracial marriage during this period was almost impossible. Perhaps Seymour believed that going through with an interracial marriage could have prematurely marked the end of the revival and brought moral disrepute on all this movement had achieved. Besides, Seymour had to consider the continuation of black leadership within Azusa as part of his decision whom to marry. Lum was apparently inconsolable at Seymour's marriage to Moore.

Although this religious community often defied the dominant modes of white racial and gendered bonding and belonging, Seymour and other Azusa members apparently feared the erotic dimensions of their own revival. Consider also Seymour's decision to force women leaders who were divorced either to stay single or remarry their expartners. Seymour had heard that some in the congregation were calling women leaders of Azusa unvirtuous because some husbands were divorcing their wives for "abandoning their homes for the sake of preaching."[52] Seymour did not want the Azusa movement to be seen as breaking up homes or taking women out of their primary roles as wives and housekeepers. He regulated women's sexuality within the movement rather than embracing the new opportunities of the revival for increased mutuality between men and women.

Yet some women leaders resisted. Just a year into the revival, Florence Crawford's husband Frank approached Seymour about his wife, claiming that her ministerial call as an Azusa leader was undermining her primary duty as a wife in the home. Because Frank felt that Florence was justifying spending so much time at church and less on taking care of her family, he filed for divorce on grounds of abandonment. With a divorced woman on pastoral staff, Seymour now felt the moral reputation of the revival was at risk. What should he do? He concluded that on biblical ground Florence should not remarry but would need to stay single.[53] Florence disagreed and soon after left the Azusa mission in Los Angeles and relocated to Portland to start her own movement and denomination.[54] While on the basis of her own writings scholars suggest there were in fact multiple reasons why Florence left, this desire of Seymour's to control Florence's marital and future sexual decisions also played a significant role in the split between them.

Probably feeling betrayed, Seymour promptly wrote a series of articles on marriage, divorce, and gender roles,[55] in which he reflects on women who disrupt and destroy their homes due to their missionary work. He invokes traditional gender roles, urging women leaders not to forget the importance of washing, ironing, scrubbing, and taking care of the little children.[56] To be fair, Seymour also admonished men in ministry to attend to their family, but Seymour made it abundantly clear that women should play the primary role. Prompted by this experience with Florence, Seymour revised his teachings on women in ministry, eventually writing in the minister's manual that "all ordination must be done by men not women," and that "women may be ministers" but not "baptize and ordain in this work." As a final move, he revised the manual to read that "women could not serve as bishop or vice bishop *since they could change these guidelines.*"[57]

Although Seymour nevertheless supported women as pastors and evangelists, he took a problematic approach to marriage and family roles, presumably deeply afraid that public charges of eroticism and wayward sexuality among Azusa women leaders would thwart the ministry—his ministry—and sully their holiness reputation. His primary means to achieve this was to control and regulate women's—not men's—sexuality within the church through a public or published institutional strategy.

Despite Azusa's own hesitancies about its erotic energies, it nevertheless disrupted the erotic life of racism in the United States. This is the complexity of this revival: that the erotic reveals both the possibilities and limitations of this movement. Azusa was what Saidiya Hartman has called a "revolution of the intimate" that fostered beautiful experiments of different, otherwise ways of desiring and living. In the first two years of Azusa, members experienced powerful transformations away from the racist patterns of disconnection and lack of intimacy, even as Seymour imposed strategies to contain specifically women's erotic urges manifesting in the church. Even if imperfectly, even if restrained by the male leadership, members of this religious community desired to remake themselves and the terms under which relationships were possible.

Erotic Fugitivity: Queering Azusa

Azusa's erotic life might be described as reflecting a broader queer sociality and fugitive practice. Here I take my cue from queer theologian Linn Tonstad, who suggests that the term "queer" moves *in and beyond* questions of sexual identity, orientation, expression, and inclusion. For Tonstad, queer more broadly refers to "visions of socio-political transformation that alter harmful practices aimed at marginalized and vulnerable populations, which include gender and sexual minorities but [is] not reduced to these groups.[58] Tonstad describes as queer "whatever is at odds with the normal, the legitimate, the dominant."[59] Queer is distance from the normative, a refusal of the normative.[60]

Throughout this chapter, my description of Azusa's erotic life has demonstrated that Azusa fostered such a queer sociality. Azusa's forms of intense intimacy and connection across racial, gender, and class lines were *lawless*. They defied the erotic life of U.S. racism. They refused to participate in America's racist and hetero-patriarchal practices of subjugation and death.

Azusa's queer sociality depended upon fugitive practices. As black feminist theorist Tina Campt notes, fugitivity is not simply an opposition to power but a refusal even to acknowledge the terms of power.[61] For Campt, fugitivity is a communal practice rather than a mere act in that it includes an entire set of everyday actions and strategies out of which marginalized subjects learn to survive and defy together. As a result, fugitivity is not some "ultimate act of rebellion but a quotidian practice of refusal by groups."[62]

Fugitivity is about "taking flight" from the hegemonic, normative boundaries of life and living. In this case, Azusa's queer life takes flight from the erotic boundaries of racist desire and practice. Azusa's erotic life might be described as a way of being that is "on the run." It is not legible within the erotic life of racist practice, as racist practice treats black and other nonwhite persons as nonsubjects, as objects and commodities within capitalist structures. It cannot make room for longing, yearning, and belonging (that is not instrumental in nature) between white and black subjects. Azusa's queer life is fugitive in the sense that it reflects quotidian practices of refusal, from interracial altar worship to egalitarian gender practices of leadership however imperfectly. Azusa's practice of erotic fugitivity disrupts the nature of desire between ethnicities, genders, classes, and more. A more liberative kind of desire and bonding is made possible. Azusa refused to settle within the borders of racist desire.

Some might retort that it is a stretch, even anachronistic, to refer to Azusa as queer and fugitive. Given what queer means today, how could any movements associated with early Pentecostalism be considered queer? Historically and even today, we know that many Pentecostal communities oppose what we now call queer people and their lifestyles/practices. While this is true of much of contemporary Pentecostalism (and Christian Protestantism in the United States as well), I am drawn by Tonstad's desire to expand the idea of queer to describe not only sexual identity, orientations, and expressions but also forms of social living that dare to transgress the harmful normative standards of society. If one accepts Tonstad's usage of the term, then Azusa is indeed queer when seeing how it refuses both the normative life of white racist desire and the dominant modes of bonding within the world of gender (women were rarely treated as equals within ecclesial and social communities).

Azusa's queer ways of being can be seen in how its liturgical life turned the erotic life of racism on its head. Azusa required that white congregants open up to black congregants on the religious terms of black members and enter into these terms in order to be transformed. Recall that slave religious practices were at the center of Azusa's religious experience. Slave religious practices invoked African rituals and ways. Yet in white American Christian discourse, Africa and its enslaved children were a metaphor for the Fall. Africa lived away from God. Africa was the essence of paganism, being the absence of discernment and truth as well as the unwillingness to seek and live into the "light." Africa was a presence that needed to be awakened and redeemed. Consequently, racial others such as Africans had to purify their soul, which meant the complete erasure of any native identity. White Christianity *allowed* blacks to *become* a civilized subject through embracing respectable white Christian religious practices. Ironically, Azusa's liturgical practices rooted in enslaved communities became the basis of religious subjectivity for *whites*. This new pattern of intimacy and belonging involved whites renouncing how blacks were culturally and religiously represented: as demonic and without divine light. They had to surrender to a religious experience with blacks not scripted by racist theological ideologies and practices. This new erotic moment was made possible through an intimacy and desire for the black religious subject that refused the terms of white racial bonding and belonging. This is what made Azusa queer: it deviated from the normative life of racist desire. And this revival's erotic patterns also created new modes of being and living not captured by American hetero-capitalist forms of life.

Azusa raises questions about the ethics of erotic relationships. What makes erotic relationships ethical is their demand upon the person to risk oneself in an encounter that transforms their very self through the other. The erotic life of Azusa is a place where the "risks of recognition are laid out."[63] It is a place where one is called upon to risk vulnerability in an encounter with the other and to take up the other person's vulnerability in their body, in their flesh. This erotic life is a fugitive practice because it is exceeds the boundaries associated with the erotic life of racism. Erotic racism bars erotic possibilities associated with the opening up to the other in noninstrumental ways. With Azusa, openness to the other is a joyful enfolding rather than a painful wound.[64] For these members, erotic connection and belonging was less about reinforcing racial trauma and inequity and more about an invitation into an intersubjective encounter of a new existential way of being that resisted and exceeded the white status quo.

The erotic life of Azusa might be understood as the site of one's *route to the other and back to one's own self*. This erotic life transforms the concept of the subject and the practice of belonging. It transforms the concept of the subject in that the subject and its ability to grasp and act morally in the world is inextricably tied to others. Subjectivity is not about a self-sufficient or self-contained individual. This atomistic understanding of human subjectivity and moral growth is challenged when turning to the erotic life of Azusa. This erotic life demonstrates that human discernment, moral judgment, and agency mature fully through intersubjective experiences that are nonobjectifying. This intersubjective mode of being then allows erotic possibilities to function as queer and fugitive against the erotic life of racism.

Azusa's erotic life generated inclusive practices of belonging. The erotic life of racism corrupts belonging, connection, and even generosity. For much of America's history, it saw slavery and segregation as constitutive of a benevolent Christianity. This compassionate paternalism was the heartbeat of white America's justification of racial hierarchy and separation. The erotic practices associated with this white supremacist system were not deemed to be cruel but generous, a "warmhearted" and morally thoughtful way of living in light of racial differences. This is the danger related to the erotic life of racism: it doesn't vacate practices of belonging but distorts these practices, fostering relationships that are built on missionary notions of "saving" the other. Azusa disrupts this corrupted mode of connection and belonging by refusing these erotic terms. Azusa creates a community that embodies erotic energy as a route to the other as subject and central to one's own sense of moral growth and humanity. Azusa's erotic life exemplifies a generosity out of which new practices of belonging could be forged. Azusa indeed fostered a queer sociality that fundamentally changed how one grows as a self in desirous relationship with diverse others.

That are many ways to challenge racist structures and practices, including erotic ones. This revival demonstrated that the erotic life of racism could be suspended temporarily, and a new kind of desire could emerge. One could experience the other as delight rather than as threat, as a subject of joy rather than an object of distrust. Azusa embodied an erotic generosity because this community knew that gifting oneself to the other constitutes the most powerful expression of communion, connection, and belonging at the deepest levels of ourselves.

5 LAWLESSNESS
A Critique of American Democracy

SO FAR IN THIS BOOK I have suggested why the Azusa Revival should not be interpreted apart from the world of politics. Now I explore how Azusa embodied a sweeping critique of American democracy under racial capitalism, and how it challenged the way in which American political institutions ordered common life. Azusa's ecclesial life shocked and contested the legal and political climate of the day. To show how Azusa critiqued American democracy, I first discuss the Azusa Revival as the activity of a lawless religious community. I foreground Azusa's suspicions about American democratic institutions, especially of citizenship. American democracy ironically sponsored un-freedoms for blacks and immigrants associated with the revival.

I next explore how Azusa's political agency was also shaped by an apocalyptic worldview and premillennial grammar which was deeply political. This apocalyptic view refashioned how Azusa enacted the political, how it embodied political agency, and *to what end the citizen was directed*. Many scholars might categorically reject the idea of the apocalyptic as sponsoring revolutionary forms of political agency. Instead, they regard the apocalyptic as apolitical, as an intentional withdrawal from and apathy toward this-worldly affairs. But that is not necessarily so, for Azusa's apocalyptic imaginary exposed the *limits* of American democracy under racial capitalism.

The politics of Azusa involved both refusing how the democratic state marked blacks and immigrants as noncitizens *and* fashioning a "politics of reexistence" that empowered them to practice freedom in ways American political and capitalist institutions forbade. Not only am I searching for a complex range of ways to understand the relationship between Azusa's ecclesial and political life that exceeds the horizon of the nation-state and racial capitalism, I also want to show how Azusa's politics reimagines "otherwise" political futures within and beyond the American capitalist state.

Against the Law

In June 1906, the *Los Angeles Times* described the erratic behavior of Azusa participants as including "rolling" and "kicking." The reporter depicted police officers being called to Azusa Street to deal with neighbors' complaints about the loud, disruptive all-night services. This article paints a full picture of the demographics of this congregation out of which the revival emerges. It estimates the congregation to number about seven hundred people, "mostly colored men and women with a sprinkling of whites" and notes that it is a "queer mixture of rich and poor." The article describes that these congregants participate in astonishing "gymnastic-like" actions and "shout so that they may be heard for blocks."[1] What is most shocking to the reporter is the participation of white wealthy individuals in this revival, embodied in his detailed description of a white tycoon wearing diamonds, and revealing that the public was genuinely taken aback at this wealthy white man's confession of conversion.[2] Patrolmen were called to this service in order to respond to both the loudness and demographic shock of the revival itself. The behavior of whites and blacks, rich and poor, men and women who attended these services did not reflect "proper" religious subjects or, by extension, proper political subjects in a segregated America across racial, class, and gender lines.

In August of that same year, the *Los Angeles Times* wrote about two evangelists who were arrested by police for holding street meetings and transported to Central Station. These evangelists understood themselves as evangelizing on the curbs, going to where people were in efforts to compel them to attend their nightly services at Azusa. Their rancorous preaching allegedly disturbed the neighborhood, resulting in police being called to the street corners where the evangelists were loudly proclaiming their message. However, one of the evangelists, sister Wiley, persisted in preaching and singing, even to the police as they took her to the police station.[3] In short, participants in this revival embodied a defiant and *lawless* religious agency. They were perceived as disregarding or breaking the law.

This lawlessness among Azusa's community took two main forms. First, they were simply noisy. At face value, this does not seem much like a problem or serious infraction. It was. Ashon Crawley reminds us that noise among marginalized communities was regarded as morally and politically problematic in the history of the West. Within the United States, from slavery onward, black noise was perceived as something to stop. Rather than being rational, coherent, and meaningful sound,[4] whites deemed black noise to be incoherent, primitive, and emotive babble.[5] Historian Mark Smith notes, "If colonial elites agreed on what produced sound, they also agreed on who produced noise. Native Americans, African Americans (slave and free), and laboring classes generally were among the greatest noise-makers in colonial America."[6] Noise is a moral and political problem, as it not only signifies nonrational and overly emotive people but also gestures politically toward people who violate law and order. So it was that in June 1906, the Los Angeles Ministerial Association wanted to silence this revival by filing a complaint with the L.A. police department against the "negro revival" on the grounds that it was disturbing the peace.[7] Police officers come to Azusa ostensibly because this revival violated noise ordinances, polluting the air with disruptive screams, cries, and shouts. Azusa was seen as "disturbing the peace," and thus in need of policing.[8]

Second, the noise of Azusa violated capitalist time or what Elizabeth Freeman refers to as chrononormativity. Chrononormativity is "the use of time to organize individual human bodies towards maximum productivity."[9] Chrononormativity aligns bodies with the rhythms of the capitalist state. It is a technique by which capitalist institutional forces seem like somatic facts.[10] Unsuspecting bodies have this temporal scheme "impressed upon them, structuring the various rhythms of their lives—from regular beats, to interruptions, rests, frenzies—to support the current social order."[11] For instance, under modern capitalism, normal "workdays" are arranged and kept distinct from "rest and family time" (weekends) in a way that provides maximum labor productivity for capitalist owners. Workdays arrange the meaning of time within society. One must be "productive" throughout the workday in order to feel healthy levels of worth and success, which means one must also privilege rest at night. Citizens find themselves simply living within this ecology, as if it were as natural to live like this as breathing the air around us when in fact it is socially constructed.

Azusa's noise of prayer, praise, and boisterous shouting late into the night and early hours of the morning transgressed such chrononormativity. Azusa in effect rejected regular capitalist bodily rhythms that ensure worker productivity and the maximization of profit. Members stayed up through the night shouting. They read scripture and tarried during the day. They made joyful noise at odd moments of the day and night. Azusa is thus a radical interruption of chrononormativity and, as Crawley notes, a fundamental critique of "a political economy of austerity and exploitation."[12] Capitalist time seeks to exploit the lives of workers through moderating and controlling where they can go and what they can do at particular times throughout the day and evening. This is done through policing and penalizing noise that is out of step with capitalist time. Azusa resisted chrononormativity through its religious practices. The rhythms and beats of Azusa's community members' lives and worship were not in service to the capitalist state.

Noise wasn't the only variety of Azusa's lawlessness. Azusa's racial and gender mixing was also deeply disruptive and subversive to the political and cultural order of the day, and therefore local newspapers commented on it frequently. The idea of black participants (and immigrant members such as Azusa's Mexican parishioners) expressing emotional intimacy with white Azusa members was not just morally reprehensible but actually unlawful in much of the United States. This led to police being regularly dispatched to watch the black participants in particular. Yet this kind of police harassment did not stop the Azusa Street movement. In fact, these clashes with law officials reinforced the community's commitment to enacting a vision of human belonging not steeped in the segregative order of America. The anxiety of the white police officers had to do with upholding the racist vision of law and order. The revival constituted a kind of lawlessness that the police felt they had to monitor for the social and political health of the city of Los Angeles.

Azusa's alleged lawlessness highlights the political crisis that it presented. Its egalitarian religious practices subversively talked back to the institutional structures and injustices of racial segregation and class disenfranchisement associated with Los Angeles and the broader nation. Azusa enacted the right *to refuse* the racial terms of the day. It refused to be incarcerated by this white nationalist vision of human community. Although the local officers sought to disrupt what was transpiring at Azusa, Azusa resisted. This entire showdown between the Azusa Revival and the police in Los Angeles gestures toward the ways in which Azusa enacted a form of political agency through its religious life.

This marking of Azusa as an overt political threat challenges interpretations of this revival as apolitical or even prepolitical. In Chapter 2 I refuted the claim that Azusa is apolitical, for those associated with the Azusa Revival did indeed embody a political agency that defied the white cultural and capitalist order of the day. However, I think some scholars might be tempted to read Azusa in another equally insidious way: as *prepolitical*. British Marxian historian E. J. Hobsbawm describes such groups as "pre-political people who have not yet found, or [have] only begun to find, specific language in which to express their aspirations about the world."[13] Hobsbawm describes "archaic" movements of social protest that might fall outside of classical patterns of Marxist agitation or movements whose political coloring is not progressive or modernist but reactionary and inarticulate. In this case, because the Azusa Revival is interpreted outside of materialist and structural visions of social change, it is seen as prepolitical and therefore politically immature and impotent.

This interpretation of Azusa is often juxtaposed with modern-liberal and liberationist theological language, which often has *Marxian* sensibilities. At the heart of classical patterns of Marxian agitation is class consciousness among workers (or the poor) that lead to political revolution and the overthrow of modern capitalist society.[14] For Marx, liberation from capitalist structures leads to *large-scale change* in society, a revolution of social and political arrangements altogether. Marxist agitation is then about structural transformation through workers coming to terms with their own exploitation and alienation due to the capitalist machinery. Although Marx has a very reductive and pejorative view of religion, and although he offers little analysis on the racial foundations of capitalism, some modern liberal and liberationist discourses see Marxian analysis as central to theorizing materialist and structuralist views of social change such as racial justice.[15] Some of modern white and black scholarship (social gospel theology and liberationist theological discourses) imagines emancipation from various oppressions in this large-scale manner. Liberation is directly connected to the upheaval and transformation of the state. Forms of resistance thus only gain their power and legitimation if they are concrete historical possibilities that effect *sweeping* systemic change.[16]

Because Azusa does not primarily envision transformation in this systemic way within the context of social and political institutions, this movement can be viewed as politically unintelligible and impotent. Hobsbawm asserts that millenarian movements often express their aspirations in "crude and clumsy" ways that are "in many respects blind and groping."[17] He states that pure millenarian movements operate differently (than modern movements) because of the "inexperience of its members or the narrowness of their horizons."[18] While he concedes that there are a few millenarian movements that engage modern methods of change, he concludes that most pure millenarian movements are not makers of revolutions. Instead, they expect the revolution to come from divine revelation or through a miracle from on high. Hobsbawm contends that such movements therefore push the logic of revolution to the point of absurdity or paradox. They are impractical and utopian.[19] Despite the impractical nature of millenarian movements, he refers to them as "primitive rebels" in need of tutoring by modern ideas of political consciousness and agency oriented toward the state. Azusa, with its holy kickers and search for the miraculous, would certainly be classified by Hobsbawm as one of these primitive movements that depend on divine revelation and opt out of modern forms of life.

However, while movements such as Azusa may not reflect classical patterns of Marxist agitation, that does not mean that they share no traits in common with Marxism. For instance, like Marxism, Azusa does not place much value in the capitalist state (in its case, the American government) as the guarantor of rights and justice. Its leaders would agree with the Marxian principle that the state, by necessity, creates various forms of inequality to maintain its own elite capitalist power and interest.[20] In fact, one could reasonably argue that Azusa affirms the ultimate abolition of the state, although the conditions under which this abolition would transpire are profoundly different from traditional Marxism. For Marxists, this revolution would be led by workers. For Azusa, the abolition of the state (and all earthly powers) would not be the result only of human efforts but also of divine cosmic activity. While Azusa thinks differently about the means under which the state is abolished, it nevertheless agrees that the state is an *irredeemable* actor in bringing lasting peace and justice.

Scholars in the social sciences such as Hobsbawm may not see movements such as Azusa mattering much to the development of modern religious history or to accounts of political action. By contrast, I suggest that we must engage movements such as Azusa, not simply as an unconnected series of episodic curiosities or as footnotes to history, but as events that have been important to the *shaping* of modern history itself.[21] For example, Azusa as a premillenarian movement does not happen in the Middle Ages but during the modern epoch, and this raises questions about practices of modernity itself.

More importantly, we must reclaim the significance of these movements as examples of different forms of political imagination. While Hobsbawm does well in attempting to reclaim millenarian movements from the peripheries of history, rejecting their treatment as marginal and unimportant, he nevertheless employs the language of primitiveness. This reinforces the very idea that such movements are archaic and therefore prepolitical—unable to articulate their political yearnings and longings within the modernist conception of revolution, which tends to hold the state at the center. Unmoored from statist aspirations, "prepolitical" movements and their practices, rituals, and idiosyncratic experiences tend to be ignored and dismissed because they are seen as irrational, primitive, and ineffective.

"Archaic" movements such as Azusa are described within evolutionary modes of consciousness, being marked as "prepolitical" in the sense that such consciousness is backward and unable to come to terms with the institutional logic of modernity. The political agency of this institutional logic is governed by reason and its aspirations are oriented toward the state and its resources and goals. Because Azusa does not do this, both then and now some people see it as unable to adapt itself to institutional strategies in order to actualize its political ends. As a result, such movements are ultimately never able to come into full revolutionary expression.

Yet these presumed primitive groups like Azusa represent the strivings of people whose irruption into history marks *our* time, whose political consciousness marks most of the societies of our time, whose political import affects the politics of our time, and whose strivings and stirrings we today must no longer ignore or dismiss.[22] One could after all turn to a number of other religious movements that do not readily express themselves in terms of the modern state, such as the Jehovah Witnesses or the Amish. To speak about these movements is to offer an account of the political that is *not* dependent on modern statist understandings of history, political agency, consciousness, the citizen subject, and more.

Azusa was under constant surveillance. The community members' forms of religious agency directly challenged the political norms and practices of the day. Rather than Azusa being prepolitical, I suggest that their forms of religious agency exposed the limits of America's market-driven state and its modern notions of political agency, particularly on the question of citizenship.

Rejecting the Citizen-Subject of American Democracy

The lawless behavior of Azusa members exposed the market-driven, democratic rhetoric through which the American state gained its political legitimacy and power.[23] The American democratic tradition has imagined itself expanding the capacity of people to govern their own lives and participate in the pursuit of the common good. Some scholars avoid speaking about democracy at the abstract level, as one always encounters "democracy" within a tradition.[24] American democracy functions not just as a political ideal but also as sets of institutional and noninstitutional practices concerned with questions of civic virtue, liberty, equality, justice, and order. On the one hand, American democracy is a complex history of institutional political arrangements in the United States that has been *overdetermined* by asymmetrical (meaning overwhelmingly white capitalist) relations of authority and power. On the other hand, marginalized or oppressed communities continue to claim and practice the ideals of American democracy.

Azusa leaders (and members) believed that American democracy was built on a series of deprivations and exclusions. The problem of American democracy is that it operates in an economy of significations—ways in which cultural language and symbols create taxonomies of meaning situated within the context of unequal power relations that are arbitrary between the signifier and signified.[25] Yet these taxonomies of meaning are stated as if they are natural perceptions and a priori knowledge when in fact they are nothing of the kind. For Long, such signification is "worse than lying because it obscures and obfuscates a moral discourse without taking responsibility for doing do."[26] Signifying discourses operate through a politics of concealment, hiding the constructed and arbitrary nature of politics. American democracy participates in these signifying games by creating taxonomies of meaning that are actually arbitrary although they are articulated as natural perceptions about the citizen-subject, law and order, justice, and so forth. The political grammar of American democracy is such a signifying discourse. Its ideas about the political world have held the white, Christian American subject at the center, and covertly locate the nonwhite, non-Christian American subject outside of the political world.

The narrative of white Christian America as the democratic savior to nonwhites in the United States and around the world has led to nonwhites being treated as primitive, savage, and uncivilized. We see this dynamic in action when white church ministers publicly described Azusa's black religious practices as pagan and primitive, and when the United States justified its exportation of American democratic values and capitalist markets by describing other cultures' non-Christian religions as hypersexual and exotic, lacking rational faculties, and unable to envision futures of progress (scientifically and technologically). We saw this in my discussion of the world fairs and how these expositions described non-European groups in America and around the world pejoratively in an effort to legitimate and cast as superior America's market-driven imperial domination. Such political logic unjustly authorized relations and institutions of racial and economic disenfranchisement and terror in this country. African Americans alongside other groups of color (such as Native Americans and Mexicans) have always been denied the political and economic privileges that should legally come with being a citizen of American society. Despite this deeply sinister history, the signifying language of American democracy has been employed in ways that represent the American state as a benevolent repository or context of fairness and impartiality.[27]

At the turn of the twentieth century, by its very way of being Azusa challenged the American democratic state and its justification of antiblack racism and violence. Religious scholars such as Cecil Robeck and Walter Hollewager recount how members of the Azusa community did not believe the state's political promises like liberty and equality because these promises ironically made possible America's racially segregated order.[28] Those black leaders who led the Azusa Street Revival would have witnessed firsthand the immediate effects of slavery and the crushing failures of Reconstruction in the South.[29] The various industrial business ventures such as the worlds fairs and their racially exploitative economic practices no doubt affected them. The state could not—would not, did not—secure the political, economic, and social rights of blacks. One can imagine the profound psychological pain and trauma African Americans endured as they yearned for a different set of opportunities in the wake of slavery's abolition but were instead met with neoslavery, a different form of slavery and dehumanization that the state itself rationalized and normalized. Jim Crow laws in the South and informal practices of segregation and racist violence in the North and West became the rule and practice of the nation. Consequently, a number of African Americans saw little hope in political promises associated with state. The state had not and would not save them.

One promise of the state was the guarantee of citizenship. In the United States, citizenship has long been an American symbol deeply linked to white purity. As a matter of law, citizens—those whom the state regarded as political subjects and therefore bearers of rights to participate in the political process—were propertied white men who enjoyed unrestricted rights to voting, housing, employment, and more.[30] Legal rights and political freedoms in the United States were distributed according to this white racial hierarchy, which meant that nonwhites were treated as peripheral and even hostile within the "democratic" order. Although Jim Crow claimed to support citizenship for African Americans by pointing to the "separate but equal" clause, African-American communities were actually disenfranchised by this clause. They were denied the benefits of citizenship as a matter of law, despite the claim that the law was neutral. Critical race theorist

Derrick Bell writes of how many whites understood this clause as settling the problem of antiblack discrimination and harm within society.[31] It did not, at all. Instead, this clause participated in the signifying games of American democracy itself. Citizenship, under the neutrality of the law (and this clause), created and maintained the conditions of black subjugation. The discourse of citizenship, underneath this clause, gestured toward who was worthy as a political subject, excluding African Americans.

While some black leaders and communities uncritically reclaimed the political symbol of the American citizen (as discussed in Chapter 2), other black communities cast a critical and suspicious eye toward the political discourse of citizenship. For example, conversations on citizenship within educated black communities tended to be framed by a politics of respectability. A black person could only be a political subject through assimilating into white Christian and political modes of becoming. Many black members of Azusa rejected white American Christian modes of being. As previously discussed, what was scandalous about the Azusa Revival is what framed experiences of the Spirit, namely slave religious practices. In *Unfinished Business: Black Women, the Black Church, and the Struggle to Thrive in America*, I have written at length that slave religious practices were being debated by white Christian communities and educated black communities during the twentieth century.[32] Many educated blacks felt similar to white Christian society that slave religious practices were antiquated, pagan retentions from Africa that were theologically demonic and socially backward. These black educated elites wanted to assimilate into American society and garner the rights that accrued to citizens. Forms of religious performativity that included or alluded to slave religious practices undermined this cause. In this case, the white dominant view of the citizen could not make room for the religious identity of blacks who employed slave religious practices in their forms of spirituality. The Azusa Revival was problematized by white and elite black Christian communities alike and undermined the goals of black respectability. The modern idea of the citizen as needing to *become a white Christian* created the conditions of black subjugation in America and interpreted members of Azusa as being beyond the pale of religious and political respectability. Members of Azusa knew that even after Reconstruction, the modern practice of citizenship was a ruse. American citizenship demonstrated the limits (or pretensions?) of American democracy itself.

Citizenship in the United States was also deeply connected to one's ability either to own property or at least to profit from America's racial capitalist institutions—neither of which impoverished black people could do. Most members at Azusa (especially black participants) certainly would not have been able to benefit from the hyperprofiteering practices of American capitalism. Recall that just a century prior to the Azusa Revival of 1906, black people *were* forms of property. For example, scholar Matthew Desmond has documented how mortgages were secured during slavery: by using enslaved people as collateral for mortgages. This method was used centuries before the home mortgage became a defining characteristic of American capitalism. Indeed, most lending was based on human property, as land wasn't worth much during the early days of slavery. As a result, the citizen was not even a category applicable to black people as they were forms of property under the law.[33] And this view of blacks lingered, revealing the deep connections between racial capitalism and antiblack racism on the question of citizenship for blacks.

These distorted histories of citizenship were part of the deep grammar of the American state and persisted into the twentieth century. Blacks continued to confront the exclusionary and signifying practices of American citizenship. Azusa members acknowledged the contradictions of American citizenship, despite the market-driven, democratic rhetoric which declared that all were welcomed as citizens. The Azusa community knew better; they knew the *limits* of the state and of its democratic discourse of freedom and justice. Their way of expressing these limits was a profoundly political act.

Political Rebellion in an Apocalyptic Key

Azusa certainly rebelled in noticeably political ways. But Azusa's political agency was also shaped by an apocalyptic worldview and premillennial grammar which was deeply political. This apocalyptic view refashioned how Azusa enacted the political, how it embodied political agency, and *to what end the citizen was directed*. Many scholars might categorically reject the idea of the apocalyptic as sponsoring revolutionary forms of political agency. Instead, they regard the apocalyptic as apolitical, an intentional withdrawal from and apathy toward this-worldly affairs. But that is not necessarily so. For Azusa's apocalyptic imaginary exposed the *limits* of American democracy under racial capitalism.

What if Azusa's premillennialism or apocalyptic sensibility were interpreted as a subversive response to the progressive millennialism that undergirded ideas of democracy in twentieth-century America? Progressive millennialism was most pronounced at the start of the twentieth century. It "is an outlook that expects society on Earth to become increasingly purified and perfected."[34] In order to achieve this perfected society, humanity must partner with a superhuman or divine authority, such as God, or some other type of secular suprahuman force or metahistorical system such as socialism or capitalism.[35] This purified, perfected society is one that adherents understand will last either a thousand years (Christian progressive millennialism) or an indefinite period of time (American capitalist and technological progressive millennialism).[36] For progressive millennialists, collective salvation occurs through political and economic progress, which are directly connected to the ever-expanding growth associated with industrial capitalism. We see this progressive millennial perspective at both the Chicago and Philadelphia World Fairs. Although American capitalists and secularists did not subscribe to theological ideas embraced by many Christian progressive millennialists, they certainly believed that American progress and economic prosperity were inevitable on the capitalist stage of world history. American leaders hailed a new age and placed the United States at the center of this unfolding global drama of peace and fortune.

But what if we understand the premillennialism of Azusa participants as being at least in part a consequence of the increasing disillusionment of this progressive millennial vision, which promised a new golden age of peace and prosperity? Azusa members were certainly disheartened by conditions of urbanization, racism, and economic inequity. The permanence of the white racial order persisted. Poverty ravaged blacks and immigrants (and poor whites). What if Azusa's Pentecostal mandate to "separate oneself" from the world was not just about spiritual and moral regeneration but also about exposing America's empty millennial promises of peace and prosperity? Certainly for Azusa congregants the expectation of Jesus Christ's second coming and the last judgment was about the destruction of existing society, which provided hope for deliverance from oppressive cultural, social, and economic relations.[37] However, in some ways this premillennial view was equally a critique of bourgeois culture, which sustained forms of racial, patriarchal, and class corruption. White bourgeois culture embraced the inevitability of a golden age of economic progress and social harmony. Azusa's premillennialism might be seen as an immanent critique of this progressive millennial view. As I discuss in *Religious Resistance to Neoliberalism*, such premillennialism represents an apocalyptic consciousness, which ought not to be interpreted merely as a retreat from the world or as apolitical and hyperindividualistic behavior. Instead, apocalyptic consciousness may be understood as radically disrupting institutional hierarchy and gross power relations that seem intractable. Azusa's apocalypticism must be historicized from within the religious and secular progressive millennial sentiments of American democracy. The American state and its democratic ideals saw history as linear and inevitably moving towards progress. By contrast, the early Azusa community assumed that history is shot through with the tragic, which necessitates an *apocalyptic* engagement with the apparatus and ideologies of the modern state.

Not that Azusa's premillennialism was responding solely to this progressive millennial view. That would be a stretch. The Azusa Revival certainly understood itself as a global awakening that would precipitate the second coming of Jesus and the last judgment. Seymour and other preachers certainly preached the "end times" at this revival. And this religious community urgently believed that they needed to prepare themselves for the consummation of history, a history that could only be redeemed through their partnership with divine action. Theologian Frederick Ware writes about this urgency Seymour expressed in one of his sermons in which he implores the congregation: "Get the baptism of the Spirit now so you will be ready for Christ's return and be spared the horrors of the Tribulation."[38] For Azusa, the modern history of the United States was shot through with *catastrophe*. One could not, they said, remedy the existential and social problems of the age through the political instruments of the current order. Rather, it would take divine interruption, a rupturing of the dehumanizing power relations that corrupted individual minds *and* generated an unjust state. Because Azusa distrusted the idea that the world could change through the apparatus of the state, social restructuring was not enough to inaugurate some golden age of justice and prosperity.

One might think that such apocalyptic sensibilities would foster a withdrawal from the social and political context and toward an otherworldliness. Not always. Azusa's apocalyptic commitments were also about *defiance* within the democratic context shaped by racial capitalism. Certain forms of apocalypticism can function as a practice of defiance.[39] But apocalyptic agency cannot be measured through modern assumptions of political action (i.e., that political agency is *only* possible through directing one's actions toward structural or institutional change). Consider how Azusa members' bodies serve as sites of subversive, defiant practice against the state. Womanist theologian JoAnne Terrell reminds us that for millennia persecuted and marginalized communities enfleshed defiance in and through their bodies, as their bodies were often the only sites where they could exert some measure of control "relative to the claims of the state."[40] Oppressed communities may choose to acquiesce to state authority or they may choose to reject state authority through claiming ownership over their own bodies, actions through which they can and have paid the ultimate price of death.

Although Azusa participants were involved in a bodily project of moral purity (i.e., through holiness codes), this was not the entire meaning of their ethics surrounding the body. Through their bodies, Azusa members defiantly rejected the moral and political injunctions associated with racial, gender, and class segregation; they enfleshed a community that fostered human intimacy and belonging across differences. This community was possible because Azusa congregants claimed their own bodies as sites of resistance against the prevailing order. Their practice of assembling their diverse racial and gendered bodies in public aroused anger and rage for contravening religious and political norms of the day. Azusa as a countercultural assembly was thus a profound act of political rebellion. The movement's apocalyptic energies were politically defiant.

I recognize that my view of the apocalyptic is only one interpretation within a broader debate over apocalypticism. Within traditional theological scholarship, the apocalyptic is often about the expectation of something imminent within history, especially the inauguration of some radical rupture within the present order of things. The apocalyptic understands history as having a definite beginning and ending, and it therefore has a futuristic orientation. Apocalyptic thinkers tend to have a concrete picture of the end of history, inaugurated by either a messiah (religious apocalypticism) or a movement like Marx's proletariat (secular apocalypticism). I instead argue that this futuristic view of a new world achieved by exposing and disrupting the present order can be interpreted as defiant, not merely otherworldly.

In short, the apocalyptic can be interpreted as something *more* than end-times ideology and withdrawal from this-world social issues. It is polyvalent in its meanings. Pauline scholar Earnest Käsemann suggests that early Christian apocalypticism functioned as a wholesale critique and condemnation of "enthusiasm," which was political action based on the fundamental belief that an order can move toward a golden age (eradication of violence, hate, ethnocentrism, etc.) through human involvement and change.[41] Early Christian communities were apocalyptic, and this apocalyptic sensibility can only be understood in relation to the particularity of their historical life-world. Christian apocalypticism was not an abstract, universal theorization of the end-times. Instead, the vision of the end and the inauguration of a new world emerged in direct relationship to the failing political, social, and economic systems of Rome. It would not be the Roman Empire that would bring salvation, and therefore any political "enthusiasm" that supported this view was spiritually false. Instead, the Christian community's hope was the return of Jesus. Yet this return was no mere appearance:

it was about Jesus as the "Bearer of the Last Judgment" in relation to the current imperial order marked by exploitation, idolatry, and pride.[42] In large part this last judgment was about holding nations accountable for their deeds, for how they treated people assigned to their care. Christian apocalypticism, then, is only anchored and qualified by the present.[43] Its vision of the future is only intelligible within the framework of a defiant rejection of what already is and of the impending judgment facing the current order. Christian apocalypticism does not understand itself as a kind of metaphysical "speculation" of end-times but is a sensibility and vision located in the concrete realm of human affairs.

Yet some scholars describe the apocalyptic as mythological and speculative. Rudolf Bultmann, for instance, finds fault with the apocalyptic for two primary reasons, says theologian David Congdon: because "it fixes the telos of history at a particular point in chronological time and [because] it claims to describe the specific form that this chronological telos will take."[44] In this account, the apocalypse is understood as literal, the culmination of history. The apocalypse therefore moves on a kind of linear historical path, suddenly punctuating the end of history like an exclamation point does a sentence.[45] Chronological time finds its singular meaning in and through the in-breaking of the apocalypse. It is a supernatural battle among cosmic powers taking place over our heads, although we ultimately are the recipients of victory from such battles. Conceived this way, the apocalyptic is the event that culminates chronological time, an event that is "in-hand." For early Christian apocalypticism, the end is "in-hand" in the sense that Jesus Christ defeats death and assures eternal victory of Christians through the resurrection.[46]

Undoubtedly, Azusa attempts to reclaim this traditional Christian apocalyptic language. The congregants believed that the Azusa Revival was an "end-times" revival in which they were inaugurating the coming of Jesus. They believed that they were living in the last and evil days. The way to make the ground ready for the coming of the Christian messiah was to prepare their own hearts through purity of thought and action (this preoccupation with individual moral purity often involved abstaining from drinking, premarital sex, etc.). On the other hand, this moral preparation entailed embodying a community of love and belonging across differences (a community that was an impossibility in the larger socio-political order for Azusa). Their way of being prepared for the apocalypse and God's coming reign (through the return of Jesus) was to live morally upright lives together in contrast to the wicked, racist culture of the era. With the coming of Jesus and the apocalypse, the end would be at hand, effecting a new world that many holiness and Pentecostal preachers speculated would be the promised thousand-year reign of God.

Although Azusa spoke of the apocalyptic in literal ways, members' view of the apocalyptic was paradoxical. This paradox is where I want to linger. Although the apocalyptic marked the end of chronological time for Azusa, it was not strictly futuristic: the apocalyptic was also about an "unveiling" of and a revelation about the present order. As British theologian Christopher Rowland states, "Apocalyptic is as much involved in the attempt to understand things as they are now as to predict future events."[47] The Azusa congregation saw the revelation of the coming reign of God and therefore of the meanings of history in the healings, wonders, and "new tongues" (or speaking in tongues) that transpired in the revival (and in other places around the world that kept up with the revival through the Apostolic newsletter). These supernatural feats were not simply about marking the end of chronological time; they were also about an invasion into the present order to rethink what was "truly real." The apocalyptic for Azusa was thus about unveiling or revealing what was "truly real" as a way to disrupt the presumed "truth" of the present racial and social order. For Congdon, this unveiling process embodies a "bifocal vision" in which the "person sees both the evil age and the new creation simultaneously."[48]

Believers at Azusa knew that one was not able to see God's actions of a new creation through the dominant everyday categories of perception, as white supremacy and racial capitalism framed that everyday existence ideologically. In fact white churches could not see precisely because the terms of white supremacy defined and framed their theological imagination. It was only through God's in-breaking and apocalyptic action that people could participate in a new kind of seeing, which revealed the current order as catastrophic and in need of redemption. For Azusa, the current order was no longer the "Truth" in terms of the way things should be. Instead, the apocalyptic age reveals and determines what is truly real or the way human relations should be. This new way of seeing the world as corrupt and in need of total repair is generated by apocalyptic invasion. Consequently, the apocalypse alters our very relation to the world in the sense that it offers a new way of seeing the world.[49] Azusa had this kind of bifocal vison, seeing both a cosmic historical ending yet the emergence of something new in creation. The Azusa community awaited the apocalypse so that it could enable others to see the evil age in light of the truth of a new creation which awaits its birth in the present age. This is the paradox of Azusa's premillennialism. It is what made this revival politically defiant.

However, one could reasonably object to my understanding of the apocalypse at Azusa, as the Azusa Revival is replete with yearnings and images of going to heaven, an apocalypse that is a break with historical time. This is a fair objection. But I wonder: must we interpret these appeals to this apocalyptic view of heaven as compensatory and otherworldly in such a singular and exclusive way? Must this apocalyptic notion of heaven be interpreted exclusively as an ideology connected to the self and individual piety, unconnected from the wider social and political order? Might we instead grasp Azusa's apocalyptic sensibilities within the aforementioned paradox—as both culminating historical time *yet* also as an unveiling of the evil present in order to see something different and transformative inside this corrupt present waiting to be born, something that shapes what is possible in the future?

I am aware that many Azusa participants foregrounded the hope of heaven within its apocalyptic rhetoric. But does this gesture disqualify Azusa's apocalypticism as politically potent? Käsemann explores the sociopolitical implications of apocalyptic thinking, refusing to reduce language about "heaven" to apolitical action. In fact, Käsemann intimates that for oppressed and persecuted communities, Christian talk about heaven has always had sociopolitical implications—and that such apocalyptic language about heaven must be demythologized. Why? Because "no one can hear the gospel without being summoned to the reality of earth from illusions about oneself, the world and especially God."[50] Käsemann argues that the language that constitutes Christian discipleship is a language that seeks to destroy illusions generated by those who govern the present order. And demythologizing in order to destroy illusions means ridding the world of the "demonic." The demonic manifests itself in the "cries of a humanity for centuries exploited by the white race, herded into the misery of slums and starved there, plagued by epidemic, and for the most part treated worse than cattle."[51] Understood in this sense, "the gospel rids [the world] of demons."[52] The apocalyptic language of heaven is about offering us an alternative sociopolitical order to that of the current imperial (or in our context, racist and capitalist) order. The apocalyptic invasion of God calls out and destroys the illusory power structures that enslave all oppressed people. And this invasion is captured in the language of heaven, which takes on sociopolitical meaning. Christopher Morse is right when he asks whether this apocalyptic view of heaven is a different kind of hopeful expectation that is not merely individualistic and apolitical. This apocalyptic form is a critique of the status quo that is being born out of prophetic rebellion against the institutions and structures of society.[53] It is a readiness for revolution through a negation of the world's exercise of corrupt and gross power.

Azusa's premillennialism is, in part, a response to the socioeconomic crisis in America. Azusa imagined its purpose being fulfilled through its revolutionary religious life, which was not in service to the apparatus of the state. Instead, this rebellion unfolds through the apocalyptic action of God, beginning with their religious action to make the ground ready for such revolution, transformation, and redemption of the world order.

Azusa can be described as challenging modern notions of political consciousness and agency through its "bifocal vision." These members reject being citizens in the making; they reject giving their energy to white supremacist visions of the state and its goals (as the world fairs did). Instead, Azusa developed an apocalyptic form of political consciousness with two goals: (1) to enact a community of racial, gender, and class solidarity as a spiritual and political practice of defiance to the racist and hetero-patriarchal, capitalist context of the day; and (2) to trust in the divine Actor of history to help remedy an order that was irredeemable. Azusa's form of political consciousness and agency is not dependent on the state at all. It enacts an "otherwise" community, one that is not beholden to white nationalistic practices of belonging. This community challenges the idea of the citizen in service to the market ends of the state. It challenges the capitalist state and its false democratic promises.

Yet, this question may persist: does Azusa really *reject* American symbols and signs of modern political consciousness and agency? What about the missionary character of Azusa? Doesn't Azusa's missionary character demonstrate that it nevertheless participates in statist forms of political consciousness and agency? When turning to Azusa's missionary practices, I am aware that this movement is the primary source of Pentecostal missions abroad in the twentieth century. American Christian missions have a very complicated history, as European and American missions have formed a central part of imperial and colonial expansionism. To speak of European Christian missiology is always to speak of the unspeakable inner life of colonial orders, a theological malpractice that continues to affect the continents of Africa and Asia. Azusa strengthened and reinvigorated Christian missions around the world.[54] This could lead scholars to question whether one can claim that Azusa is truly rejecting the will of the State, as this will was deeply tied to Christian forms of colonial practice fueled by missiological logic and endeavors.

Azusa was indeed mission-oriented. But the Christian practice that spread abroad through Azusa was highly syncretistic, integrating indigenous religious and cultural norms into a community's expression of Christian Pentecostal practice. Religious scholar Harvey Cox writes about the many kinds of Pentecostalisms that have been forged around the world, in part because Azusa's kind of Pentecostalism was highly narrative-driven, experiential, and experimental. Communities encountering this Pentecostalism were able to meld their Pentecostal encounter with indigenous religious and cultural patterns and expressions. These Pentecostal encounters around the world were not driven by U.S. colonial elites or economic corporations but by those who felt disinherited within the context of the United States. The desire motivating many missionaries that the Azusa community sent abroad by the Azusa community was for each person to experience their own inherent dignity as a human being. Many missionaries (although not all) going abroad did not have the instrumental interests that the American state and white Christian religion possessed (namely to expand American cultural and economic power). Instead, those coming from Azusa wanted to empower those abroad with spiritual power to discern their own inherent dignity. Cox has tracked how Azusa's message has affected global communities, fueling subversive spiritual and political practices of defiance and transformation.[55]

A Politics of Reexistence

Azusa also imagined a different political future outside of America's white capitalist order. Azusa's idea of the future is not encased and measured by modern capitalist ideas of millennial progress. Azusa does not dream of its future through the language and the ends of the capitalist state. Instead, Azusa understands that promises of freedom and liberation are fragile, as they are situated within the contingencies, tragedies, and contradictions of history itself. And when strategies of freedom and liberation *depend* upon the goodwill or inclusive disposition of the state, one is already entangled in liberal hopes—that the state ultimately secures one's future.

The Azusa community fashioned a "politics of reexistence" that allowed its members to refuse how the state marked them as apolitical (or prepolitical). Azusa members were interpreted by broader society as people without proper political consciousness and agency to shape America's democratic future. But Azusa resisted through its cultivation of a politics of reexistence. Here I draw on Adolfo Alban Achinte's notion of reexistence as "the mechanisms that human groups implement as a strategy of questioning and making visible the practices of racialization, exclusion and marginalization, procuring the redefining and re-signifying of life in conditions of dignity and self-determination, while at the same time confronting the bio-politic that controls, dominates and commodifies subjects and nature."[56] Achinte imagines marginalized groups redefining the terms under which they confront practices of exclusion and disenfranchisement politically not at the site of state institutions but through everyday aesthetic practices and senses.[57] For Achinte, the egalitarian everyday practices of marginalized groups make visible and question the death-dealing conditions under which people experience duress. So, for instance, Azusa's everyday religious and aesthetic practices of tarrying and laying on of hands among people across diverse racial and gender affiliations revealed and fought back against the racially segregative postures of the state. These everyday religious practices can be understood as modes of self-determination and resistance, which seek to remake how this community existed. Azusa therefore embodied a politics of reexistence. A politics of reexistence does not depend on appeals to the state, for Achinte. I think this politics of reexistence allows us to rethink how we actualize different political futures from racial capitalism, particularly when the most vulnerable are excluded from such conversations. How we become more democratic is not simply a matter of the state. Counterpublics, to use Nancy Fraser's words, create alternative publics where the search for common goods happens at the site of everyday practices instead of in and through the state.[58]

Also notice that Achinte employs a Foucauldian idea of politics, being the quest to participate in practices of freedom that allow the subject to challenge the disciplinary power associated with the bio-political order in efforts to reimagine the conditions of dignity and worth under which all people can exist. As Foucault reminds us, disciplinary power is not coercive but productive. It normalizes the terms under which we exist as moral agents.[59] The normalization of such power writes itself upon our bodies, and our bodies participate in the rhythms and beats of such normalization and domination. Moreover, this disciplinary power does not punish; instead, it understands certain moral behaviors and activities as being inherent to nature and innate to what it means to be human, so that individual agents regulate their own actions in accord with normative terms of social and political existence. Consequently, individuals are controlled by terms they believe to be their own. And this process of normalization is embedded in everyday aspects of living, beginning with how we move through the world as embodied beings.

At the start of the twentieth century in the United States, disciplinary power could be seen in how it shaped both black and white political subjects. Whites regarded the white racial order as a given; it shaped how they normalized racist ideas and practices. While black communities rejected such racist views, many did embrace the innocence and virtues of American democratic participation, particularly on the question of citizenship. Many black communities did not question the basic assumption that political action should be directed toward the ends and resources of the state. But Azusa did and this was radical. To be sure, I understand why black communities (and other marginalized populations) appeal to America's official political institutions. In a society where black Americans have always fought for basic resources to survive and thrive, the state becomes essential in the face of life and death realities. This is a legitimate position. However, this view has often *overdetermined and even dismissed* other ways to exist politically in the face of the state and its death-dealing practices.

Even among some Pentecostal scholars, religious action and agency are seen as harmful if such actions are not directing their energy toward the state and its resources. Pentecostal scholar Frederick Ware rejects the premillennial predispositions (apocalyptic sensibilities) of Pentecostalism because it has led to "experiments in social activism and reform" that "have been sporadic and limited."[60] Because Pentecostals are waiting on the imminent return of Jesus, they tend to overspiritualize social issues (poverty, racism, etc.) by describing such social problems as demonic, only remedied through the coming *eschaton* instead of through their direct political engagement with political institutions and structures. For Ware, social engagement is then justified as a tool for evangelism rather than as intrinsically central to Christian witness and identity. This apocalyptic position leads to apolitical postures.

I agree with Ware on the impotent political action (or inaction) of many neo-Pentecostal communities today. But I am dubious about applying this argument to the political practices of Azusa (and certain early Pentecostal communities). I am interested in the political assumptions that undergird Ware's evaluation. Ware seems to operate with the black postmillennial view that there is utility in appealing to America's social and political institutions in transforming the world. He says this appeal is necessary in order to establish a new era of earthly equality and justice. Ware believes that this is what black liberation theology offers: the historical possibility of a new age of justice. Though I agree that there is virtue in the structuralist approach black liberation theology offers, Ware employs black theology *as a way to negate* the political potency and possibilities of otherwise political imaginaries among early Pentecostals. He states: "Black Pentecostalism falls short of . . . renewing the Black Church by not articulating a *sound* eschatology."[61] Ware's logic appears to conclude that Azusa does not have an adequate politics because of its apocalypticism. His argument infers that Azusa's premillennialism is backward and apolitical, literally incompatible with meaningful political agency and action.

In fact there are many possibilities for political agency and practices associated with "otherwise" political futures. Black liberation theology offers one account—but it is not an exhaustive account. Even Ware admits (in footnote 3) that there are themes and categories other than liberation through which to interpret meaningful social action and political existence, such as transcendence, mystery, joy, fulfillment, and friendship.[62] The politics of Azusa is about offering *forms of reexistence* by which to challenge disciplinary power and its bio-political order of race in order for individuals to take up practices of freedom toward self-actualization, dignity, and worth. Not every account of politics needs to be singularly material or structural in scope; there are accounts that address questions of freedom and transcendence, who we understand ourselves to *be* and how we should move about in the world in efforts to challenge disciplinary modes of normalization. Revolution in relation to our subjectivities is an equally important *political* issue. Azusa embodied a humbler notion of how we shape political futures: through refashioning oneself and the collective life one is part of, which has profound social and political implications.

Through its countercultural way of forming community and religious practices of intimacy and belonging across race, gender, and class, Azusa sought to practice freedom. Black members of Azusa at least would not learn to accept their subordinate status and forgo their cultural and religious identity in efforts to become the proper American citizen within the matrices of segregation and racial capitalist violence. Similarly, within the first few years of the revival, many white members made decisions to refuse the psychosocial world of white supremacy that regarded black migrants and diverse immigrants as threats and outsiders. Instead, they initiated themselves into a way of being that honored the full humanity of nonwhites as *subjects*. This community made decisions to embody revolutionary intimacy. Their countercultural modes of life together drew reporters, police authorities, religious leaders, and others to this revival. There, such observers watched with anxiety and angst as this community in a variety of ways acted out their rejection of white notions of political and social belonging.

The Azusa community did not offer grand promises of liberation because it knew the fragile nature of America's political institutions and the limited reach of any efforts to fight racial capitalism. Instead it enabled practices of freedom through which people could self-actualize in community. Practicing freedom was a way for Azusa members to assert their own religious and moral agency against racial violence and economic injustice, so that *this assertion of religious and moral agency was the political victory*. Highlighting Azusa's alternate forms of political agency radically changes who we imagine the political agent to be. Most of the poor blacks and immigrants that made up the revival were *no longer citizens in the making or humans in the making, according to broader white capitalist society*. They were people who survived, even joyously, on the assumption that the statist instruments of domination will always belong to somebody else and so they never aspired to control them, and that *these instruments could not save them*. Instead, they aspired to a different way of enacting human intimacy and belonging, demonstrating that practices of citizenship unburdened by divisive, insider/outsider logic are indeed possible, no matter how fleeting such practices may be.

Most importantly, Azusa's religious life and forms of political agency ask more radical questions about political belonging. Some scholarship has focused on narrow notions of political belonging, noting how exclusionary ideas of citizenship harm. I ask: doesn't every statist notion of citizenship imply an insider/outsider, friend/enemy logic? States are invested in territories, boundaries, and lines that clearly demarcate what is inside and outside its proper scope of power. Can statist notions of political belonging ever be nonexclusionary? State projects of political belonging tend to demand primary loyalties that do not always resonate with the kind of radical democratic formation Azusa's religious life represents. And projects of political belonging represent a range of standpoints that nevertheless demand complete loyalty by marking those who are a threat from those who are friends. Unfortunately, it marks individuals according to affiliations they appear to represent. This kind of correlation does not always map onto reality and, more importantly, it doesn't enable a new moment of radical community that transcends tribal loyalties.

Azusa's politics of reexistence gestures toward something other than statist and sovereign ideas of political belonging: the conditions for the possibility of *human belonging*. I think Azusa allows us to linger on how to move beyond the largely modern-statist political terms that the concept of citizenship represents. I suggest that theological and religious studies can usefully theorize beyond modern statist and sovereign notions of political belonging, amplifying the importance of a politics of human belonging. The politics of human belonging is most certainly political, but it is not political in the sense of depending on the logic of boundaries and outsiders in order to secure its own definition. We desperately need a new practice of democratic citizenship as human belonging. Azusa attempted to be a prefigurative community, bearing witness to more radical practices of community and citizenship. Perhaps we can learn from Azusa other ways of envisioning democratic belonging.

6 A DEMOCRACY TO COME
Embracing Azusa's Political Moodiness

DURING A 2019 TELETHON, White House advisor and televangelist Paula White told viewers that there is a "Department of Treasury in Heaven" and that their name would be written on the list if they gave money to Jim Bakker to build a new TV studio.[1] Her statement certainly communicates that faith is transactional in nature. White imagines God as a "divine vending machine: you put in your coin of faith (check or credit also accepted) and out pops your health, wealth, and victory, the latter degraded from a cosmic triumph to positive feelings about your personal life."[2] She speaks of Christian faith as primarily about wealth and health, an unfolding experience of attaining things. Her materialistic attitude and visibility make it really hard to remember how some current Pentecostal communities are part of a historical tradition of attending to the vulnerable and marginalized, as Azusa did. She reminds us of the gross materialism that abounds in charismatic, Evangelical, and neo-Pentecostal churches today, that they are more often than not part of the status quo, not sponsors of a revolution within broader society.

Yet Pentecostals are not the only religious group that privileges prosperity today. Many Christian churches, instead of modeling Jesus' teachings of radical belonging, warrant censure both for their uncritical support of inequitable capitalist practices disguised as routes to prosperity, and for subtly or not so subtly encouraging parishioners to measure the quality of their faith through their material advancement.

Moreover, these churches tend to condemn those who are poor. If individuals do not have a certain level of financial stability or success, such churches blame them for their economic deprivation. By looking down on the poor, churches easily become insulated centers of middle-class welcoming. Unfortunately, the poor are disproportionately brown and black people, disenfranchised by contemporary processes of racial capitalism. Current capitalist structures, in large part, reinforce cycles of structural racism and economic exploitation that many white and black churches wittingly or unwittingly leave unquestioned and even deliberately perpetuate.

This chapter is about how religious communities might imagine a democracy to come by rethinking the modes and moods of democratic belonging for today in light of Azusa's example and legacy. Azusa's religious life not only radically critiques early modern capitalism; it also offers a way for contemporary religious communities to envision democratic practices of belonging against the backdrop of neoliberal capitalism's deep racial divisions and material inequalities. A large part of participating in such a democracy to come involves *embracing a political moodiness about current practices of American democracy.* Azusa was moody about democratic life. It was suspicious about America's cluster of democratic promises. This chapter argues that we must practice what religious scholar Karen Bray calls "grave attending" to those trapped in the demonic circuits of racial capitalism in order to cultivate political moodiness. Part of practicing such grave attending is acknowledging the political moodiness of those who continue to suffer under racial capitalism and how such moodiness enables us to envision new practices of democratic belonging not beholden to racialized structures of capital. Religious communities might imagine a democracy to come which rethinks possibilities human belonging.

A Democracy to Come

Poststructuralist thinker Jacques Derrida speaks about a "democracy to come." For him, this "coming" is not some linear, evolutionary process in which democracy is destined to unfold neatly in a more perfect way within history. It is not the "democracy of the state" as such, with its rules, procedures, and norms. Instead, this democracy is a coming event, an advent and invocation in which people are compelled to tap into the relational character and potentiality of radical inclusion, belonging, and intimacy—in short, a radically democratic life. A democracy to come is about the endless transformations of "we the people" who constitute democratic life. Derrida's idea of democracy to come stresses the *potential* and *aspirational quality* of democracy. Democracy to come interprets democracy not as some permanent state but as something open-ended and unfinished. Democracy is never fully actualized in the present, but is always deferred, as Derrida reminds us. Though it is never fully achieved, it does have a future disruptive potential that can manifest in the present through the people.[3]

Democracy to come primarily focuses on a transformation of what is meant by "we the people," because it is the people who form the realities and possibilities of democratic life. Yet, what exactly do we mean by "we the people"? Although "we the people" is often understood as a unified will that grants legitimacy to political actions and decisions, this is far from the truth. "We the people" is heterogeneous and diverse, often possessing *multiple wills* and desires that collide and contrast. What kind of people are "we the people"? Are these people who "like to bludgeon, maim, or destroy people—and maybe even do it for or 'in the name of' the people?"—do such people claim an absolute right to everything, including the right to harass, insult, and demean?[4] Are these people driven by a desire to pursue their own self-interests with few or any restrictions? Are these people who simply want the freedom to amass great amounts of wealth without an attendant sense of social responsibility? Are these people bent on transforming democratic life into the few elite that "represent" the many? These questions challenge the meaning of democracy under the state, which is often about a way to maximize private interests and benefits while requiring a minimal commitment to public goods or shared common life.[5]

For Derrida, we the people gestures toward a humanity that is radically open to being refashioned in light of justice.[6] A democracy to come is about attending to the suffering and to mourning the vulnerable. It functions as a call to justice. Democracy to come gives rise to "what is called a coming event" (or advent), which is not some actualization and final point of justice in history that is engineered and made possible by political heads but is a call that is taken up by a radically democratic people, a people who are willing to participate in a transgressive and transformational critique of the existing order beyond homogeneity and conformity. In other words, democracy to come also means "democrats to come" in the sense that the people, through their practices and deliberations, are willing to become steadily democratized, that is, to become humanized by encountering others.[7] This *kind* of people must be radically open to new thoughts, new horizons, and new practices that privilege the humanizing of our social and political worlds.

Azusa might be understood as answering a call for a "democracy to come" beyond the dehumanizing machinations of racialized capitalism in which "we the people" in the United States operated according to white supremacist ideology and capitalist logic. I want to challenge the assumption that Azusa can only be interpreted as invoking individualistic piety, as if Azusa can only be interpreted in this narrow religious way. As I have demonstrated throughout this book, Azusa's religious modes and practices reflect a humanizing and democratizing way of being in the face of racially segregationist institutions and ways of life. Through its liturgical and communal performances, Azusa's religious life was infused with democratic vitalities, enacting revolutionary modes of life together, even if these modes of life were episodic and fleeting. This democracy to come involved Azusa critiquing and condemning white capitalist systems of oppression and rejecting their segregated, exploitative modes of living and relating. In this sense while Azusa certainly imagined itself ushering in the biblical kingdom that Jesus preached about, we also can interpret Azusa as a prefigurative community of radical democratic relations that are not bound to America's segregated "democratic" systems of racial capitalism. Azusa was an event and movement that embodied a call to justice, to mourning with and for those crushed by the religious, social, and political structures and practices of society. This religious community imperfectly sought to reform its members away from violent, exclusionary ways of being and towards more radical forms of belonging and embrace across lines of alterity and difference.

Azusa as a community that invoked a democracy to come also helps religious communities rethink the moods they need in order to embody radical political critique, and in order to prepare the way for more radical forms of democratic belonging in light of contemporary experiences of racial capitalism. A large part of cultivating democratic practices of belonging involves embracing a political moodiness about current practices of American democracy under neoliberal capitalism and its racializing practices. Azusa was moody about democratic life. It was suspicious about America's cluster of democratic promises. But Azusa's moodiness did not translate into hopelessness. Through their apocalyptic sensibilities, Azusa's members envisioned an eschatological community of persons that could politically defy the racial-capitalist order. As discussed at length in the previous chapter, these members saw a possibility of a new creation being birthed in the midst of a failed political system. This creation was a community of radical belonging, inclusion, and revolutionary intimacy. They envisioned a democracy to come.

To be at Azusa was to encounter the moods of those who were deeply marginalized by America's racial and capitalist order. We have seen how this revival privileged the religious practices of black communities and leaders of this movement (such as black women domestics and men like Seymour), practices through which they articulated Azusa as a direct challenge to the racial-capitalist order of the day. Whites could only authentically participate in this revival through entering religious life on *black terms*. Moreover, Chinese, Mexicans, Armenians, Russians, and other nationalities were present at Azusa and their yearnings and longings for a better world also had to be heard. That this religious community listened to the moods of its members in order to envision alternative practices of belonging helps us to imagine what a democracy to come might entail today.

Grave Attending to the Unredeemed

If a democracy to come seeks to reform and refashion the character of the people who issue calls to justice, this means we have to *pay attention to the moods* of those who are devastated by neoliberal racial capitalism today,[8] and that disproportionately means people who are black and brown. When I speak of paying attention, I am invoking Bray's idea of grave attending within contemporary capitalism. Grave attending is about listening to the "political moodiness" of those who experience grief, pain, trauma, and lament within current capitalist processes. Bray talks about a certain kind of political moodiness that is present among the vulnerable, especially racial, gendered, and disabled communities.[9] Moods such as grief, rage, depression, anxiety, and pessimism tell us something about the unhappiness that neoliberal racial structures and practices produce.[10] However, neoliberal capitalism doesn't allow for these kinds of moods. Instead, it demands that we embrace productive, optimistic, and happy moods in order to be worthy within market structures.

Consider a young black boy in a low-income neighborhood who hears through all kinds of social and political messaging that he is only as successful as what he can buy, who his friends are, what he owns, and where he lives. Economic and political leaders also constantly remind him that he is a threat and menace because of who he is (black) and where he lives (his low-income neighborhood). It is hardly surprising that as a result of these unfair circumstances, he becomes moody within this white-dominated political and economic context. This might lead him to participate in an underground economy in order to attain all the economic and social things that make human beings "worthy" within broader society.

Unfortunately, our market systems define worthiness. Though this young man's actions are often interpreted as defying and breaking the law, that is not an accurate interpretation. His actions reflect his moodiness, grief, and unhappiness within a system that produces and is responsible for this very unhappiness. He is unable to feel his own sense of dignity within a system that measures human worth through material things and financial advancement. What would it mean to explore how these moods are signs of economic inequality and social brokenness within America's supposedly democratic institutions?

This young black man might be characterized as part of the unredeemed within late capitalism. As Bray notes, the unredeemed are those who refuse to "go with the flow" of late capitalism because capitalist promises reflect relations of cruel optimism. As discussed in the Introduction, such people reject the redemptive narratives that market capitalism espouses—that one will be saved if one embraces the democratic promises of capitalism. The promise of capitalism is that the poor and "broken" can be made whole through participation in a free market society.[11] All people can become happy, healthy, and productive by embracing the unbridled economic and social freedom that markets create. In fact, neoliberal capitalism uses the same providential logic as industrial markets did—that capitalism is tied to America's divine role as a country that will bring progress and flourishing to a world. The unredeemed refuse to see these promises as salvific. They exercise their freedom to be suspicious, pessimistic, and unhappy about these promises because they experience these promises as illusions. The aforementioned black boy expresses pessimism and unhappiness in American democracy and its market practices, finding social worth and acceptance in alternative, underground economies. He experiences mainstream democratic promises as cruel because they deny him an opportunity to advance within society.

Grave attending thus means paying attention to the political moods of the unredeemed and exhibiting "a caring for the gravity, the pulling down to the material world, the listening and feeling for what all its myriad emotions have to tell us and where they lead us."[12] What would it mean to listen to the moods of the unredeemed? What questions, insights, and breakthroughs might we experience if we wrestled with their pessimism about American democracy and its capitalist promises? As Bray notes, to attend gravely to the moral weightiness of the unredeemed is to "stick with those who have been marked as without worth and moody."[13] Their moodiness can also help us wander away from demands to be optimistic, happy, productive within a racial-capitalist system that causes structural exploitation and existential unhappiness and see other aspects of life as having value.

Grave attending alters to *whom* we pay attention. It means we pay attention to the unredeemed, the ones who refuse the redemptive narratives of capitalism because of the effects such structures have. It allows us to ask how contemporary capitalism *feels* to people. Capitalism produces material inequality and racial stigmatization and exploitation among those who are classified as losers within a market system. How does this constant loss feel for people who are vulnerable? What are the moods of those crucified by late capitalism? And how might this reshape our own democratic visions of social and political becoming and belonging?

I think Bray is right that being moody leads to different theological and political landscapes. The moodiness of the unredeemed become strategies for them in the face of structural unhappiness and despair. A "micro tactic of the self has macro political implications."[14] This was certainly the case for the Azusa community. Azusa evinced this political moodiness. Azusa was moody about the economic and political fabric of early twentieth-century America. It did not embrace the promises of industrialism as seen through the world fairs and expositions. It did not see redemption in the providential theology undergirding American white Evangelicalism and its embrace of early capitalism. It categorically rejected the racist forms of belonging—the moods of fear, mistrust, hatred—that industrial capitalism maintained and exacerbated. Azusa instead evinced a moodiness—a pessimism and distrust—toward the white nationalist, capitalistic structure that created intense forms of racial, gendered, and economic fragmentation and trauma.

Many people called Azusa mad and irrational. I suggest that Azusa being seen as moody, irrational, and mad carries theological and political weight and even virtue. According to capitalist leaders, the salvific narratives of industrial progress could redeem workers if these workers oriented themselves toward an optimistic belief in the American democratic and market systems. In other words, Azusa members could be redeemed through being profitable as workers. I have discussed at length in earlier chapters how black and immigrant labor was commodified, how these workers were objectified and treated as mere cogs in the machine of racial capitalism. Azusa members can be seen rejecting this capitalist anthropology of human worth and meaning. Through their religious practices and forms of human belonging, Azusa articulated a different anthropological vision of community in which people were accorded inherent worth and dignity because they were made in the divine image. Human worth could never be something obtained through capitalist processes. Instead, human dignity is *a priori*. Azusa members refused to be redeemed as workers within America's racial capitalist institutions.

Azusa then offers different theological and political landscapes of becoming as the unredeemed, a community that was politically moody about American institutions. Recall the apocalyptic sensibilities of Azusa. In part, this apocalypticism can be seen as defiance toward the white supremacist and market order of the day, refusing to see the world redeemed through endless economic and technological progress. The apocalyptic which marks Azusa is not just about reaching for other worlds; it is also an *immanent critique and refusal* of white, market conditions of human and political becoming.

Azusa's religious life might be described as a moody praxis that wanders away from the atomistic, fear-based forms of community that racial capitalism engenders in order to wander toward firmer cultural spaces of democratic belonging and communal connection.

I think Azusa offers moral resources for religious communities today in fostering democratic practices of belonging, intimacy, and connection. Being politically moody about American democracy and its reproduction of racial capitalism is a sensibility we need in order to cultivate real practices of social and political togetherness, beyond the commodified ways of relating that late racial capitalism offers.

A Moody Democracy of Suffering: Beyond White Working-Class Sympathy

How might religious communities follow Azusa in paying grave attention to the unredeemed? Although many answers might emerge for different communities, I propose only one here, the answer that I think is central: religious communities must acknowledge that we live in a moody democracy of suffering that cannot be reduced to white working-class pain. Over the last decade, there has been increasing discussion on economic dislocation in our country. But this conversation tends to grant empathy to white working-class pain in ways that black communities have yet to experience. And this focus on white working-class trauma and dislocation obscures the insidious realities of racial capitalism.

Near the end of Barak Obama's final term as president, conversations were already being amplified on the growing economic suffering of white working- and middle-class America. By 2020, a particular book swept onto the scene of academia and American politics about white working-class despair fostered by late capitalist systems. American economists Anne Case and Angus Deaton document what they refer to as the explosion of "deaths of despair" in the last decade among white working-class Americans. In *Deaths of Despair and the Future of Capitalism*, Case and Deaton document the epidemic of such deaths among white, middle-aged, working-class Americans. Among whites aged forty-five to fifty-four, deaths of despair tripled from 1990 to 2017.[15] In the first part of this study Case and Deaton introduce us to Becky Manning, who talks about how her husband died: after a long bout of alcohol addiction and failed employment opportunities, he "blew his head off."[16] She described the fateful night she discovered him in their home, and she notes that he felt deep failure over their son's drug addiction, his inability to make the money he needed to keep the family afloat, and his alcohol addiction.[17] Case and Deaton note that suicide rates are rising rapidly among this particular group and that its members report being in greater emotional pain than before, and in poorer health.[18] There has been a steep decline, giving rise to an explosion of deaths caused by suicide, drug overdoses, and alcoholic liver disease.[19]

Incidents like Becky husband's death have economic and social roots. Case and Deaton discovered that the vast majority of these cases were white middle-aged Americans without a bachelor's degree, people who have been locked out of employment opportunities due to how American markets structure labor and prospects for jobs.[20] They note that the four-year college degree increasingly divides America, pointing to the widening gap in economic and social well-being between those with a bachelor's degree and those without. Since the end of the 2008 Great Recession, "between January 2010 and January 2019 nearly sixteen million new jobs were created, but fewer than three million were for those without a four-year degree. Only fifty-five thousand were for those with only a high school degree."[21]

Through careful documentation, Case and Deaton further discovered that "those without a degree are seeing increases in their levels of pain, ill health, and serious mental distress, and declines in their ability to work and socialize."[22] The degree becomes the key marker of economic well-being and social status. As a result, people without a degree report being devalued, disrespected, and treated in dismissive ways, even being encouraged to think of themselves as losers in a system they feel is rigged against them.[23]

This creates contexts of depression and suicide in which white working-class groups are turning to drugs and alcohol. They also isolate themselves socially.

Case and Deaton note that what characterized a great number of these deaths was that such persons were typically not embedded within communities such as unions, organized religion, or intimate partnerships. They do not feel a sense of belonging or connection. Those that turned to drugs and alcohol also reported that the drugs produced "warmth, euphoria and belonging" in response to feelings of trauma, loneliness and shame, and worthlessness.[24] They felt alienated and disconnected, profoundly stressed by not being able to work or make a living wage to care for themselves and those they love. Such despair is not only psychological and social but also economic. It is rooted in the machinations of neoliberal economy. Rather than bringing calamity on themselves, it is the ways in which American capitalism structures employment, wages, education, healthcare, and more that burdens them. They do not feel they belong.

Although white working classes indeed have been deeply affected by current capitalism and are politically moody about such structures, it is important to note that they have often deflected their sense of despair by embracing racial hostility and animosity. Many working white communities blame immigrants and blacks for their economic and social decline. In political discussions, working-class whites often claim reverse racism in education and employment, as they chafe at people of color being given consideration as a way to meet diversity standards. Moreover, white religious communities like white Evangelical churches reinforce this sense of white persecution. This is a mistake. While neoliberal capitalism has undoubtedly generated poverty and pain in white working-class communities, people of color cannot be scapegoated for such pain. Black communities have endured decades of disenfranchisement by white society and economy. In fact, the kind of generosity that Case and Deaton apply to the inequities associated with working-class white communities *has often been denied to black communities*. The moods of the white working class, specifically their emotions of anger and acquiescence, can be felt within our economic and social context. Such people are grappling with what American democracy *is not*. This gross structural disenfranchisement associated with contemporary capitalism simply demonstrates that American capitalism directly affects, not only people of color (through forms of racial capitalism), but also the prospects and possibilities of working-class whites, although many of these white communities reject the need to be in solidarity with poor and working-class communities of color due to their own participation in structural racism.

What is interesting to me is which group is heard in such discussions over the inequities and inequalities of contemporary capitalism. White working-class stories are gravely attended to, as if the economic and cultural problem of market structures have finally been revealed through *this* population's deprivation, angst, and despair. Why not the same passion for communities of color who have experienced the devastating effects of *racial capitalism* for centuries? Why not treat with equal care the countless stories of how markets have created despair, anxiety, and intergenerational cycles of deprivation for black communities? Why haven't immigrants been given empathy in the way that working-class whites are, as they stare down profound economic and cultural precarity? What might it mean to attend gravely to people of color who disproportionately endure duress under current U.S. forms of racial capitalism?

As I am writing this text, the world is experiencing a historic pandemic caused by a novel coronavirus. Alongside the physical devastation of hundreds of thousands of deaths in the United States alone, the global economy has gone into a steep depression. Unemployment in the United States is at an all-time high since the 1930s Great Depression era. While many communities in the United States have experienced job loss and deep economic precarity, this pandemic has particularly intensified economic and racial disparities that have been present for decades. Consider the "essential worker" that made headlines in many major news outlets. Essential workers are heroes or sheroes of our society right now, as they have put themselves on the line to care for the basic needs of citizens who are sheltering in place during this pandemic. Many reporters highlight the absence of healthcare and living wages associated with these essential workers in order to shame our society for not taking care of the very people who are preserving our basic forms of existence in this moment. Oddly, news outlets make this seem like breaking news, information we didn't have before. But this is not the case. Workers in the service industry have for decades suffered forms of deep economic disenfranchisement, of not being paid well, and of being without sufficient health care coverage.

These workers also happen to be disproportionately people of color. Racial capitalism continues to operate in covert ways today, as our postindustrial economy thrives from the expropriation and exploitation of black and brown labor. No wonder many of these essential workers made their voices heard during this time, even threatening not to show up at work if companies and businesses did not attend to the flagrant injustices they were enduring. This pandemic produced moods among those who suffer like essential workers. What would it mean to pay attention to the moods of those who are devastated within the matrices of racial capitalism today? When we attend to the moods of the vulnerable, how does this reorient how we think about possibilities for democratic becoming and belonging?

A number of vulnerable communities are moody about the way in which contemporary capitalism is lauded for its unprecedented economic growth and inevitable march towards progress. They disagree that this is a virtue. Scholars have documented how capitalism has rolled back relative gains made over the last several decades among economically disadvantaged communities of color. Black economists such as Julianne Malveaux, Dania Francis, and Marcellus Andrews assert that capitalism is not simply generating rising prosperity and better health. Instead, capitalism today is exacerbating racial inequalities and creating cultures of frustration and despair.

For instance, working-class black communities feel betrayed in the wake of technological advancements surrounding automation. Consider how artificial intelligence and automation are increasingly leading to large unemployment rates for blacks as well as creating a crisis of disappointment and despair among blacks who tend to reside in neighborhoods that are unemployed or underemployed. *Business Insider* reports that artificial intelligence and automation will disrupt 4.5 million jobs for African Americans by 2030 without any intervention.[25] Blacks also have a 10 percent greater likelihood of automation-based job loss than other workers.[26] Moreover, because of historic discrimination and disenfranchisement, black workers have a higher rate of job displacement, as they are overrepresented in jobs that will be cut due to automation, such as fast food restaurant workers, office secretary support, service workers, retail workers, and mechanical support.[27] Automation will contribute to and exacerbate an already widening racial wealth gap.

Some black workers lament that growing automation has also caused companies to treat them as dispensable within an economy that no longer needs them. They are treated as commodified labor that can be easily discarded for more efficient pathways toward profit. Unfortunately, companies do not need to care for automated programs in ways that they care for human workers. Automated programs do not need healthcare, childcare, and a living wage. The political moodiness of black workers with respect to the objectification and discarding of their labor and livelihoods demonstrates that contemporary capitalism still deeply devalues the labor and lives of blacks. For the business owner, how black workers have been treated in the wake of automation is seen as part of the general processes of capitalism attempting to become more efficient in order to produce greater wealth and well-being. When turning to the political moods of these black workers, we encounter another story about American neoliberal racial capitalism and its dehumanizing treatment of black lives. Black labor (and hence black life) only has value with respect to how well it can be used towards America's machinery of unhindered profit.

In *Unfinished Business: Black Women, the Black Church, and the Struggle to Thrive in America*, I discussed at length how black communities have been treated in disposable ways within the context of American economy. White Americans disproportionately own more homes and owe less debt than blacks. Economically disadvantaged black communities continue to experience poor educational outcomes, as schools in these residential areas are underfunded, ill-equipped, and lack the resources on par with predominantly white peer schools. Poor access to high quality medical care persists among working black communities, as they are often unable to pay for the medical care (regular doctors, office visits, prescriptions, etc.) needed to survive and thrive. This country has recently been shocked by the high rates of maternal mortality among black women. Many studies report that black pregnant mothers are often not believed when they experience pain or physical duress before, during, and after birth.[28] Even more insidious, the medical community assumes that black women can inherently endure more physical pain than white women, which wittingly or unwittingly leads medical practitioners to generate deadly outcomes for black mothers. The racial logics that continue to fuel uneven, inequitable outcomes for black people, create a context of discontent and even despair among poor working-class blacks. Black workers have endured this kind of dehumanizing treatment since the founding of this nation. Why should they embrace the illusive promises of happiness that American democracy and its neoliberal capitalist apparatus articulate? Why should black citizens go with the flow of the redemptive democratic narratives on the salvific nature of American capitalism (American dream, meritocracy, etc)? Why shouldn't black workers feel rage and anger over such de-humanizing capitalist practices surrounding labor, education, healthcare, and more? What can we learn by listening to such anger?

American democracy promises equal political participation and voice, yet allows racial-capitalist institutions to make adverse economic decisions that disproportionately affect people of color. Structural racism can especially be seen in the basement wages working-class blacks experience. As reported by Mitchell Hartman in 2019 on the Marketplace podcast, while unemployment numbers are at historic lows and wages have been rising, the Bureau of Labor Statistics shows that the African-American working class has benefited much less than white and Asian workers. While inflation adjustment for wages are up 5 percent for white workers, 6 percent for Asian workers, and 10 percent for Hispanic workers, it is up by only 1.2 percent for black workers.[29] State and local hikes in minimum wages have been helpful, but federal laws on increasing minimum wage would address where the majority of black workers reside: in midwestern and southern states that resist increases in wages.

One might think that black workers' wages are just the result of midwestern and southern states' business practices. This would be misleading: it is also about *racial* exploitation. Terrance Wise, a thirty-one year-old black man, works at a McDonalds restaurant in Kansas City, Missouri. He notes that he has asked his employer for a raise for once every three years, only to be met with refusals each time. After Terrance started organizing with the labor movement, Fight for $15, and went on strike, he got a raise immediately. For Terrance, racial discrimination was a key factor in his employer refusing his previous requests.[30] But imagine all the black workers like Terrance who are never heard. How will they survive? Imagine their anger when faced with these realities.

Middle-class blacks are also politically moody in the face of current racial-capitalist practices. We see the general gutting of the black middle class particularly clearly from the 2008 recession onward. Black home ownership was pillaged after the crash and revealed racist strategies and practices among mortgage companies toward African-American individuals and entire communities. Understandably this has led poor and working-class black communities to distrust the system, and has further deepened the anger that bubbles up among economically disadvantaged black youth. If the market system does not offer basic dignity to black workers, how can these workers feel a sense of security and belonging in the American system? These are basic questions being asked by social movements such as Black Lives Matter. Young people are protesting in the streets the unequal conditions fueled by neoliberal practices and their racist logics. Racial capitalism persists. So many black communities still feel they do not belong within our current capitalist society. Particularly among disadvantaged black youth, racial capitalism makes them feel angry and ashamed that they have to show rage to get the nation's attention and be treated with basic dignity and respect. What might we learn by listening to the moods—the anger, rage, and depression—of so many black workers and citizens who feel betrayed by America? What use is the rhetoric of American democracy if it is not truly democratic?

In addition, immigrants endure suffering and are politically moody when confronting the racist logics and inequitable economic practices that affect them. Immigrants are often targeted in public discourse and policy as criminal and immoral, especially Latinx immigrants. One can just turn to the conversations and policies surrounding the U.S. border and witness racist, xenophobic rhetoric used to criminalize poor immigrants from diverse countries. These immigrants are seen as breaking the law as "foreign aliens," even as attempting to attain economic benefits from the U.S. system unlawfully. The dominant capitalist discourse has characterized immigration (among people of color) as symptomatic of the brokenness of other countries and of the criminality of immigrants themselves. However, why do poor or working-class Latinx immigrants get mischaracterized in this way (especially when European immigrants from professional classes constitute a large portion of immigrants coming to the United States)? Why do we not talk about the structural reasons why Latinx immigration has skyrocketed, reasons to which the United States has contributed through its trade policies, wars and military interventions, and so forth?

Listen to this stories of two immigrants, Naomi and Mireya. Naomi, at ten years old, decided to cross the Mexico-U.S. border. Immigrating from Central America, Naomi was surrounded by violence and corruption in her home country and feared for her life. She was also an abused child, not receiving the care she needed from her family. After she had applied as an asylum seeker she connected with World Relief, an organization that helps immigrants seek refuge.[31] Naomi challenges our ideas of who we believe the average immigrant to be. Some Americans depict the average immigrant as a lazy man, bent on raping women and taking away jobs from hard-working blue-collar white citizens. This is untrue: over half of immigrants who are detained at the border are women and children. But also consider Mireya's story, a young Mexican woman who has been living in the United States for twenty-five years undocumented. In order to apply for permanent citizenship, she would have had to return to Mexico and appear before the U.S. consulate. With plenty of justification, she feared that if she did this, she would not be allowed to come back to her home or be detained by ICE if she returned to her home. For well over two decades, she has made her life in the United States and has contributed to society through working and paying taxes. She has a husband and five children whom she did not want to leave.[32] These stories challenge the idea of the immigrant as troubled and a financial burden to U.S. taxpayers. These two stories also demonstrate that women and children are often disproportionately represented among immigrants who are seeking better lives in the United States.

Most importantly, we rarely address the myth that American corporations and companies contribute positively to other nations around the world. For the truth is that whatever wealth the United States helps to produce for other nations is often concentrated in the hands of an elite few. I have already written at length about the impact of the 1996 NAFTA trade agreement on vulnerable nations like Mexico.[33] Nor do we talk about the primary cause of job erosion and impoverishment of hardworking farmers and agricultural producers in Mexico which led many of them to the United States in the first place: the 1996 NAFTA treaty which directed almost all corn production to transnational U.S. corporations. Small farmers could not compete with these corporations, leaving such farmers to economic devastation and dislocation. These trade agreements often exacerbate dislocation, poverty, and despair. There has been little to no discussion of the ways in which American corporations then brought Mexican workers to America in order to "cheapen" the labor pool, although American corporate practices were in large part the very reason why Mexican workers were forced to work abroad. American businesses praise international trade agreements and the unprecedented wealth these treaties create. However, such trade agreements are profoundly immoral, ignoring entire indigenous economies and ways of life for the sake of profit.

In short, Naomi and Mireya are affected by the Machiavellian processes of racial capitalism sponsored by the neoliberal economy. Yet racist worldviews that undergird global capitalist practices either measure and value immigrants such as these women according to their labor value or declare them to be criminal because they do not meet the market bottom line. Meanwhile, countries like the United States do not take responsibility for how their actions have helped spur international economic crises, contributing to movement across borders.

What would it mean to listen to the laments and political moodiness of Naomi and Mireya? How might we learn from their emotional exhaustion and suspicion over the perception that America is a country of democratic belonging?

These narratives of anger, angst, and despair among communities of color demonstrate that they are crushed by the machinations of racial capitalism. They are moody about democratic practices. The United States' neoliberal capitalism disproportionately fosters alienation and existential despair among communities of color, although they are extended less empathy than economically disadvantaged whites. Forms of racial capitalism create precarious situations of inequality among black and other ethnic communities. Blacks and other ethnic (as well as immigrant) communities continue to experience severe exploitation and commodification. Religious communities must grapple with these realities and moods, as they teach us something about the moral failures of capitalism and American democracy and what we might do to foster otherwise communities of democratic belonging.

Being Taught by the Unredeemed: A Political Project

The political project I am commending is to gravely attend to the vulnerable, mourn with those who suffer under racial capitalism, and fight for a more compassionate way of seeing those who are disenfranchised. We might linger and mediate on these kinds of questions: What does it mean for society to listen, integrate, and be *taught* by the political moodiness of the unredeemed (suffering people who refuse to be integrated into neoliberal racial capitalism because it fails to actually meet their social and economic needs)? How do our political commitments change when the unredeemed and marginalized truly feel like they are heard and *belong*? Even political liberals might acknowledge the pain of those who suffer under racial capitalism but *can we be taught by them* in order to know what is needed in terms of political agency and action? Democratic belonging is about being taught by those who are politically moody. We can only know what is of political importance when we attend to their suffering in this way. The political program I am suggesting is less about lobbying or voting (an institutional program oriented towards the state) and more about *how we live well together, the quality of our relationships within society, how we are produced as subjects, and how we are transformed through encounters with others who suffer* (which we see at Azusa). This political project suggests cultivating a way of listening and living, a way of encountering and embracing those who suffer *on their terms*, allowing these encounters to transform what we politically value and work toward.

What does it mean to be taught by the unredeemed or those who refuse to settle for America's political project of cruel optimism? How can we transform our political ways of seeing when the unredeemed, disgruntled, politically moody, and disenfranchised truly feel like they belong? Being taught by the unredeemed suggests that *the unredeemed know something we don't know about suffering under neoliberal forms of racial capitalism*. Being taught by the unredeemed means renewing our commitment to listen to the socially alienated within our cultural and economic institutions. As Bray remarks, "To [attend] emotionally . . . to the alienated is to be willing to have our terrain up-tilled, reshaped and differently plotted."[34] This is how radical possibilities of democratic belonging unfold: through a process in which we allow our own assumptions, ideas, and projections about alienated groups to be up-tilled, reshaped, and differently plotted as we seek to live into contexts of justice and embrace. In large part, this means gravely attending to the political moods of the unredeemed and becoming moody ourselves about American democracy under racial capitalism today.

One might counter that listening to the unredeemed doesn't necessarily motivate people to *act with and on behalf* of those who are alienated. This is somewhat true. When I speak of being taught by the unredeemed, I do not mean this simply in an educational sense—as in a white person simply learning the facts of black people's existence within the current context of racial capitalism. More specifically, being taught by the unredeemed involves letting the vulnerable *lead the way* in how I (and society more broadly) advocate for institutions that are nonracist and equitable. Being taught by the marginalized means paying attention to their suffering and acting in solidarity with those who are political moody. As one might discern, hastily attempting to articulate a political agenda without first paying attention to the unredeemed cuts against what I am commending. Society doesn't even know what it *should* be doing until these voices are taken into account. This is risky business. Listening to the unredeemed challenges hyperprofit markets that depend on the exploitation of black and brown classes. It challenges the state and its political apparatus, as being in solidarity with the unredeemed means aiming *toward the abolition* of many state-sponsored institutions and practices (i.e., minimum wage, prisons, policing, etc.). This is what makes being taught by the alienated risky business. Listening to the unredeemed is a radical vision of democratic belonging because it directly challenges state and market forces that (re)produce neoliberal racial capitalism and its subsequent forms of suffering.

Being taught by the unredeemed also suggests that democratic belonging is *fragile* and must constantly be remade within the context of being taught by those who are impacted by America's political project of cruel optimism. Contemporary experiences of racial capitalism reveal the enduring fragility of democratic belonging because the lingering effects of structural racism continue to shape the terrible racial and economic experiences that black and brown communities endure. Democratic belonging is the impossible possibility, a necessary ideal that is never fully achieved yet might morally guide our own forms of social togetherness. As a result, there must always be a rethinking, a redoing, a reformulating, a reexperimenting to cultivate the conditions for the possibility of radical belonging.

A radical vision of religious and democratic belonging is about imagining the not-yet. How might religious communities cultivate transformation within themselves in order to discern the not-yet, beyond racial-capitalist machinations? We need a *transformed people* to envisage different political imaginations and horizons. Political imagination is not simply thinking in ways that reform the racial-capitalist system and white-dominated democratic contexts. Political imagination is envisioning alternate worlds in which we can *begin again*, where *revolution beyond our present structures is possible*. Azusa members attempted to imagine and even at times inhabit such worlds, even if their attempts were fleeting and incomplete. Azusa's religious life proposed a revolution of the existing order. Likewise, religious communities can lead in proffering radical social and political imaginations and actions in response to the status quo. Being taught by the unredeemed is a necessary political project to imagining the not-yet.

Azusa's religious life stands as an invitation to all religious communities to orient themselves toward a democracy to come. New worlds await to be imagined and born beyond the confines of neoliberal, racial capitalism. It is up to religious communities to accept the challenge and articulate the possibilities of a not-yet.

NOTES

Introduction

1. Vinson Synan, *The Century of the Holy Spirit: 100 Years of Pentecostal and Charismatic Renewal, 1901–2001* (Nashville, TN: Thomas Nelson Publishers, 2001), 42–45.

2. Harvey Cox, *Fire from Heaven: The Rise of Pentecostal Spirituality and the Reshaping of Religion in the Twenty-First Century* (Boston: Da Capo Press, 1995), 46–47.

3. See N. T. Wright, *Acts for Everyone, Part One* (Louisville, KY: Westminster John Knox Press, 2006); Peter Wagner, *The Book of Acts: A Commentary* (Ada, MI: Chosen Books, 2008); and Douglas Jacobsen, *A Reader in Pentecostal Theology: Voices from the First Generation* (Bloomington: Indiana University Press, 2006). These texts do well in providing good exegetical work on the Acts 2 narrative of Pentecost I briefly talk about.

4. See Willie Jennings, *Acts: A Theological Commentary on the Bible* (Louisville, KY: Westminster John Knox Press, 2017). Jennings mines the Pentecost narrative in Acts for its socially transformative dimensions. He argues that Pentecost precipitated a "revolution of the intimate" whereby groups torn apart by hatred and fear within empire become communities who overcome these bitter divisions. Another such text is Ben Witherington's, *Acts of the Apostles: A Socio-Rhetorical Commentary* (Grand Rapids, MI: Eerdmans Publishing, 1997).

5. Texts that plumb the social character of early Azusa include: Amos Yong, *The Spirit Poured Out on All Flesh: Pentecostalism and the Possibility of Global Theology* (Ada, MI: Baker Publishing Group, 2005); Cheryl Sanders, *Saints in Exile: The Holiness-Pentecostal Experience in African American Religion and Culture* (Oxford: Oxford University Press, 1999); Nimi Wariboko, *The Pentecostal Principle: Ethical Methodology in New Spirit* (Grand Rapids, MI: Eerdmans Publishing, 2011), and *The Charismatic City and the Public Resurgence of Religion: A Pentecostal Social Ethics of Cosmopolitan Urban Life* (New York: Palgrave Macmillan, 2014); and Estrelda Alexander, *Black Fire: One Hundred Years of African-American Pentecostalism* (Downers Grove, IL: IVP Academic Publishing, 2011).

6. For the most extensive accounts of this history of interracial radicalism and inclusion and the poor reception of this interracialism among white ministers and the local press, see Cecil Robeck, *The Azusa Street Mission and Revival: The Birth of the Global Pentecostal Movement* (Nashville, TN: Nelson Publishers, 2006).

7. To read more about the egalitarian gender norms of this revival, refer to chapter 5 in Ian Macrobert, *The Black Roots and White Racism of Early Pentecostalism in USA*, 2nd ed. (Eugene, OR: Wipf & Stock Publishers, 2003; originally published by St. Martin's Press, 1988); and Estrelda Alexander, *The Women of Azusa Street* (Laurel, MD: Seymour Press, 2012).

8. Cheryl Gilkes, *If It Wasn't For the Women: Black Women's Experience and Womanist Culture in Church and Community* (Maryknoll, NY: Orbis Books, 2000). Explore part 2 of this text, especially chapter 5, to read about the history of Baptist and Methodist women flocking to holiness and Pentecostal churches.

9. Frank Bartleman, *Azusa Street: An Eyewitness Account to the Birth of the Pentecostal Revival* (New Kinsington, PA: Whitaker House, 2000), 51. Originally published in 1962 by Voice Christian Publications.

10. Seymour eventually preached restrictions on married women's ministries in order to satisfy the charge that the Azusa Revival was encouraging the breaking apart of nuclear families, which would have supported the confusion of gender roles. Refer to chapters 4 and 5 in Gaston Espinosa, *William J. Seymour and the Origins of Global Pentecostalism: A Biography and Documentary History* (Durham, NC: Duke University Press, 2014).

11. Refer to James Goff, *Fields White unto Harvest: Charles F. Parham and the Missionary Origins of Pentecostalism* (Fayetteville: University of Arkansas Press, 1988). Goff challenges interpreting Azusa as a transgressive space that expands early Pentecostalism's social imaginary on questions of racial, gender, and class inclusion.

12. Cedric Robinson, *Black Marxism: The Making of the Black Radical Tradition*, 2nd ed. (Chapel Hill, NC: University of North Carolina Press, 2000), xxxii.

13. See some of Cone's texts that address themes of freedom, joy, communion, and justice, texts such as *The Spirituals and the Blues: An Interpretation* (Maryknoll, NY: Orbis Books, 1992). He talks about the *diversity* of black experiences and desires as blacks attempted to hold themselves together within the context of American racism.

14. Robinson, *Black Marxism*, xxxi.

15. Ibid.

16. Gargi Bhattacharyya, *Rethinking Racial Capitalism: Questions of Reproduction and Survival* (London: Rowman & Littlefield, 2018), x.

17. Ibid., 7.

18. Ibid., ix.

19. Ibid.

20. Robinson, *Black Marxism*, 10.

21. Ibid.

22. Ibid., 11.

23. Ibid.

24. Ibid., 4.

25. Ibid.

26. Bhattacharyya, *Rethinking Racial Capitalism,* 52.

27. Lauren Berlant, *Cruel Optimism* (Durham, NC: Duke University Press, 2011), 1.

28. Ibid.

29. Ibid., 9.

30. Ibid., 20.

Chapter 1: Capitalist Visions

1. Cited in Robert Rydell, *All the World's a Fair* (Chicago: University of Chicago Press, 1984), 9.

2. Ibid., 39.

3. James Green, *Death in the Haymarket: A Story of Chicago, the First Labor Movement, and the Bombing that Divided Gilded Age America* (New York: Pantheon Books, 2006), 3.

4. Ibid.

5. Stanley Buder, *Pullman: An Experiment in Industrial Order and Community Planning* (New York: Oxford University Press, 1967), 141. For an extended discussion of Pullman's feeling concerning the tensions prior to the Haymarket riot, refer to chapters 11 and 12.

6. "A Dynamite Bomb Thrown into a Crowd of Policemen," *Chicago Daily Tribune*, May 5, 1886, as quoted in Green, *Death in the Haymarket*, 5.

7. Ibid.

8. Ibid.

9. Ibid.

10. Ibid.

11. Ibid.

12. Green, *Death in the Haymarket*, 11.

13. Ibid.

14. Rydell, *All the World's a Fair*, 48.

15. J. S. Norton, "Blessings of American Liberty," *Chicago Tribune*, July 5, 1893, 2. Cited in Rydell, *All the World's a Fair*, 48.

16. Walter Besant, "A First Impression," *Cosmopolitan Magazine* 15 (1893): 536–37. Cited in Rydell, *All the World's a Fair*, 48.

17. Rydell, *All the World's a Fair*, 3.

18. Ibid., 13.

19. Ibid.

20. Ibid., 45.

21. Harvey Cox, *Fire from Heaven: The Rise of Pentecostal Spirituality and the Reshaping of Religion in the Twenty-First Century* (Boston: Da Capo Press, 1995), 22.

22. Ibid., 20.

23. Ibid., 30.

24. George Townsend, "People and Impressions of the World's Fair," MS in the Chicago Historical Society, George Alfred Townsend Papers. Cited in Rydell, *All the World's a Fair*, 41.

25. Rydell, *All the World's a Fair*, 19.

26. Ibid., 14.

27. Ibid., 46.

28. Kelly Brown Douglas, *Stand Your Ground: Black Bodies and the Justice of God* (Maryknoll, NY: Orbis Books, 2015), 6–16.

29. Henry Harris Jessup, "The Religious Mission of English-Speaking Nations," *The Dawn of Religious Pluralism: Voices from the World's Parliament of Religions, 1893*, ed. Richard Hughes Seager (La Salle, IL: Open Court, 1993), 37. Originally published in Walter Houghton, *Neely's History of the Parliament of Religions* (Chicago, IL: Nelly Publishing, 1894).

30. Ibid.

31. Ibid., 38–39.

32. Ibid., 41.

33. Ibid.

34. *Plessy v. Ferguson* was a landmark decision made in 1896 by the U.S. Supreme Court that upheld as constitutional legal segregation in public facilities as long as those facilities were "separate but equal." For more reading on this decision and its deleterious effects that lasted throughout the twentieth century, see Steve Luxenberg, *Separate: The Story of Plessy v. Ferguson, and American's Journey from Slavery to Segregation* (New York: W. W. Norton, 2019).

35. Rydell, *All the World's a Fair*, 40.

36. Ibid., 67.

37. Ibid., 25.

38. Ibid.

39. Edward B. McDowell, "The World's Fair Cosmopolis," *Frank Leslie's Popular Monthly* 36 (October 1893): 415. Cited in Rydell, *All the World's a Fair*, 66.

40. John C. Eastman, "Village Life at the World's Fair," *Chautauquan* 17 (1893): 602–4. Cited in Rydell, *All the World's a Fair*, 66.

41. Paul Robinson, "Race, Space, and the Evolution of Black Los Angeles," in *Black Los Angeles: American Dreams and Racial Realities*, ed. Darnell Hunt and Ana-Christina Ramon (New York: New York University Press, 2010), 22.

42. Ibid.

43. Ibid.

44. Ibid., 24.

45. See Douglas Monroy, *Thrown Among Strangers: The Making of Mexican Culture in Frontier California* (Berkeley: University of California Press, 1990). This text challenges the depiction of Los Angeles and other early Californian settlements as savage prior to U.S. intervention.

46. See ibid., chapters 1 and 2. Monroy details some of the horrible punishments settlers in early pueblo L.A. (including priests) inflicted on Native Americans (Indians) as a way to teach them reason and the natural laws of God. For instance, punishment was inflicted upon Native Americans for not seeing time, animals, and tools within an economic framework or as things that allow one to be productive and profitable in the larger public square. To the contrary, Native Americans saw this kind of European rationale about time and animals as a despiritualization of such things (51–52).

47. Robinson, "Race, Space, and the Evolution of Black Los Angeles," 24.

48. Ibid.

49. Scholars chart how different ethnicities married each other. Mestizos and mulattos began to outnumber Spaniards who relocated to this frontier. In large part, mixed race individuals had greater social mobility because they were providing leadership within this colony. See ibid., 25–27.

50. Ibid.

51. Ibid., 25.

52. Ibid., 25–27.

53. Ibid., 27.

54. Ibid.

55. Ibid.

56. Ibid., 30. Southerners were so intent on fostering slaveholding sentiments and practices in L.A. that the Fugitive Slave Law of California was passed in 1852. This law protected southerners who brought slaves into California, making it illegal for slaves to run away from their owners while residing in California. The act made it clear that these slaves maintained the status of "property," despite other laws being on the books outlawing slavery itself. Even more insidious, this act endangered free blacks. Many free blacks were known for offering help, escape, and refuge to runaway slaves.

57. Ibid., 32.

58. Ibid. Also see Gordon Wheeler, *Black California: The History of African Americans in the Golden State* (New York: Hippocrene Books, 1993), for more on Bidy Mason's life and response to such laws.

59. Robinson, "Race, Space, and the Evolution of Black Los Angeles," 32. The White Witness Only Law was passed in 1850. This law was harmful in that it banned court testimonies given by nonwhite witnesses. This banning of court testimony by blacks was a common practice throughout the United States but not a practice that marked early L.A. I am not asserting that early L.A. was some racial utopia where persons of African descent had complete freedom. But I do maintain that people of African descent in early L.A. *pueblos* and then Mexico experienced greater social and legal standing in political institutions such as the courts. This banning of court testimony by blacks allowed whites to commit violent crimes against blacks with impunity, as there was no longer any legal system that held whites accountable. Whites who perpetrated crimes or violent attacks knew that they could behave any way they wanted toward blacks, as long as there were no witnesses to testify against them. Consequently, blacks had to use extreme caution. After this law passed, there are numerous accounts of unprovoked attacks, such as beatings, rape, and other violent crimes against black people in L.A., many of these attacks at the hands of white southerners.

60. Rydell, *All the World's a Fair*, 42.

61. Ibid.

62. Booker T. Washington, "The Standard Printed Version of the Atlanta Exposition Address," September 18, 1895, in *The Booker T. Washington Papers*, vol. 3, ed. Louis Harlan (Urbana: University of Illinois Press, 1972), 586.

63. Ibid., 585–87.

64. Ibid.

65. Ibid., 74.

66. Ibid., 80.

67. Walter Cooper, *Cotton States and International Exposition and South Illustrated* (Atlanta: Illustrator Company, 1896), 29. Cited in Rydell, *All the World's a Fair*, 80.

68. Booker T. Washington, "The Story of My Life and Work," in *The Booker T. Washington Papers*, vol. 1, ed. Louis Harlan (Urbana: University of Illinois Press, 1972), 67–68.

69. Rydell, *All the World's a Fair*, 84.

70. Ibid., 52. Also see Ida B. Wells, *The Reason Why the Colored American Is Not in the World's Columbian Exposition: The Afro-American Contribution to Columbian Literature*, ed. Robert Rydell (Urbana: University of Illinois Press, 1999); originally published as a pamphlet in 1893.

71. Rydell, *All the World's a Fair*, 52.

72. Ibid.

73. Ibid.

74. Josh Sides, *L.A. City Limits: African American Los Angeles from the Great Depression to the Present* (Los Angeles: University of California Press, 2003), 11.

75. Jefferson Edmonds, "The Greatest State for the Negro," *The Liberator*, 1911, archives at Los Angeles Library. As quoted in Lonnie Bunch, "The Greatest State for the Negro: Jefferson L. Edmonds, Black Propagandist of the California Dream," in *Seeking El Dorado: African Americans in California*, ed. Lawrence Graaf, Kevin Mulroy, and Quintard Taylor (Seattle: University of Washington Press, 2001), 129, 135–36, 140. .

76. W. E. B. Du Bois, *The Crisis*, July 1913, as quoted in Sides, *L.A. City Limits*, 11.

77. Sides, *L.A. City Limits*, 12.

78. Ibid.

79. Ibid., 26.

80. Ibid.

81. Ibid.

82. Robinson, "Race, Space, and the Evolution of Black Los Angeles," 35.

83. Ibid.

84. Sides, *L.A. City Limits*, 12.

85. Gilbert Osofsky, *Harlem: The Making of a Ghetto-Negro Mew York, 1890–1930* (New York: Harper and Row, 1968), 11.

86. Sides, *L.A. City Limits*, 16.

87. Charlotta Bass, *Forty Years: Memoirs From the Pages of Newspaper* (Los Angeles: California Eagle Press, 1960), 14.

88. Sides, *L.A. City Limits*, 16.

89. Ibid., 17.

90. Ibid., 13.

91. "Colored Cooperative," *Los Angeles Times*, November 20, 1901, 9.

92. "First Negro to Practice," *Los Angeles Times*, September 3, 1903. As cited in Robinson, "Race, Space, and the Evolution of Black Los Angeles," 36.

93. Robinson, "Race, Space, and the Evolution of Black Los Angeles," 36.

94. Sides, *L.A. City Limits,* 14. Also see Grace Stimson, *Rise of the Labor Movement in Los Angeles* (Berkeley: University of California Press, 1955). One would only need to ask blue-collar workers (black and Mexican) about the racism that existed among unions that were forming in early twentieth-century L.A. Blue-collar whites joined all-white craft unions and lived in working-class suburbs that were thoroughly race restricted. This was often true also of white-collar workers.

Chapter 2: Toppling Orthodoxies

1. Fannie Williams, "What Can Religion Do to Advance the Condition of the American Negro," in *Neely's History of the Parliament of Religions,* ed. Walter Houghton (Chicago: Neely Publishing, 1894), 623, as cited in *The Dawn of Religious Pluralism: Voices from the World's Parliament of Religions, 1893,* ed. Richard Hughes Seager (La Salle, IL: Open Court, 1993), 149.

2. See Wanda Hendericks, *Fannie Barrier Williams: Crossing the Borders of Region and Race* (Champaign: University of Illinois Press, 2013). Fannie's contributions have been underarticulated, especially her stringent critique of racial capitalism associated with early industrialization as well as how white Evangelical churches made possible the gross market exploitation of black bodies. Hendericks's text picks up on these important themes.

3. See Lyle Dorsett, *A Passion for Souls: The Life of D. L. Moody* (Chicago: Moody Publishers, 2003). Dorsett not only describes his early life before his turn toward Christian evangelism but also details the global scope of his ministry as a premier white Evangelical voice.

4. James Gilbert, *Perfect Cities: Chicago's Utopias of 1893* (Chicago: University of Chicago Press, 1991), 176. Gilbert cites accounts of Moody preaching in the D. L. Moody Sermon Series at Yale Divinity School Library. This comment was taken from Box 8 of this archive.

5. Ibid., 177.

6. Ibid., 181.

7. Ibid., 185.

8. Ibid.

9. Ibid., 179.

10. Turlington Harvey, "Letter to a Friend," November 17, 1888, from Harvey File, Moody Bible Institute Library, Chicago. As cited in Gilbert, *Perfect Cities,* 179.

11. James Findlay, *Dwight L. Moody: American Evangelist, 1837–1899* (Eugene, OR: Wipf & Stock Publishers, 2007), 327.

12. In order to reach the millions of people attending the Columbian Exposition, Moody shifted his views on what he previously saw as sin, being attending theaters and reading Sunday newspapers (which showed amusements advertisements oriented toward dance halls/clubs, drinking, etc.). In order to reach the masses creatively, Moody decided to hold his revivals in theaters, public amusement centers, and public halls. His favorite spot to preach on Sundays was the infamous Haymarket Theatre in downtown Chicago

(the site of class violence). Much to the consternation of many white Christian preachers, he believed that these alternative spaces could gather the masses to hear his gospel message. Moody felt that holding services in these spaces "moved religion out of the church building to find audiences wherever they might be found." Another strategy of Moody's within the white Christian clergy establishment was publishing his services in the amusement columns of newspapers. As discussed, amusement columns were avoided by respectable Christians, especially Evangelicals, because such columns advertised drinking, sex, dancing clubs, and other "worldly activities." Moody made a decision to advertise his revival services precisely in these columns to draw crowds from the Chicago Exposition. He knew that Americans and foreigners attending the fair read these newspapers. He even remarked to a reporter for the *Chicago Tribune* that advertising his services in these amusement sections "paid" and "brought in the crowds." He believed that his advertising was "in the service of the Lord." See Gilbert, *Perfect Cities*, 187–95.

13. Ibid., 189.

14. Ibid., 192.

15. Refer to Timothy Gloege, *Guaranteed Pure: The Moody Bible Institute, Business, and the Making of Modern Evangelicalism* (Chapel Hill: University of North Carolina Press, 2015). See chapter 7, in which Gloege asserts that many said of Moody that he did not discriminate against blacks in the North but did not have the "courage of his convictions" in the South.

16. Dennis E Graf, "Dwight L Moody and the 1893 Chicago World's Fair Campaign" (master's thesis, Wheaton College, 1965), as quoted in Gilbert, *Perfect Cities*, 179.

17. Gilbert, *Perfect Cities*, 170–72.

18. Ibid., 193–95.

19. Ibid., 198.

20. Moody stands in a long line of Christian evangelists who contributed toward a "nation of consumers," to use Rodney Clapp's words. Clapp explores how Christian revivalists of the nineteenth and twentieth centuries were, in part, the architects of consumerism in the United States. Clapp notes that Evangelical revivalism encouraged "rapturous feelings and a malleable self that is open time and again to the changes of conversion and reconversion." This religious conversion "translated into a propensity toward conversion to new products, a variety of brands, and fresh experiences." Clapp connects advertisement and consumerist strategies among Christian revivalists to larger trends of consumerism in the United States. He is not arguing that revivalists are responsible for a culture of consumerism in United States. Rather, he maintains that evangelists and revivalists played a key role in how consumerism would grow in the United States—through religious rationale and choice. See Clapp's essay, "Why the Devil Takes VISA: A Christian Response to the Triumph of Consumerism," in *Christianity Today*, October 7, 1996, available at www.tyler.net/triddorus/devil_takes_visa.html (accessed September 24, 2021).

21. Fannie Williams, "Religious Duty to the Negro," in *The New Woman of Color: The Collected Writings of Fannie Barrier Williams, 1893–1918*, ed. Mary Jo Deegan (DeKalb: Northern Illinois University Press), 73.

22. Ibid., 73.

23. Ibid., 75–77.

24. Kelly Brown Douglas, *Stand Your Ground: Black Bodies and the Justice of God* (Maryknoll, NY: Orbis Books, 2015), 54.

25. Williams, "Religious Duty to the Negro," 77.

26. Perry Duis, *The Saloon: Public Drinking in Chicago and Boston, 1880–1920* (Chicago: University of Illinois Press, 1998), 5.

27. Ibid., 95–97.

28. Ibid., 155–58.

29. Ibid., 143.

30. Iain MacRobert, *The Black Roots and White Racism of Early Pentecostalism in the USA*, 2nd ed. (Eugene, OR: Wipf & Stock Publishers, 2003), 15.

31. Estrelda Alexander, *Black Fire: One Hundred Years of African-American Pentecostalism* (Downers Grove, IL: IVP Academic Publishing, 2011), 41.

32. Ibid., 42.

33. Cecil Robeck, *The Azusa Street Mission and Revival: The Birth of the Global Pentecostal Movement* (Nashville, TN: Thomas Nelson Publishing, 2006), 137.

34. Refer to Albert Raboteau, *Slave Religion: The "Invisible Institution" in Antebellum South* (Oxford: Oxford University Press, 1978), especially chapters 2 and 5. These chapters not only thickly describe the religious live of the enslaved but also concentrate on depict particular slave religious practices and how they diverge from broader white Evangelical views taught as part of plantation missions.

35. Robeck, *Azusa Street Mission and Revival*, 150.

36. Alexander, *Black Fire*, 48.

37. Robeck, *Azusa Street Mission and Revival*, 22–23.

38. Ibid., 23.

39. Ibid., 37.

40. Ibid., 38.

41. Ibid.

42. Ibid., 39.

43. African *influences* certainly shaped slave religious practices in the United States. I emphasize "influences" as a way to push-back against the argument that Africanisms arrived in North America intact. In *The Birth of African American Culture: An Anthropological Perspective*, anthropologists Sidney Mintz and Richard Price offer a compelling account of the genesis of African-American culture, which includes slave religious practices. Arguing against sociologists such as Melville Herskovits that Africanisms survived intact in the United States, Mintz and Price insist that there were never pure African retentions or survivals when the African enslaved arrived on American shores. No pure Africanisms survived the Middle Passage without profound transformation and change. There was no direct importation of African religions, especially in the United States, although the Caribbean would see the highest number of African religious traditions make it to their land virtually unaltered, among them Haitian *Vodun*. Moreover, African religious traditions were diverse and polyvalent, not

given to a cohesive system of beliefs. Although there are thousands of ethnolinguistic and religious communities in Africa, one might argue that there are some common "orientations" among many African societies, particularly religious cultures in West Africa. Diverse African religions were danced and sung, enacted and performed through music, rhythm, and dance as feet stomped on the floor and bodies swayed. African music with its polyrhythmic character and heterophony in conjunction with African dance had moral and religious significance, expressing a *performed* way of engaging questions of divinity and community. This expression of faith and belief in West African societies involved one's entire being. In *Slave Religion*, Albert Raboteua aptly remarks that "so essential are music and dance to West African religious expression that it is no exaggeration to call them 'danced religions'" (15). Such danced religions were less about dogma and more about the "grammar of culture," a cultural vocabulary that understood the spirit to pervade all of life as well as the universe creatively. How one experienced truth was through somatically enacted worship with and for the collective, even as one experienced one's own sense of divine consciousness. As religion scholar Iain MacRobert suggests, African religion is a religion of the spirit and only in a secondary sense a religion of the book.

44. Raboteau, *Slave Religion,* 30–35.

45. Ibid., 35.

46. Alexander, *Black Fire*, 36.

47. James Goff interprets Azusa as part of a broader Pentecostal movement which was doctrinally marked by debates over sanctification and the doctrine of initial evidence (being speaking in tongues). For Goff, Seymour's Azusa Revival stands in the tradition of Parham's Pentecostal revivals in Topeka, Kansas, and Houston, Texas. For Goff, at the center of the Pentecostal movement was the doctrine of initial evidence. He interprets those who left Methodist and Baptist Churches (including black Pentecostals) as doing so because of this doctrinal difference. See James Goff, *Fields White unto Harvest: Charles F. Parham and the Missionary Origins of Pentecostalism* (Fayetteville: University of Arkansas Press, 1988), especially the introduction where he offers an interpretation of the historical development of North American Pentecostalism.

48. Also see Barbara Savage, *Your Spirits Walk Beside Us: The Politics of Black Religion* (Cambridge, MA: Harvard University Press, 2008), 6.

49. Raboteau, *Slave Religion*, 67.

50. Ibid., 66.

51. John Watson, *Methodist Error or Friendly Advice to Those Methodists Who Indulge in Extravagant Religious Emotions and Bodily Exercises*. As cited in Raboteau, *Slave Religion*, 67.

52. Cited in Alexander, *Black Fire*, 28–29.

53. Goff, *Fields White unto Harvest*, 130.

54. Ibid., 219, see n. 7.

55. See ibid., chapter 2, where Goff spends time explaining the mixed reception of Parham's Pentecostal community in Topeka and other parts of Kansas. His community was charged with irrational emotionalism by reporters and other ministers.

56. See ibid., especially the introduction and chapter 3, where he elucidates Parham's turn to tongues as *xenolalia* to evangelize the world during the end times.

57. Frank Macchia, "Sighs Too Deep for Words," *Journal of Pentecostal Theology* (1992): 56–60.

58. William Seymour, *The Doctrines and Discipline of the Azusa Street Apostolic Faith Mission,* ed. Larry Martin (Pensacola, FL: Christian Life Books, 2000), 77–78.

59. See chapter 1 in James Richardson, *With Water and Spirit: History of African American Apostolics from the Beginning Until 1980* (Laurel, MD: Seymour Press, 2019).

60. Alexander, *Black Fire*, 32–33.

61. R. W. L. Moberly, "How Appropriate is 'Monotheism' as a Category for Biblical Interpretation?" in *Early Jewish and Christian Monotheism*, ed. Loren Stuckenbruck and Wendy E. S. North (New York: T & T Clark International, 2004), 219–20.

62. Willie James Jennings, *The Christian Imagination: Theology and the Origins of Race* (New Haven, CT: Yale University Press, 2011), 24.

63. Ibid., 40.

64. Alexander, *Black Fire*, 33.

65. Christopher Ehret, *The Civilizations of Africa: A History to 1860* (Charlottesville: University of Virginia Press, 2016), 41–42.

66. Ibid., 41. Also see Ehret, *History and the Testimony of Language* (Berkeley: University of California Press, 2010).

67. Charles Long, *Significations: Signs, Symbols, and Images in the Interpretation of Religion* (Aurora, CO: Davies Group Publishers, 1999), 9.

68. Michael Jackson, *Paths Toward a Clearing: Radical Empiricism and Ethnographic Inquiry* (Bloomington: Indiana University Press, 1989), 127.

69. Ibid., 12.

70. A really good example of religious experience at Azusa that sat between experience and category is Charles Harrison Mason's experience. From a phenomenological perspective, Mason doesn't describe his experience at Azusa in terms of confirming conceptual truths but rather he rids himself of objective facts as he opens himself up to the religious experience itself. Mason is clear that he goes to Azusa praying and desiring to receive spiritual power to address the "ungodly deeds among the races." Mason writes in a journal: "That night the Lord spoke to me that Jesus saw all of this world's wrongs but did not attempt to set it right until God overshadowed him with the Holy Ghost." Mason concluded that he "had to do the same thing." For Mason, the "doctrinal" Pentecostal view (taught by Parham and other white ministers) emphasized tongues at the center of the Spirit experience. Mason arrives in Los Angeles and brackets this doctrinal position and opens himself up to anticipation and surprise in what his spiritual experience will reveal about the form and content of his Christian faith moving forward, how he needed to address the "ungodly deeds of the races" and remedy "wrongs of the world." When Mason arrives at Azusa, what his experience of the Spirit will disclose is an *open question*. His openness doesn't assume that tongues and healing are the only outcomes of his experience. He brackets dominant theological statements about the Pentecostal experience in order potentially to witness and experience something new

and unexpected. Mason's experience lies between experience and category, as it is not a completely unmediated experience *or* completely doctrine alone that shapes his understanding of the Spirit at Azusa. See Ithiel Clemmons, *Bishop C. H. Mason and the Roots of the Church of God in Christ* (Bakersfield, CA: Pneuma Life Publishing, 1996), 46–50.

71. Robeck, *Azusa Street Mission and Revival*, 111.

72. Ibid.

73. Ibid., 112.

74. "Police Asked to Raid Reds: Azusa Street Residents Are Annoyed by Anarchists," in *Los Angeles Times*, August 6, 1906, 11, https://latimes.newspapers.com/search/#query=police+asked+to+raid+reds%3A+Azusa+Street&dr_year=1906-1906 (accessed November 4, 2021).

75. Melvyn Dubofsky, *"Big Bill" Haywood* (New York: St. Martin's Press, 1987), 16–17.

76. See Joseph Conlin, *Big Bill Haywood and the Radical Union Movement* (New York: Syracuse University Press, 1969).

77. Grace Stimson, *Rise of the Labor Movement in Los Angeles* (Los Angeles: University of California Press, 1955), 289–93.

78. Ibid., 288–94.

79. Ibid., 233.

80. Conlin's text *Big Bill Haywood and the Radical Union Movement* narrates how union organizing in the Rocky Mountain states made its way to Los Angeles in the form of protests. To understand the Charles Moyer case, one would need to understand the labor situation in these Rocky Mountain states. Much of the labor war was located in Idaho. Idaho possessed some of the largest mines rich in lead. The miners would work up to fourteen hours a day in the smelter mines around deadly arsenic fumes. These arsenic fumes inevitably led to the poor health of miner workers, specifically to paralysis in arms and legs, and to hair and teeth falling out. Men working in the mines would have gaunt, sickly faces with a strange green tone, often without eyebrows or eyelashes. The conditions were abominable and insufferable. The WFM responded to these inhumane conditions by forming unions to represent the interests of the miners against the death-dealing exploitation of the mine owners. Through the help of the WFM, mine workers organized strikes. The mine owners fought back, even bringing in gunmen (or "troops") to maintain order among the mine workers. This face-off grew more and more violent, as the president of WFM urged miners to arm and defend themselves in response to the flagrant violence of the mine owners. A number of strikes continued, which created severe violent engagement between owners and workers, which resulted in the governor of Idaho calling in troops. Mine workers were arrested and thrown into jail without a trial or due process. One thousand men were even herded into a bull pen. One night, a bomb was attached to Governer Steunenburg's home and the governor was killed. A reward of several thousand dollars was offered in connection with the solving of the murder. Tom Hogan "came forward" to confess that he had carried out the murder, also implicating mining union officials such as the WFM. While traveling, Charles Moyer, along with other WFM officials, were arrested and brought back to Idaho to stand trial. Many groups felt that Tom Hogan had falsely implicated Moyer.

There was another narrative surrounding the confession of Tom Hogan who implicated the leaders of WFM. It was believed that detectives forced Hogan to falsely accuse labor leaders through intimidation tactics. Detectives assigned to this case were able to get Hogan to admit that he was really "Harry Orchard" and that he had been hired by the leaders of WFM to carry out the murder of the governor. This then implicated Moyer in the plot to kill Steunenburg. Moyers (along with other WFM leaders) were in Colorado when "Harry Orchard" confessed. However, Colorado was a state that was friendly to unions and so would not extradite Moyer and others based on this confession. Governmental officials in Idaho decided the only way to make Moyer and other union leaders stand trial was to concoct a plan to kidnap them, bringing them to Idaho to stand trial. Governmental officials succeeded. Based on the insidious manner in which Moyer was caught and detained, workers and labor union leaders felt as if *labor* was being put on trial. This trial was called the first "Trial of the Century." In particular, workers around the nation who heard about the arrest and trial of Charles Moyer were incensed. How this case was handled caused national outrage. The growing labor movement contended that how governmental officials were handling this case was biased. Because Los Angeles was slowly becoming an important context for the growing labor movement due to its record number of immigrants, this city was one among a number of cities that decided to stage a protest.

81. I do think one could offer up an alternative understanding of the August incident recorded in the *Los Angeles Times*. One could question altogether whether the neighbors were even truthful in the charge that Azusa members were threatening to join the protests in the streets. As I discussed earlier in the text, the Azusa Revival was seen as loud, crude, and violating both racial and class norms. The police authorities received a number of complaints against Azusa participants, which led to the police often patrolling the area as a "precautionary" measure. Many in the surrounding neighborhood wanted to see the revival leave their area, so the complaint that Azusa members were about to participate in a law-breaking demonstration, even if patently false or believed to be true, is possible. My point in raising this incident as an example of false reporting is not meant to nullify other interpretations that may arise. Rather, I raise the possibility of false reporting to ground the tentative character of my own assertion on what the August incident truly means for the political activity and consciousness of Azusa Street participants. While false reporting is a possibility, I think this article challenges monolithic readings of political agency among Azusa participants. Most Azusa participants were domestics, janitors, agricultural or industrial workers. This community would have had a keen sense of the poor conditions and inhumane circumstances that California workers endured. In part, they experience Azusa as a social safeguard, a world that offered them meaning and hope within the context of exhaustion and potential despair. Members of this community would have been very familiar with the labor movements during this time and would even have discussed labor leaders who were attempting to be in solidarity with exploited workers on the growing Los Angeles scene. Given the widespread social dislocation and alienation that migrants and immigrants experienced on arriving and residing in California, it seems plausible that the charge (Azusa members

threatening to join the labor protest) is potentially true. It is clear that the Azusa Revival as a whole did not take this same position. However, I have argued throughout this text that the meanings of Azusa to those actually participating in this revival are highly contested. This point of contestation extends to this moment. Even though the newspaper reports a few Azusa members threatening to join the protest, one could surmise that these participants' potential participation in the march demonstrates *diverse viewpoints already present on the practices of political action.* As a result, the August incident does shed light on potentially different kinds of social agency operating at Azusa.

82. Michel Engh, *Frontier Faiths: Church, Temple, and Synagogue In Los Angeles, 1846–1888* (Albuquerque: University of New Mexico Press, 1992), 14.

83. Ibid., 16.

84. James Woods, "The Diary of Rev. James Woods," in *Historical Society of Southern California Quarterly* 23 (June 1941): 83–84. As quoted in Engh, *Frontier Faiths,* 17.

85. Engh, *Frontier Faiths,* 26.

86. Ibid., 27.

87. Ibid.

88. Ibid., 60.

89. Espinosa, *Seymour and the Origins of Global Pentecostalism,* 57.

90. Ibid.

91. Ibid.

92. Ibid.

93. Ibid., 55–58.

94. Cecil Robeck, "The Azusa Street Mission and Historic Black Churches: Two Worlds in Conflict in Los Angeles' African American Community," in *Afro-Pentecostalism: Black Pentecostal and Charismatic Christianity in History of Culture* (New York: New York University Press, 2011), 30.

95. Ibid.

96. Ibid., 31.

97. Frank Bartleman, *Azusa Street: An Eyewitness Account to the Birth of the Pentecostal Revival,* originally published in 1925 (New Kensington, PA: Whitaker House, 2000), 55.

98. William Seymour, "The Holy Spirit: Bishop of the Church," in *Apostolic Faith* 3, no. 1 (July–September 1907), as quoted in Robeck, "Azusa Street Mission and Historic Black Churches," 32.

99. Ibid.

100. William Seymour, "Money Matters," in *The Words That Changed the World: Azusa Street Sermons,* ed. Larry Martin (Joplin, MO: Christian Life Books, 1999), 35.

101. Ibid., 36.

102. Ibid.

103. Ibid.

104. Espinosa, *Seymour and the Origins of Global Pentecostalism,* 301.

105. Robeck, *Azusa Street Mission and Revival,* 106.

106. Ibid.

107. See Oscar Garcia-Johnson, *Spirit Outside the Gate: Decolonial Pneumatologies of the American Global South* (Downers Grove, IL: Intervarsity Press, 2019). Refer to chapter 6 where he describes in detail how he uses this concept of "outside the gate" with reference to how certain discourses and communities challenge orthodox forms of theological knowledge.

Chapter 3: Black Female Genius

1. Trena Armstrong, "The Hidden Help: Black Domestic Workers in the Civil Rights Movement" (master's thesis, University of Louisville, December 2012), 20.

2. Saidiya Hartman, *Wayward Lives, Beautiful Experiments: Intimate Histories of Social Upheaval* (New York: W. W. Norton, 2019), 47.

3. Ibid.

4. Ibid.

5. Ibid.

6. Ibid., 77.

7. Ibid.

8. In Zora Neale Hurston's novel *Their Eyes Were Watching God,* she put this statement, that "black women are the mules of the world," in the mouth of the protagonist Janie Crawford. Mules were conditioned to serve the needs of others and similarly, black women were expected to serve the needs of everyone else in American society but their own needs.

9. Tamura Lomax, *Jezebel Unhinged: Loosing the Black Female Body in Religion and Culture* (Durham, NC: Duke University Press, 2019), 14–22. Lomax provides a thick description of Black Venus and biblical Jezebel, which would meld together in creating the modern trope of Jezebel in the United States from slavery through present day. She traces the Black Venus trope in Europe to the objectification of black women's bodies such as Saartjie Baartman who was also known as Hottentot Venus. She was exhibited in a zoo in Paris and London. When she died, her vagina and buttocks were examined, dissected, and ultimately displayed in a museum in Paris (15). The Black Venus trope signified sexual savagery and cursed. This trope legitimated the objectification of black women and eventually would inform the Jezebel trope in the United States.

10. Ibid., 21.

11. Ibid., 23.

12. Ibid.

13. A number of scholars have written about the gendered forms of slavery black women experienced, which not only included field and house duties but also entailed breeding children for their white masters in order to expand units of free slave labor. See these three texts on black women's reproductive labor being the linchpin of slavery and plantation economics in the United States: Jennifer Morgan, *Laboring Women: Reproduction and Gender in New World Slavery* (Philadelphia: University of Pennsylvania Press, 2004); Alys Weinbaum, *The Afterlife of Reproductive Slavery: Biocapitalism and Black Feminism's Philosophy of History* (Durham, NC: Duke University Press, 2019); and Ned and Constance Sublette, *The American Slave Coast: A History of Slave-Breeding*

Industry (Chicago: Lawrence Hill Books, 2017). They not only provide reviews of historical research on black women reproduction during and after slavery in the United States but also explore the effects of this lingering slave-market legacy on black women's reproductive lives within American culture and economy today.

14. Refer to Kathleen Brown, *Good Wives, Nasty Wenches, and Anxious Patriarchs: Gender, Race, and Power in Colonial Virginia* (Chapel Hill: University of North Carolina Press, 1996). See especially chapter 3, pages 75–106.

15. Marvel Cooke and Ella Baker, "The Bronx Slave Market," *The Crisis*, November 1935, as quoted in Alana Erickson Coble, *Cleaning Up: The Transformation of Domestic Service in Twentieth Century New York City* (New York: Routledge Press, 2006), 52.

16. Cooke and Baker, "Bronx Slave Market," as quoted in Hartman, *Wayward Lives,* 341.

17. Coble, *Cleaning Up*, 52.

18. Ibid., 55.

19. See Jacqueline Jones, *Labor of Love, Labor of Sorrow: Black Women, Work, and Family, from Slavery to Present* (New York: Vintage Books, 1985), 209.

20. Brian Lanker, interview, "Queen Mother Audley Moore," in *I Dream a World: Portraits of Black Women Who Changed America* (New York: Stewart, Tabori, and Chang, 1989), 103. Also see Phyllis Palmer, *Domesticity and Dirt: Housewives and Domestic Servants in the United States, 1920–1945* (Philadelphia: Temple University Press, 1989), 71–75.

21. Ibid., 55. Also see "Wages and Hours of Labor," *Monthly Labor Review* 32, no. 5 (May 1931): 137–38.

22. Armstrong, *Hidden Help*, 15.

23. Hartman, *Wayward Lives,* 297.

24. Ibid., 299.

25. Ibid.

26. Ibid., 306.

27. Adrienne M. Israel, *Amanda Berry Smith: From Washerwoman to Evangelist* (Lanham, MD: Scarecrow Press, 1998), 40–42.

28. Ibid., 43. Originally published in Amanda Berry Smith, An *Autobiography: The Story of the Lord's Dealings with Mrs. Amanda Smith (Chicago: Meyer & Brother Publishers, 1893), 79–84.

29. Church of God in Christ Official Website, "COGIC History: Amanda Berry Smith," *Historical Perspectives in the Church of God in Christ*, www.cogic.org/blog/cogic-history-amanda-berry-smith (accessed March 16, 2018).

30. *The Helper*, newsletter, ed. Amanda Smith (November 1907), 2, as quoted in Israel, *Amanda Berry Smith*, 127.

31. Israel, *Amanda Berry Smith*, 128.

32. Amanda Smith's industry, determination, and self-reliance is what she wanted to teach the children at her orphanage. I recognize that the language of self-reliance draws suspicion and even critique to the modern progressive mind. For certain, discourses on self-reliance within the early industrial period and in our contemporary market-driven

culture is morally problematic, seeking to blame individuals for not being self-reliant and industrious if they are poor or economically struggling rather than turning to structural inequalities that create the very conditions of economic disadvantage. However, Smith's language of self-reliance should be seen as somewhat radical within the time period she lived. In much of the South, sharecropping was a form of neoslavery that many blacks were subjugated to, which did not allow them to practice independence and economic self-determination. In similar ways, the North and West had a different system of economic disenfranchisement, which was paying blacks inhumane wages. One can concede that Smith's discourse of self-reliance participated in the Victorian white moral order of the day that reinforced black respectability, but her language of self-reliance also directly critiqued American racist institutions that made it impossible for blacks to be self-reliant and economically self-determined.

33. Refer to chapter 4 in Israel, *Amanda Berry Smith,* as Israel speaks at length about the ties she formed with white Methodist churches, which also was responsible for catapulting her career as a holiness preacher. However, black churches did not like this, particularly AME churches out of which she emerged. Many felt she had been a sell-out for not using her gifts in the AME church to help her own communities. Black Methodist leaders also felt that white Methodist churches had resources and gifts to do well, whereas so many black churches were languishing and in need of Smith's gifts and acumen. Smith resisted this description of her as a sell-out and probably knew that her white networks were central in allowing her orphanage to stay viable, although she never directly stated this to black churches.

34. Israel, *Amanda Berry Smith*, 127.

35. bell hooks, *We Real Cool: Black Men and Masculinity* (New York: Routledge Press, 2004), 4.

36. Estrelda Alexander, *The Women of Azusa Street* (Laurel, MD: Seymour Press, 2012), 10.

37. Ibid., 39.

38. Ibid.

39. Ibid., 41.

40. Ibid., 42.

41. Ibid.

42. Emma Cotton, "The Inside Story of the Outpouring of the Holy Spirit-Azusa Street, April 1906, *Apostolic Faith* 1, no. 1 (April 1936): 1–3; Alexander, *Women of Azusa Street*, 42–43; and also refer to Frank Ewart, *The Phenomenon of Pentecost* (Hazelwood, MO: World Aflame Press, 1947), 74–76.

43. Seymour is referred to as the chief person or Pioneer throughout Vinson Synan, *William J. Seymour: Pioneer of the Azusa Street Revival* (Alachua, FL: Bridge Logos Publishers, 2012).

44. Cecil Robeck, *The Azusa Street Mission and Revival: The Birth of the Global Pentecostal Movement* (Nashville, TN: Nelson Publishers, 2006), chapters 1 and 2. Also see Gaston Espinosa's framing of Azusa through Seymour in his book *William J. Seymour and the Origins of Global Pentecostalism: A Biography and Documentary History*

(Durham, NC: Duke University Press, 2014). While Espinosa's treatment of Seymour is to center him in early Pentecostalism that foregrounds the black origins of Azusa and its impact on the global growth of Pentecostalism, Espinosa nevertheless primarily interprets the meanings of this movement through Seymour's leadership.

45. In Mark Anthony Neal, *New Black Man* (New York: Routledge, 2015), he has an extended discussion of this strong black man archetype as the black man ideal. See chapter 1.

46. hooks, *We Real Cool*, 6.

47. Neal, *New Black Man*, 28.

48. Ibid., 29.

49. Ibid.

50. Ibid., 60.

51. Espinosa, *Seymour and the Origins of Global Pentecostalism*, 106.

52. Ibid.

53. Ibid.

54. Ibid., 107.

55. Yvonne Chireau, *Black Magic: Religion and the African American Conjuring Tradition* (Oakland: University of California Press, 2003), 22.

56. Ibid.

57. Ibid.

58. W. C. Rucker, "Gatekeepers Between Two Worlds: Female Conjurers, Healing Traditions, and African Spirituality in the American South," paper presented as the annual meeting of the Association for the Study of African-American Life and History, Westin Convention Center, Pittsburg, Pennsylvania, May 26, 2009.

59. Ibid.

60. Alonzo Johnson, "'Pray's House Spirit': The Institutional Structure and Spiritual Core of an African American Folk Tradition," in *Ain't Gonna Lay My 'Ligion Down: African American Religion in the South* (Columbia, SC: University of South Carolina Press, 1996), 8.

61. Ibid., 8.

62. In chapter 4 of *The Azusa Street Mission and Revival*, Robeck talks about black women leading prominent white men in the worship experience at Azusa, a surprising and even embarrassing reality for whites reading about the Azusa Revival in newspapers.

63. Historian of Christianity David Daniels notes that tarrying finds its roots in nineteenth-century African-American spirituality. Pentecostal adherents believed that through tarrying, God offered the seeker salvation, cleansing, and deliverance. Through a dramatic and ecstatic encounter with the divine, conversion and baptism would come. Before tarrying, the African-American seeker was transformed within the context of the mourner's bench or ring shout associated with camp meetings or revivals. Through these religious encounters, the seeker was able to cross spiritual thresholds. These thresholds ranged from visions and dreams to overwhelming awe and glossolalia. These religious experiences were very dramatic and determined the seeker's religious encounter and

spiritual identity. Only through religious rituals and practices like the ring shout and eventually tarrying could one experience true conversion and spiritual power. See Daniels, "Until the Power of the Lord Comes Down," in *Contemporary Spiritualities: Social and Religious Contexts* (New York: Continuum, 2001), 173–91.

64. Ibid., 175.

65. Ibid., 178.

66. Ibid.

67. Ibid.

68. Ibid.

69. Ibid.

70. It is important to note that although tarrying was an African-American spiritual practice, it also reflected historic Christian practices of contemplative prayer. Tarrying as a prayer form involves the recitation of a word or phrase that Christians have practiced throughout centuries within Catholic and Orthodox traditions. Tarrying reflects spiritual aims associated with contemplative prayer such as communion and union with God. Tarrying also mirrors prayer forms that stress verbalizing specific prayer words rather than silent mediation and contemplation while waiting on God. Although some forms of contemplative prayer limit the body, tarrying is distinctive in that it actively engages the body in enacting prayer. The body is the vehicle through which the prayer is embodied and brought to life. Moreover, tarrying (and its bodily expression) is not a private affair. Tarrying is a communal event, a communal form of prayer, through which the spirit is invited and union is achieved between God and the community within which an individual is situated. Read more about this point in ibid., 178.

71. Iain MacRobert, *The Black Roots and White Racism of Early Pentecostalism in the USA*, 2nd ed. (Eugene, OR: Wipf & Stock Publishers, 2003), 60.

72. William Seymour, *The Doctrines and Discipline of the Azusa Street Apostolic Faith Mission,* ed. Larry Martin (Pensacola, FL: Christian Life Books, 2000), 77–78.

73. This paragraph on Fisher is taken from Cecil Robeck, "William Seymour and 'The Biblical Evidence,'" in *Initial Evidence: Historical and Biblical Perspectives on the Pentecostal Doctrine of Spirit Baptism*, ed. Gary B. McGee (Eugene, OR: Wipf & Stock Publishers, 1991), 82.

74. Roberts Liardon, *The Azusa Revival: When the Fire Fell* (Shippensburg, PA: Destiny Image Publishers, 2006), 189–90.

75. Ibid., 191.

76. Margaret Nash, "Thoughts on the History of Women's Education, Theories of Power, and This Volume: An Introduction," in *Women's Higher Education in the United States: New Historical Perspectives*, ed. Margaret Nash (New York: Palgrave Macmillan, 2018), 6.

77. What is a founder? This is not just a historical question. This query is also a philosophical, social-theoretical and religious question. It is a philosophical question in the sense that the idea of "founder" grows out of the quest for neatly delineated "origins," a way of looking back in order to definitively identify *the* individual behind the movement. This search for "the figure," in part, is grounded in how modernity has

increasingly framed the quest for origins in highly *individualistic* ways. The assumption is that you secure the meaning of a movement in large part by turning to the founder. This question is also social, as the idea of founder is situated within cultural and social forms that are always and already hetero-sexist, racist, and more. The historical conversation about "the founder" is replete with erasures, invisibility, and silences even as it simultaneously makes room for openings, discoveries, and illuminations. Moreover, this question is theological, often pointing to the limits of religious epistemologies that exclude subjects like women who are central to the formation of religious production itself. "What is a founder?" might be understood as a historiographical question that finds its antecedents in social, philosophical, and political agendas, interests, and end goals.

78. The perennial problem with the debate surrounding "the founder" of Azusa is that the socio-cultural *habitus* out of which scholars think about *how* the production of knowledge emerges is deeply flawed. Modern scholarship tends to locate the production and ownership of knowledge in the *individual or the figure of the founder* (and more specifically, in the European hetero man). In these scholarly estimations, the way in which knowledge is produced and understood is determined by particular figures, which are seen as offering explanatory power to phenomena being researched. I would like to challenge this view of the knowledge production process. To speak of the knowledge production process is already to be engaged in a conversation about how collectivities and the relations of power that undergird these communities give way to particular phenomena that we come to explain and classify. In other words, one must ask what collective structures and networks of power and authority give rise to the possibility of certain kinds of knowledge related to social, religious, and/ or political movements.

79. Hartman, *Wayward Lives*, 62.

80. Ibid., 65.

Chapter 4: Azusa's Erotic Life

1. "Rolling and Diving Fanatics 'Confess,'" *Los Angeles Times*, June 23, 1906, 7, www.newspapers.com/search/#query=%22Rolling+and+Diving+Fanatics+%27Confess%27%22+Los+Angeles+Times.&t=4312&ymd=1906-06-23 (accessed November 4, 2021).

2. Jennifer Nash, *Black Feminism Reimagined: After Intersectionality* (Durham, NC: Duke University Press, 2019), 30.

3. Audre Lorde, "Uses of the Erotic," in *Sister Outsider: Essays and Speeches* (Berkeley, CA: Crossing Press, 1984), 56–57.

4. Ibid.

5. Refer to my book *Religious Resistance to Neoliberalism: Black Feminist and Womanist Perspectives* (New York: Palgrave Macmillan, 2015), particularly chapter 3, "Loss of the Erotic." Drawing upon Christian theologian Paul Tillich and black feminist Audre Lorde, I draw a distinction between the erotic and the pornographic, holding the erotic as a pure, liberating form of desire as opposed to the death-dealing character of the pornographic. I now find this distinction actually obscures the multiple, even contradictory aspects of the erotic.

6. Sharon Holland, *The Erotic Life of Racism* (Durham, NC: Duke University Press, 2012), 3. .

7. Ibid., 3.

8. Ibid., 3–4.

9. Ibid.

10. Ibid., 6.

11. Ibid.

12. Ibid.

13. Ibid.

14. Ibid., 4–5.

15. Ibid., 9.

16. Dionysian visions of the world are about embracing the chaotic, grotesque nature of experience itself in understanding the world instead of searching for some kind of primordial unity that brings order to chaos within the world. Although Friedrich Nietzsche uses this term in order to understand the aesthetics of the world, it also applies more broadly to how we interpret the meaning of human experience. I understand the erotic (human desire) to be Dionysian in character, which compels us to trace the ambiguities and contradictions (possibilities and limitations) of the erotic rather than proclaiming the erotic as simply life-giving. For more on the Dionysian idea, see Friedrich Nietzsche, *The Dionysian Vision of the World*, trans. Ira Allen (Minneapolis: Univocal Publishing, 2013); and Bruce Ellis Benson, *Pious Nietzsche: Decadence and Dionysian Faith* (Bloomington: Indiana University Press, 2008).

17. A couple of queer theorists who do this work are: Rosemary Hennessey, *Profit and Pleasure: Sexual Identities in Late Capitalism* (New York: Routledge, 2000); and Kevin Floyd, *The Reification of Desire: Towards a Queer Marxism* (Minneapolis: University of Minnesota Press, 2009).

18. Robert Rydell, *All the World's a Fair* (Chicago: University of Chicago Press, 1984), 66.

19. Friends of the White City, "Origin of the Midway Plaisance," www.friendsofthewhitecity.org/architecture/buildings/the-midway-plaisance (accessed July 24, 2019).

20. Rydell, *All the World's a Fair*, 66.

21. Friends of the White City, "Origin of the Midway Plaisance."

22. See Kelly Brown Douglas, *Sexuality and the Black Church* (Maryknoll, NY: Orbis Books, 1999), 56–59.

23. Refer to Ida B. Wells-Barnett, *The Red Record*, originally published in 1895 (New York: Open Road Media, 2015). Through investigative journalism, Wells writes about thousands of lynching that took place down in the postbellum South and the real racist reasons why lynching occurred, which rarely involved black men raping white women.

24. Douglass, *Sexuality and the Black Church*, 58.

25. Friends of the White City, "Origin of the Midway Plaisance."

26. Edward B. McDowell, "The World's Fair Cosmopolis," in *Frank Leslie's Popular Monthly* 36 (October 1893): 415. As quoted in Rydell, *All the World's a Fair*, 66.

27. John C. Eastman, "Village Life at the World's Fair," *Chautauquan* 17 (1893): 602–4. As cited in Rydell, *All the World's a Fair*, 66.

28. Refer to Ralph Waldo Emerson, "Self-Reliance," originally published in 1841. Emerson unfolds his philosophy of human freedom through self-reliance, which is about an individual's duty to self-actualize by thinking her own thoughts rather than merely conforming.

29. Harvey Cox, *Fire from Heaven: The Rise of Pentecostal Spirituality and the Reshaping of Religion in the Twenty-First Century* (Boston: Da Capo Press, 1995), 20.

30. Ibid.

31. John Winthrop, "A Model of Christian Charity," in *A Library of American Literature: Early Colonial Literature, 1607–1675*, ed. Edmund Clarence Stedman and Ellen Mackay Hutchinson (New York: Charles L Webster and Company, 1892), 304–7.

32. John O'Sullivan, "Annexation," *United States Magazine and Democratic Review* 17, no. 1 (July–August 1845): 7.

33. William Bacon Stevens [to members of the clergy], February 14, 1873, HSP Centennial Collection, Box 1, Folder 10, as quoted in Rydell, *All the World's a Fair*, 19.

34. White leaders at the exposition were attempting to envision a more hospitable future for non-European citizens in America and around the world, especially through notions of Christian friendship. The discourse on friendship posited as its goal the ending of racial hostility and violence characteristic of the nation's past. America had ended a civil war just two decades prior. The nation needed to decide the role non-whites would have in modern America. Unfortunately, white political and economic leaders believed that they had to determine this role while maintaining the old racial order which benefited so many white Americans. Consequently, this exposition used the discourse of friendship. This discourse on friendship supported concerns for formal equality through the law. The Emancipation Proclamation and the Thirteenth Amendment were cited as evidence of white Christian Americans' good will toward black citizens. However, blacks believed that his Christian call for friendship was steeped in white American national interest, especially in light of increasing protest among newly freed blacks in the face of continued white brutality. White America's notion of friendship was based on capitalist and political interests.

35. See Edward Baptist, *The Half Has Never Been Told: Slavery and the Making of American Capitalism* (New York: Basic Books, 2014). Refer to the introduction and chapter 1, where he refutes the idea that northern states were simply attempting to compromise with southern states over slavery when crafting the Constitution. The history is more complex. Instead, the three-fifths compromise allowing the expansion of slavery to burgeoning southern states was expected to make the entire nation an economic superpower within a century.

36. See Debra Bergoffen, *The Philosophy of Simone De Beauvoir: Gendered Phenomenologies, Erotic Generosities* (Albany: State University of New York Press, 1997), 184–88. In these pages, she expounds on erotic desire as a generosity rather than an appetite.

37. Ashon Crawley, *Blackpentecostal Breath: The Aesthetics of Possibility* (New York: Fordham University Press, 2017), 5.

38. Ibid., 11.

39. See Albert Raboteau, *Slave Religion: The "Invisible Institution" in Antebellum South* (Oxford: Oxford University Press, 1978); Richard Newman, *Freedom's Prophet: Bishop Richard Allen, the AME Church, and the Black Founding Fathers* (New York: New York University Press, 2008); and Stephen Ochs, *Desegregating the Altar: The Josephites and the Struggle for Black Priests, 1871–1960* (Baton Rouge: Louisiana State University Press, 1990).

40. Gaston Espinosa, *William J. Seymour and the Origins of Global Pentecostalism: A Biography and Documentary History* (Durham, NC: Duke University Press, 2014), 56.

41. Ibid.

42. Ibid., 96.

43. Alma White, *Demons and Tongues* (Zarapeth, NJ: Alma White [1910] 1949), 67–70. As quoted in Espinosa, *Seymour and the Origins of Global Pentecostalism*, 96.

44. Parham, "Free Love," in AF (October 1912), 6. As quoted in Espinosa, *Seymour and the Origins of Global Pentecostalism*, 99.

45. Ibid.

46. Ibid.

47. Espinosa, *Seymour and the Origins of Global Pentecostalism*, 113.

48. Ibid.

49. Ibid.

50. Ibid., 114.

51. Ithiel Clemmons, *Bishop C. H. Mason and the Roots of the Church of God in Christ* (Bakersfield, CA: Pneuma Life Publishing, 1996), 50.

52. Espinosa, *Seymour and the Origins of Global Pentecostalism*, 107.

53. Ibid., 106–7. Espinosa expounds on why Seymour forbade Florence to remarry. Seymour felt that scripture forbade a divorcee remarrying while the exspouse lived. If the divorcee remarried, she would be committing adultery, as she and her exhusband were still seen as married in the eyes of God.

54. Ibid.

55. Ibid., 107.

56. Ibid.

57. Ibid., 108. My emphasis.

58. Linn Tonstad, *Queer Theology* (Eugene, OR: Cascade Books, 2018), 3.

59. Ibid., 64. She borrows this definition of queer from David Halperin; he discusses this definition in *Saint Foucault: Towards a Gay Hagiography* (Oxford: Oxford University Press,1995), 61.

60. Tonstad, *Queer Theology*, 64.

61. Tina Campt, "Black Feminist Futures and the Practice of Fugitivity," talk given at Barnard College, available at the Barnard Center for Research on Women website, http://bcrw.barnard.edu/bcrw-blog/black-feminist-futures-and-the-practice-of-fugitivity (accessed November 17, 2017).

62. Ibid., 1.

63. Bergoffen, *Philosophy of Simone De Beauvoir*, 184.

64. Ibid., 205.

Chapter Five: Lawlessness

1. "Rolling and Diving Fanatics "Confess," in *Los Angeles Times*, June 23, 1906, 7, www.newspapers.com/search/#query=%22Rolling+and+Diving+Fanatics+%27Confess %27%22+Los+Angeles+Times.&t=4312&ymd=1906-06-23&lnd=1 (accessed November 4, 2021).

2. Ibid.

3. "Holy Roller Has It Bad," *Los Angeles Times*, August 14 1906, 12, www.newspapers. com/search/#query=%22Holy+Roller+Has+It+Bad%22+Los+Angeles+Times&t=4312& ymd=1906-08-14 (accessed November 4, 2021).

4. Ashon Crawley, *Blackpentecostal Breath: The Aesthetics of Possibility* (New York: Fordham University Press, 2017), 139.

5. Ibid.

6. Mark Smith, *Listening to Nineteenth-Century America*, illus. ed (Chapel Hill: University of North Carolina Press, 2001), 10. As quoted in Crawley, *Blackpentecostal Breath*, 140.

7. Crawley, *Blackpentecostal Breath*, 145.

8. Ibid., 144.

9. Elizabeth Freeman, *Time Binds: Queer Temporalities, Queer Histories* (Durham, NC: Duke University Press, 2010), 3.

10. Ibid.

11. James Hoke, "Unbinding Imperial Time: Chrononormativity and Paul's Letter to the Romans," in *Sexual Disorientations: Queer Temporalities, Affects, and Theologies*, ed. Kent Brintnall et al. (New York: Fordham University Press, 2018), 68.

12. Crawley, *Blackpentecostal Breath*, 144.

13. E. J. Hobsbawm, *Primitive Rebels: Studies in Archaic Forms of Social Movement in the Nineteenth and Twentieth Centuries* (Manchester: Manchester University Press, 1978), 2.

14. Karl Marx was writing in the context of censorship within Prussia and contemplating with other intellectual and political groups the conditions under which social reform is possible. By 1844, he was a self-identified communist and argued that free market competition will give way to capitalist monopoly leading to economic crisis and the alienation of workers from their labor. Just as Marx was finishing this project, an uprising of textile workers in Silesia, Germany, took place in June 1844. While the strike was small by French or English standards of the time, it represented the first serious collective action by workers inside Germany protesting against the social and working conditions imposed on them by the new system of factory production. The workers smashed machines and even demolished several of their bosses' mansions. The king of Prussia sent in soldiers, who fired into the crowd, killing at least eleven workers and injuring many more. Marx championed this revolt and was shocked when some of his former friends from radical philosophical circles in Germany downplayed or ignored it. For him, what sits at the heart of capitalist revolt is

the collective political agency of workers themselves to overthrow modern capitalist society.

15. Marx's idea of class consciousness is *humanistic* and nonreligious in character. For Marx, after the Silesian uprising, the Prussian state attempted to argue that only through religious feeling or Christian hearts coming together could society respond effectively to the social crisis associated with the uprising. Marx disagreed. He argued that this response does not honestly grapple with how religion functions in relation to bourgeois domination. Religion has been used as a tool of bourgeois ideology, legitimating the capitalist oppression reinforced by the state. Religion then led to worker's self-estrangement, as they could not see themselves as the agents of their own future. For certain, Marx's reductive view of religion was based on how Christianity was used as a tool of hegemony by the Prussian state. Moreover, his view of religion was based on Feuerbach's observation of Christianity. For Feuerbach, when human species project an idealized image of itself onto God and worships this imaginary being, the person becomes estranged from herself; one's earthly existence becomes alien and hateful. Religion supports the alienated laborer within capitalist societies. Religion supports the capitalist state by not allowing humans to produce freely as a form of self-actualization. Consequently, emancipation or liberation within classical Marxian analysis is more secular and humanist in character, although numerous scholars have employed neo-Marxian methods that rethink the generative uses of religion in social change.

16. For instance, the Social Gospel Movement was postmillennial, believing that the reign of God will expand within history through human efforts. The expansion of God's reign comes through social transformation of human relations, leading to an era of peace and righteousness prior to Christ's return. This long era of peace and righteousness is grounded in the preaching of the gospel, the saving work of the Holy Spirit, and the Christianization of the world's cultures and institutions. It is a golden age of spiritual and material prosperity, which might be understood as the culminating work of the Holy Spirit. While salvation is eschatological and beyond history, salvation is also unfolding within the historical processes, waiting to be realized in a society governed by love and justice. The underlying theological rationale of the social gospel movement assumed that improving social conditions had to be worked out concretely within the socioeconomic institutions of early twentieth-century America. For Social Gospel thinkers such as Walter Rauschenbusch, Christian political agency is best captured in actualizing the reign of God here on earth, within the context of modern political and economic institutions and organizations. Consequently, the Social Gospel, as an example of theological liberalism, largely frames salvation in this-world, structural terms. This salvation involves a form of political consciousness and agency that must come to terms with the apparatus of the state and its political and economic processes, working within and/or restructuring modern institutions to realize God's kingdom.

17. Hobsbawm, *Primitive Rebels*, 3.

18. Ibid., 58.

19. Ibid., 59.

20. After the Silesia uprising, Marx was angered that the Prussian state asserted that

this uprising was about a shortage of food and water alongside the failure of administration and charitable institutions to respond properly. Marx rejected this rationale. He said that this diagnosis misreads the principle of the state (or nature of the state) as *creating* poverty through class structure, competition, and alienation of workers from labor. For Marx, what was needed was a complete revolution of the state, which for him was centered on its abolition.

21. Hobsbawm, *Primitive Rebels*, 10.

22. Ibid.

23. When I refer to the "state," I am not referring to it as a singular, homogenous institution. The state is too complex and contradictory to be defined. It is a diverse, diffuse set of institutions, rules, techniques, practices, and powers that may even be contradictory in relation with one another. For me, the state is not so much a system or a subject as a complex diversity of techniques, powers, rules, and practices that find institutional expression in all kinds of local ways, with a central aim of securing, enforcing, and preserving physical territory and social order. Historically, the American state has exercised techniques and powers in order to normalize, secure, and protect its racialized market-driven order. One technique of statecraft has been describing America's democratic institutions and processes as objective and fair. One need only to turn to much of democratic political theory and the multiple ways in which it treats power and authority quite apart from "objective" procedures that are used to secure fairness within deliberative decision-making processes (rather than demonstrating how such rules are constituted by uneven relations of power and authority from the start). The American state and its democratic institutions are imagined as a context of liberalism and impartiality in pursuit of individual fulfillment and the search for the common good. The ideal of democracy is about the capacity of people to govern their own lives, but the American state often diminishes such capacities. Refer to Wendy Brown, "Finding the Man in State," *Feminist Studies* 18, no. 1, 1992, especially pages 12–13.

24. We cannot speak about democracy outside of a specific tradition(s). American democracy has traditions and genealogies. See Jeff Stout, *Democracy and Tradition* (Princeton, NJ: Princeton University Press, 2004).

25. Charles Long, *Significations: Signs, Symbols, and Images in the Interpretation of Religion* (Aurora, CO: Davies Group Publisher, 1986), 1–2.

26. Ibid., 1–2.

27. John Hoffman, *Citizenship Beyond the State* (Thousand Oaks, CA: Sage Publications, 2004), 12.

28. Refer to chapter 1 in Walter Hollenwager, *Pentecostalism: Origins and Developments Worldwide* (Ada, MI: Baker Academic, 2005).

29. On the failures of Reconstruction, see Henry Louis Gates, *Stony the Road: Reconstruction, White Supremacy, and the Rise of Jim Crow* (New York: Penguin Books, 2019); and Adam Fairclough, *The Revolution That Failed: Reconstruction in Natchitoches* (Gainesville: University of Press Florida, 2018).

30. There is a plethora of books in black studies, history, political philosophy and Christian ethics on the problem of American citizenship. For this book, see David

Theo Goldberg, *Racist Culture: Philosophy and the Politics of Meaning* (Oxford: Black-well Publishers, 1993); and Judith Shklar, *American Citizenship: The Quest for Inclusion* (Cambridge, MA: Harvard University Press, 1991).

31. See Derrick Bell, *Silent Covenants: Brown v. Board of Education and the Unfulfilled Hopes of Racial Reform* (Oxford: Oxford University Press, 2005). See chapter 1 on how the "separate but equal" clause was articulated by whites as providing equal and just social arrangements among black and white communities, although this clause actually reinforced and intensified black subjugation.

32. Refer to chapter 1 in Keri Day, *Unfinished Business: Black Women, the Black Church, and the Struggle to Thrive in America* (Maryknoll, NY: Orbis Books, 2012).

33. Matthew Desmond, "American Capitalism and the Plantation," 1619 Project, *New York Times Magazine,* www.nytimes.com/interactive/2019/08/14/magazine/slavery-capitalism.html (accessed January 20, 2020).

34. Michael Ashcraft, "Progressive Millennialism," in *The Oxford Handbook of Millennialism,* ed. Catherine Wessinger (Oxford: Oxford University Press, 2016), 44.

35. Ibid., 44. See *The Oxford Handbook of Millennialism,* chapters 3 and 25, where scholars Michael Ashcraft and Jon Stone provide an in-depth historical discussion of progressive millennialism or postmillennialism (among other millennialisms) in the United States. For these scholars, unlike premillennialism, Christian postmillennialists believed that the second coming of Jesus and the last judgment would occur after the Millennium, that is, after the world has achieved a thousand-year period of peace and progress. This age of peace would be ushered in by Christian social and political action. Postmillennialists also believed that this age of peace would be ushered in by the New World, specifically the United States. Secular and business leaders did not subscribe to this religious type of postmillennialism but they did have a secular view of progressive millennialism (postmillennialism), in which industrial and technological progress would usher the world into a more perfect unity and lasting peace.

36. Ashcraft, "Progressive Millennialism," 44.

37. See John Stone's conversation on premillennialism in, "Nineteenth-and-Twentieth Century American Millennialisms," in *Oxford Handbook of Millennialism,* 492–513.

38. Frederick Ware, "The Church of God in Christ and the Azusa Street Revival," in *Azusa Street Revival and Its Legacy,* ed. Harold Hunter and Cecil Robeck (Eugene: OR: Wipf & Stock Publishers, 2009), 254.

39. This apocalyptic attitude rejects faith in the state and the market and chooses instead to practice a defiant faith in what they believe to be God's power and benevolence. It is a defiant faith against empire and the empty promises that imperial institutions offer to the masses. The Azusa Revival affirmed God as the creator and ruler of human relations in the world, not governmental institutions associated with the state. Many white American churches had a very Calvinistic view of state authority, urging Christian communities to pray for and obey those whom God has placed in positions of authority. While the Azusa movement certainly prayed for leaders, they also defiantly rejected the authority of worldly rulers who embodied the wicked, corrupted character of the era.

Azusa announced that their citizenship was not "of this world" but of another impending world about to break into history. This religious view might not simply be read as compensatory or "otherworldly" but as a radically defiant challenge to the truth of current social realities constructed and maintained by American empire.

40. JoAnne Terrell, *Power in the Blood? The Cross in the African American Experience* (Eugene, OR: Wipf & Stock Publishers, 2005; originally published by Orbis Books, 1998), 26.

41. Ernst Käsemann, "The Beginnings of Christian Theology," in *New Testament Questions of Today*, trans. W. J. Montague (London: SCM Press, 1969), 92. As cited in David Congdon, "Eschatologizing Apocalyptic: An Assessment of the Present Conversation on Pauline Apocalyptic," in *Apocalyptic and the Future of Theology: With and Beyond J. Louis Martyn* (Eugene, OR: Cascade Books, 2012), 121.

42. Congdon, "Eschatologizing Apocalyptic," 121–23.

43. Ibid., 122.

44. Ibid.

45. Ibid.

46. Ibid., 124.

47. Ibid.

48. Ibid., 132.

49. Ibid., 125.

50. Ernst Käsemann, *On Being a Disciple of the Crucified Nazarene: Unpublished Lectures and Sermons*, ed. Wolfgang Kraus and Rudolf Landau, trans. Roy Harrisville (Grand Rapids: Eerdmans Publishing, 2010), 177. As cited in Congdon, "Eschatologizing Apocalyptic," 126.

51. Ibid., 201.

52. Ibid., 203.

53. Congdon, "Eschatologizing Apocalyptic," 128.

54. To read more about how Azusa strengthened American missions around the world, refer to Gaston Espinosa, *William J. Seymour and the Origins of Global Pentecostalism: A Biography and Documentary History* (Durham, NC: Duke University Press, 2014), chapter 3.

55. Harvey Cox, *Fire from Heaven: The Rise of Pentecostal Spirituality and the Reshaping of Religion in the Twenty-First Century* (Boston, MA: Da Capo Press, 1995), chapters 9–14, where Cox traces how Azusa shaped the practices of burgeoning Pentecostal communities around the world.

56. Adolfo Achinte, "Interculturadad Sin Decolonialidad? Colonialidades Circulantes y Practicas de Re-existencia," in *Diversidad, Interculturalidad y Construccion de Ciudad*, ed. Wilmer Villa and Arturo Grueso (Bogota: Universidad Pedagogica Nacional / Alcaldia Mayor, 2008), 85–86. Trans. and cited in Catherine Walsh and Walter Mignolo, "The Decolonial For: Resurgences, Shifts and Movements," in *On Decoloniality: Concepts, Analytics, and Praxis* (Durham, NC: Duke University Press, 2018), 18.

57. Walter Mignolo and Rolanda Vazquez, "Decolonial Aesthesis: Colonial Wounds/Decolonial Healings," *Social Text Online*, published July 13, 2013, https://

socialtextjournal.org/periscope_article/decolonial-aesthesis-colonial-woundsdecolo-nial-healings (accessed September 24, 2021).

58. See Nancy Fraser's essay *Rethinking the Public Sphere* (CreateSpace Independent Publishing Platform, 2016), in which she defines counterpublics as discursive arenas that develop outside of the official public sphere where members of marginalized groups and invent and circulate counter discourses that serve as oppositional interpretations to the how the state (official public sphere) defines them. Counterpublics are formed in response to exclusion from official dominant publics associated with the state.

59. Michel Foucault, *Discipline and Punish: The Birth of the Prison,* 2nd Vintage Book ed. (New York: Random House Publishing, 1995), 202–14.

60. Frederick Ware, "On the Compatibility/Incompatibility of Pentecostal Premi-llennialism with Black Liberation Theology," in *Afro-Pentecostalism: Black Pentecostal and Charismatic Christianity in History and Culture* (New York: New York University Press, 2011), 200.

61. Ibid., 201. Emphasis added.

62. Ibid., 192.

Chapter 6: A Democracy to Come

1. David Robertson, "Paula White's New Book *Something Greater* Is Revealing, Dis-turbing and Depressing," in *Christianity Today*, October 19, 2019, https://christiantoday.com/article/paula-whites-new-book-something-greater-is-revealing-disturbing-and-depressing/133464.htm (accessed September 24, 2021).

2. Bonnie Kristian, "Why Televangelist Paula White Is the Perfect Trump Adminis-tration Hire," in *The Week*, November 1, 2019, https://theweek.com/articles/875819/why-televangelist-paula-white-perfect-trump-administration-hire (accessed September 24, 2021).

3. Jacques Derrida, *Rogues: Two Essays on Reason*, trans. Pascale-Anne Brault and Michael Naas (Stanford, CA: Stanford University Press 2005), 37–38. Derrida refers to "democracy to come" as "the other democracy" in the sense that democracy to come doesn't refer to a democratic ideal expressed within nation-states or simply among ideo-logical groups. Instead, it "suggests the incompletion and delay, the self-inadequation of every present and presentable democracy, in other words, the interminable adjourn-ment of the present democracy." Rather than democracy as a procedural idea of delib-erative consensus or a substantive notion of freedom and agency, he emphasizes the unending experience of alterity as marking the democratic moment, as characterizing a democracy to come. This unending experience of alterity or experience of the other reveals the unfinished character of democracy, not as a system but as *a way of life that is shaped by and for diverse community*. This event as an ongoing experience of alterity is a radical form of relationality that can potentially disrupt structural injustices and democratize or humanize social relations.

4. Fred Dallmayr, *Democracy to Come: Politics as Relational Praxis* (Oxford: Oxford University Press, 2017), 23.

5. Ibid., 27.

6. Derrida, *Rogues*, 87–90. On p. 87, beginning with point #3, Derrida links "the democratic" beyond nation-state sovereignty" to an "international juridico-space that, without doing away with every reference to sovereignty, never stops innovating and inventing new distributions and forms of sharing, new divisions of sovereignty." Derrida hopes to connect the democratic to a space where practices of human rights constantly refashion social contexts of intimacy, friendship, and belonging that make way for a more humanizing, democratizing humanity. Derrida's democracy to come is in pursuit of justice, which is often undermined by the law (the law that is often expressed through institutional power relations, interests, and agendas that strive for homogeneity and conformity). It is important to remember, for Derrida, that a democracy to come involves the pursuit of justice but Derrida's idea of justice is paradoxical in that it is a justice that "cannot wait" yet a justice that is always deferred (coming to us as potentiality) and never actualized perfectly in the present.

7. Dallmayr, *Democracy to Come*, 40.

8. Neoliberal capitalism has received widespread attention in the humanities and is increasingly being discussed in religious scholarship. When I speak of neoliberal capitalism, I am not only referring to a set of economic policies oriented toward unregulated markets and the dismantling of social welfare policies to mitigate the undesirable consequences of markets on the poor. I am also referring to it as a *market morality* and cultural ideology that attempts to mold and govern our moral conduct and behavior. Neoliberal capitalism and its market morality (i.e., privileged values of competition, rabid individualism, and the endless pursuit of profit) try to provide the *moral* terms of our existence. They demand that individuals relate to each other in instrumental ways in order to achieve success and fulfillment. They turn social relations into market relations in which persons primarily relate to each other in economic terms. Friends only have meaning if they help one accrue social standing. People's economic success and meaning are measured by in what zip code they reside or by what kind of car they drive. Neoliberal capitalism and its market morality together create a different community of persons that weighs the value of human life according to how such life is measured by the accumulation of material things and success. I discuss at length the category of neoliberalism and explore its philosophical, economic, and critical-theoretical understandings in *Religious Resistance to Neoliberalism: Black Feminist and Womanist Perspectives* (New York: Palgrave Macmillan, 2015), 5–14.

9. Karen Bray, *Grave Attending: A Political Theology for the Unredeemed* (New York: Fordham University Press, 2020), 3.

10. Ibid., 3.

11. Ibid., 12.

12. Ibid., 4.

13. Ibid.

14. Ibid., 9.

15. Anne Case and Angus Deaton, *Deaths of Despair and the Future of Capitalism* (Princeton, NJ: Princeton University Press, 2020), 45.

16. Ibid., 37.

17. Ibid.

18. Ibid., 1.

19. Ibid., 3.

20. Ibid.

21. Ibid., 7.

22. Ibid., 3.

23. Ibid., 3–4.

24. Ibid., 95.

25. Allana Akhtar, "Artificial Intelligence Slated to Disrupt 4.5 million Jobs," in *Business Insider Online*, October 7, 2019, www.businessinsider.com/mckinsey-finds-black-men-will-lose-more-jobs-automation-2019-10 (accessed September 24, 2021).

26. Ibid.

27. Ibid.

28. Please see Helen Arega et al., *Battling over Birth: Black Women and the Maternal Health Care Crisis* (Amarillo, TX: Praeclarus Press, 2017). This book offers a comprehensive study of the deep disparities associated with black maternal health and mortality and provides updated studies on this issue.

29. Jeanna Smialek and Ben Casselman, "Black Workers' Wages Are Finally Rising," in *New York Times*, February 7, 2020, www.nytimes.com/2020/02/07/business/black-unemployment-wages.html (accessed September 24, 2021). These authors write that black workers' wages are finally rising in our American economy but they do not demonstrate that this increase in black wages in any way closes the *racial disparities* in wages. Does it close the inequitable gap between white and black wages? Unfortunately, it has not, despite the explosion of articles that praise the increase in wages among blacks.

30. Mitchell Hartman, "African-American Wages Nearly Stagnant over a Decade," in *Marketplace*, April 18, 2019, www.marketplace.org/2019/04/18/african-americans-wages-nearly-stagnant-over-decade (accessed September 24, 2021).

31. To read Naomi's full story, see Dana North, "Stories from the Border: Naomi," in *World Relief News Online*, July 10, 2019, https://worldrelief.org/blog/stories-from-the-border-naomi?gclid=EAIaIQobChMIt5yaor6a6AIVBmKGCh15oQJ8EAAYAiAAEgIEvPD_BwE (accessed September 24, 2021).

32. Darcy Courteau, "Mireya's Third Crossing," *The Atlantic* (online), June 2019, www.theatlantic.com/magazine/archive/2019/06/border-crossings-one-immigrants-journey/588064 (accessed September 24, 2021).

33. Day, *Religious Resistance to Neoliberalism*, 8.

34. Bray, *Grave Attending*, 106.

SELECTED BIBLIOGRAPHY

Alexander, Estrelda. *Black Fire: One Hundred Years of African-American Pentecostalism*. Downers Grove, IL: IVP Academic Publishing, 2011.

———. *The Women of Azusa Street*. Laurel, MD: Seymour Press, 2012.

Ashcraft, Michael. "Progressive Millennialism." In *The Oxford Handbook of Millennialism*, ed. Catherine Wessinger, 44–65. Oxford: Oxford University Press, 2016.

Bartleman, Frank. *Azusa Street: An Eyewitness Account to the Birth of the Pentecostal Revival*. New Kensington, PA: Whitaker House, 2000.

Bass, Charlotta. *Forty Years: Memoirs from the Pages of Newspaper*. Los Angeles: California Eagle Press, 1960.

Bergoffen, Debra. *The Philosophy of Simone De Beauvoir: Gendered Phenomenologies, Erotic Generosities*. Albany: State University of New York Press, 1997.

Berlant, Lauren. *Cruel Optimism*. Durham, NC: Duke University Press, 2011.

Bhattacharyya, Gargi. *Rethinking Racial Capitalism: Questions of Reproduction and Survival*. London: Rowman & Littlefield, 2018.

Bray, Karen. *Grave Attending: A Political Theology for the Unredeemed*. New York: Fordham University Press, 2020.

Brown Douglas, Kelly. *Stand Your Ground: Black Bodies and the Justice of God*. Maryknoll, NY: Orbis Books, 2015.

Buder, Stanley. *Pullman: An Experiment in Industrial Order and Community Planning*. New York: Oxford University Press, 1967.

Case, Anne, and Angus Deaton. *Deaths of Despair and the Future of Capitalism*. Princeton, NJ: Princeton University Press, 2020.

Campt, Tina. "Black Feminist Futures and the Practice of Fugitivity." Talk given at Barnard College, available at the Barnard Center for Research on Women website, http://bcrw.barnard.edu/bcrw-blog/black-feminist-futures-and-the-practice-of-fugitivity (accessed November 17, 2017).

Chireau, Yvonne. *Black Magic: Religion and the African American Conjuring Tradition*. Oakland: University of California Press, 2003.

Clemmons, Ithiel. *Bishop C. H. Mason and the Roots of the Church of God in Christ*. Bakersfield, CA: Pneuma Life Publishing, 1996.

Coble, Alana Erickson. *Cleaning Up: The Transformation of Domestic Service in Twentieth Century New York City*. New York: Routledge, 2006.

Congdon, David. "Eschatologizing Apocalyptic: An Assessment of the Present Conversation on Pauline Apocalyptic." In *Apocalyptic and the Future of Theology: With and Beyond J. Louis Martyn*, 118–36. Eugene, OR: Cascade Books, 2012.

Cox, Harvey. *Fire from Heaven: The Rise of Pentecostal Spirituality and the Reshaping of Religion in the Twenty-First Century*. Boston: Da Capo Press, 1995.

Crawley, Ashon. *Blackpentecostal Breath: The Aesthetics of Possibility*. New York: Fordham University Press, 2017.

Dallmayr, Fred. *Democracy to Come: Politics as Relational Praxis*. Oxford: Oxford University Press, 2017.

Daniels, David. "Until the Power of the Lord Comes Down." In *Contemporary Spiritualities: Social and Religious Contexts*, 173–91. New York: Continuum, 2001.

Day, Keri. *Religious Resistance to Neoliberalism: Black Feminist and Womanist Perspectives*. New York: Palgrave Macmillan, 2015.

———. *Unfinished Business: Black Women, the Black Church, and the Struggle to Thrive in America*. Maryknoll, NY: Orbis Books, 2012.

Derrida, Jacques. *Rogues: Two Essays on Reason*. Trans. Pascale-Anne Brault and Michael Naas. Stanford, CA: Stanford University Press, 2005.

Dubofsky, Melvyn. *"Big Bill" Haywood*. New York: St. Martin's Press, 1987.

Duis, Perry. *The Saloon: Public Drinking in Chicago and Boston, 1880–1920*. Chicago: University of Illinois Press, 1998.

Ehret, Christopher. *The Civilizations of Africa: A History to 1860*. Charlottesville: University of Virginia Press, 2016.

Engh, Michel. *Frontier Faiths: Church, Temple, and Synagogue in Los Angeles, 1846–1888*. Albuquerque: University of New Mexico Press, 1992.

Findlay, James. *Dwight L. Moody: American Evangelist, 1837–1899*. Eugene, OR: Wipf & Stock Publishers, 2007.

Foucault, Michel. *Discipline and Punish: The Birth of the Prison*. 2nd Vintage Book ed. New York: Random House Publishing, 1995.

Freeman, Elizabeth. *Time Binds: Queer Temporalities, Queer Histories*. Durham, NC: Duke University Press, 2010.

Gilbert, James. *Perfect Cities: Chicago's Utopias of 1893*. Chicago: University of Chicago Press, 1991.

Goff, James. *Fields White unto Harvest: Charles F. Parham and the Missionary Origins of Pentecostalism*. Fayetteville: University of Arkansas Press, 1988.

Green, James. *Death in the Haymarket: A Story of Chicago, the First Labor Movement, and the Bombing that Divided Gilded Age America*. New York: Pantheon Books, 2006.

Hartman, Saidiya. *Wayward Lives, Beautiful Experiments: Intimate Histories of Social Upheaval*. New York: W. W. Norton, 2019.

Hendericks, Wanda. *Fannie Barrier Williams: Crossing the Borders of Region and Race*. Champaign: University of Illinois Press, 2013.

Hennessey, Rosemary. *Profit and Pleasure: Sexual Identities in Late Capitalism*. New York: Routledge, 2000.

Hobsbawm, E. J. *Primitive Rebels: Studies in Archaic Forms of Social Movement in the Nineteenth and Twentieth Centuries*. Manchester: Manchester University Press, 1978.

Hoffman, John. *Citizenship Beyond the State*. Thousand Oaks, CA: Sage Publications, 2004.

Hoke, James. "Unbinding Imperial Time: Chrononormativity and Paul's Letter to the Romans." *Sexual Disorientations: Queer Temporalities, Affects, and Theologies*, ed. Kent Brintnall et al., 68–89. New York: Fordham University Press, 2018.

Holland, Sharon. *The Erotic Life of Racism*. Durham, NC: Duke University Press, 2012.

Hollenwager, Walter. *Pentecostalism: Origins and Developments Worldwide*. Ada, MI: Baker Academic, 2005.

hooks, bell. *We Real Cool: Black Men and Masculinity*. New York: Routledge, 2004.

Israel, Adrienne M. *Amanda Berry Smith: From Washerwoman to Evangelist*. Lanham, MD: Scarecrow Press, 1998.

Jackson, Michael. *Paths Toward a Clearing: Radical Empiricism and Ethnographic Inquiry*. Bloomington: Indiana University Press, 1989.

Jennings, Willie James. *The Christian Imagination: Theology and the Origins of Race*. New Haven, CT: Yale University Press, 2011.

Jessup, Henry Harris. "The Religious Mission of English-Speaking Nations." In *The Dawn of Religious Pluralism: Voices from the World's Parliament of Religions, 1893*, ed. Richard Hughes Seager, 37–42. La Salle, IL: Open Court, 1993.

Johnson, Alonzo. "'Pray's House Spirit': The Institutional Structure and Spiritual Core of an African American Folk Tradition." In *Ain't Gonna Lay My 'Ligion Down: African American Religion in the South*, 8–38. Columbia, SC: University of South Carolina Press.

Jones, Jacqueline. *Labor of Love, Labor of Sorrow: Black Women, Work, and Family, from Slavery to Present*. New York: Vintage Books, 1985.

Käsemann, Ernst. "The Beginnings of Christian Theology." In *New Testament Questions of Today*, trans. W. J. Montague, 82–107. London: SCM Press, 1969.

———. *On Being a Disciple of the Crucified Nazarene: Unpublished Lectures and Sermons*. Ed. Wolfgang Kraus and Rudolf Landau. Trans. Roy Harrisville. Grand Rapids: Eerdmans Publishing, 2010.

Lanker, Brian. Interview: "Queen Mother Audley Moore." In *I Dream a World: Portraits of Black Women Who Changed America*, 103. New York: Stewart, Tabori, and Chang, 1989.

Macchia, Frank. "Sighs Too Deep for Words." *Journal of Pentecostal Theology* (1992): 56–60.

Liardon, Roberts. *The Azusa Revival: When the Fire Fell*. Shippensburg, PA: Destiny Image Publishers, 2006.

Lomax, Tamura. *Jezebel Unhinged: Loosing the Black Female Body in Religion and Culture*. Durham, NC: Duke University Press, 2019.

Long, Charles. *Significations: Signs, Symbols, and Images in the Interpretation of Religion*. Aurora, CO: Davies Group Publishers, 1999.

Lorde, Audre. "Uses of the Erotic." In *Sister Outsider: Essays and Speeches*, 54–65. Berkeley, CA: Crossing Press, 1984.

MacRobert, Iain. *The Black Roots and White Racism of Early Pentecostalism in the USA.* 2nd ed. Eugene, OR: Wipf & Stock Publishers, 2003.

Moberly, R. W. L. "How Appropriate is 'Monotheism' as a Category for Biblical Interpretation?" In *Early Jewish and Christian Monotheism*, ed. Loren Stuckenbruck and Wendy E. S. North, 216–34. New York: T & T Clark International, 2004.

Nash, Jennifer. *Black Feminism Reimagined: After Intersectionality*. Durham, NC: Duke University Press, 2019.

Nash, Margaret. "Thoughts on the History of Women's Education, Theories of Power, and This Volume: An Introduction." In *Women's Higher Education in the United States: New Historical Perspectives*, ed. Margaret Nash, 1–22. New York: Palgrave Macmillan, 2018.

Neal, Mark Anthony. *New Black Man*. New York: Routledge, 2015.

Osofsky, Gilbert. *Harlem: The Making of a Ghetto-Negro Mew York, 1890–1930*. New York: Harper and Row, 1968.

O'Sullivan, John. "Annexation." *United States Magazine and Democratic Review* 17, no. 1 (July–August 1845): 5–10.

Raboteau, Albert. *Slave Religion: The "Invisible Institution" in Antebellum South*. Oxford: Oxford University Press, 1978.

Robeck, Cecil. *The Azusa Street Mission and Revival: The Birth of the Global Pentecostal Movement*. Nashville, TN: Nelson Publishers, 2006.

———. "The Azusa Street Mission and Historic Black Churches: Two Worlds in Conflict in Los Angeles' African American Community." In *Afro-Pentecostalism: Black Pentecostal and Charismatic Christianity in History of Culture*, 21–42. New York: New York University Press, 2011.

———. "William Seymour and 'The Biblical Evidence.'" In *Initial Evidence: Historical and Biblical Perspectives on the Pentecostal Doctrine of Spirit Baptism*, ed. Gary B. McGee, 72–95. Eugene, OR: Wipf & Stock Publishers, 1991.

Robinson, Cedric. *Black Marxism: The Making of the Black Radical Tradition*. 2nd ed. Chapel Hill, NC: University of North Carolina Press, 2000.

Robinson, Paul. "Race, Space, and the Evolution of Black Los Angeles." In *Black Los Angeles: American Dreams and Racial Realities*, ed. Darnell Hunt and Ana-Christina Ramon, 21–59. New York: New York University Press, 2010.

Rydell, Robert. *All the World's a Fair*. Chicago: University of Chicago Press, 1984.

Savage, Barbara. *Your Spirits Walk Beside Us: The Politics of Black Religion*. Cambridge, MA: Harvard University Press, 2008.

Seymour, William. "Money Matters." In *The Words That Changed the World: Azusa Street Sermons*, ed. Larry Martin, 35–38. Joplin, MO: Christian Life Books, 1999.

———. *The Doctrines and Discipline of the Azusa Street Apostolic Faith Mission*, ed. Larry Martin. Pensacola, FL: Christian Life Books, 2000.

Sides, Josh. *L.A. City Limits: African American Los Angeles from the Great Depression to the Present*. Los Angeles: University of California Press, 2003.

Stimson, Grace. *Rise of the Labor Movement in Los Angeles*. Los Angeles: University of California Press, 1955.

Synan, Vinson. *The Century of the Holy Spirit: 100 Years of Pentecostal and Charismatic Renewal, 1901–2001*. Nashville, TN: Thomas Nelson Publishers, 2001.

Synan, Vinson. *William J. Seymour: Pioneer of the Azusa Street Revival*. Alachua, FL: Bridge Logos Publishers, 2012.

Terrell, JoAnne. *Power in the Blood? The Cross in the African American Experience*. Eugene, OR: Wipf & Stock Publishers, 2005.

Tonstad, Linn. *Queer Theology*. Eugene, OR: Cascade Books, 2018.

Walsh, Catherine, and Walter Mignolo. *On Decoloniality: Concepts, Analytics, and Praxis*. Durham, NC: Duke University Press, 2018.

Ware, Frederick. "The Church of God in Christ and the Azusa Street Revival." In *Azusa Street Revival and Its Legacy*, ed. Harold Hunter and Cecil Robeck, 243–58. Eugene: OR: Wipf & Stock Publishers 2009.

———. "On the Compatibility/Incompatibility of Pentecostal Premillennialism with Black Liberation Theology." In *Afro-Pentecostalism: Black Pentecostal and Charismatic Christianity in History and Culture*, 191–208. New York: New York University Press, 2011.

Washington, Booker T. "The Standard Printed Version of the Atlanta Exposition Address." In *The Booker T. Washington Papers*, vol. 3, ed. Louis Harlan, 583–87. Urbana: University of Illinois Press, 1972.

———. "The Story of My Life and Work." In *The Booker T. Washington Papers*, vol. 1, ed. Louis Harlan, 1–210. Urbana: University of Illinois Press, 1972.

Williams, Fannie. "Religious Duty to the Negro." In *The New Woman of Color: The Collected Writings of Fannie Barrier Williams, 1893–1918*, ed. Mary Jo Deegan, 73–77. DeKalb: Northern Illinois University.

INDEX

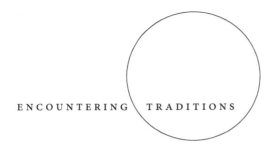

ENCOUNTERING TRADITIONS

CPSIA information can be obtained
at www.ICGtesting.com
Printed in the USA
JSHW020420240223
R12355300004B/R123553PG38102JSX00007B/1